YOU GUYS ARE HISTORY!

YOU GUYS ARE HISTORY!

Devon Malcolm

CollinsWillow

An Imprint of HarperCollins*Publishers*

First published in 1998
by CollinsWillow
an imprint of HarperCollins*Publishers*
London

© Devon Malcolm 1998

1 3 5 7 9 8 6 4 2

A CIP catalogue record for this book is
available from the British Library

ISBN 0 00 218840 6

Printed in Great Britain by Clays Ltd, St Ives plc

PHOTOGRAPHIC ACKNOWLEDGEMENTS
Allsport picture no. 13 (Adrian Murrell), 14 (Chris Cole), 15 (Ben
Radford), 27 (Adrian Murrell), 29, 30, 33 (Graham Chadwick); **Patrick
Eagar** 16, 17, 24, 25, 26, 28, 35, 40; **Empics** 20 (Graham Chadwick),
31, 32 (Lawrence Griffiths), 38 (Chris Turvey), 39 (Brendon Monks);
Express Syndication 41 (Douglas Morrison); **Keith Moon** 8, 23;
Sportsline/David Munden 9, 10, 11, 12, 18, 19, 21,
34 (Paul Sturgess), 36, 42

To my four beautiful girls – my wife Jenny and daughters Natalie, Erica and Stephany

CONTENTS

ACKNOWLEDGEMENTS

So many kind and caring folk have helped me over the years; above all, my beloved parents and grandparents, who taught me such a lot. I just wish my dear mother had lived long enough to see me achieve something in my chosen profession. I know she would have been so proud. My three lovely daughters are a constant joy, and give me valuable perspective away from cricket. Above all, my lovely wife, Jennifer, who has been a constant source of encouragement and sound advice over the years, as well as being a brilliant wife and mother. I haven't forgotten her excellent organisational skills either!

There are many at Derbyshire CCC whom I should thank, especially my first coach, Phil Russell, for having faith in me, and my first captain, Kim Barnett, for a vital, early grounding in what was needed to make the grade in county cricket. Not forgetting all those marvellous Derbyshire supporters, who always supported me unstintingly. Throughout the world of cricket, I've been very fortunate to have the support and affection of the cricket-loving public, whose sense of fair play has helped sustain me during difficult and painful times. My respect and gratitude to you all; your kind words and actions over the years have been deeply appreciated.

To Naynesh Desai, a good friend and invaluable legal and business adviser, who was a rock during some traumatic periods.

Finally, to Derby County Football Club and BBC Radio's Patrick Murphy. The football club's public relations officer, Jim Fearn, kindly provided me sanctuary away from three lively children to work on this book – and thanks to the *Derby Evening Telegraph* for use of their executive box – while Pat Murphy battered his way through the Midlands traffic network to record my thoughts on tape, then put them into print. Any errors are all Pat's fault, while I'll take the credit for the bits that the reader liked!

Devon Malcolm
Oakwood, Derby

ONE

FROM JAMAICA TO SHEFFIELD

It was the radio commentaries that really brought cricket to life for me. Growing up in Jamaica we were aware of our local cricket heroes like Lawrence Rowe and Michael Holding, and of the supremacy of the West Indies side under Clive Lloyd's captaincy, but life was full for me, with lots of other sports to be played. Cricket wasn't my ruling passion until I was about thirteen. I was good at athletics, particularly sprinting, and I loved football. But then I heard Tony Cozier on the radio commentating on the West Indies fast bowlers running in and bowling fast. He'd talk about them pushing off the sightscreen to run long distances, then delivering the ball at the speed of light. I loved the drama of it all – over the radio the excitement of the crowd came across readily; the sense that the batsman was hanging on for dear life against the quickies; the roar from the spectators if the batsman hooked a bouncer, or was hit by one. It was typically West Indian: noisy, passionate and dramatic. Being a fast bowler seemed to be the summit of your sporting ambitions if you were from the Caribbean, especially as the West Indies kept bowling out the opposition in the mid-seventies. To this day, I prefer following cricket on the radio, rather than television. Somehow, the feel of the game comes over better; you can sense what it's like at the ground and drink in the atmosphere, especially when it's coming from the Caribbean, where the spectators are so animated.

I was only daydreaming about playing cricket for a living, though, as I rushed into the school playground, listening to the commentary and pretending I was a great fast bowler. In Jamaica at that time, Michael Holding was an icon, the local boy made good. I was just thirteen when he bowled out England at the Oval in 1976, making his name in world cricket with his devastating speed and gloriously smooth action. His nickname was 'Whispering Death' because of his graceful yet deadly hostility, and we were all so proud of him. A few years later, I was privileged to join Michael in English county cricket, playing for Derbyshire. He was a fantastic help to me – but as a young boy, such a notion never entered my head. I was set on getting a good education and working in a well-respected profession. A doctor or an accountant, yes. A cricketer? You must be joking! In the West Indies, most families have high hopes for their children in education. You are expected to progress up the ladder through academic achievements and make something of yourself. Sporting prowess may give you social status but doesn't get you a job. Besides, everybody plays some kind of sport in the Caribbean, and it's rare to find a child so single-minded about making it to the top in the sporting world. I certainly had no such burning ambitions as a boy, and my family kept my nose to the academic grindstone, just in case I faltered!

I grew up in a quiet part of Jamaica called St Elizabeth, a beautiful area about 80 miles west of the capital, Kingston. I was the oldest of two children, with a sister, Karen. My mother, Brenda Lee, died when I was six years old. We were a loving, close-knit family, and – as usual in the Caribbean – an extended family, with my grandparents very influential. My grandmother Maudlyn was a remarkably calm, capable woman who never seemed to be fazed by all the usual domestic crises going on around her. She just kept smiling, oblivious to any chaos. My family reckon I've inherited Maudlyn's laid-back temperament, although I do have to stress that I'm not Mister Cool when I've got a ball in my hand! Dorrel, my grandfather, was a huge cricket fan. As well as playing it keenly, he'd get distracted easily by the game. Time and again, he'd go to the market to buy livestock, see that a game of cricket was going on nearby, settle down to watch the match and eventually come home without going anywhere near the market. He'd talk cricket to me, but it was only after he died when I was twelve that I really got involved with the game.

At the age of fourteen, I won a scholarship to the St Elizabeth Technical High School where I specialised in science subjects, as well as English. I joined the army cadets at school and the discipline instilled there and by my family has undoubtedly helped me through various crises subsequently. Early on, I learned how important it is to keep your dignity, not to make a fuss in public, and to have your own personal standards. That was particularly vital all those years later, when I went through so much mental anguish on the 1995 England tour to South Africa. Our tour manager, Ray Illingworth, made my life a misery then, but I was able to draw on those early lessons. Growing up in a close-knit village was very valuable to me, because it was such a disciplined community. If you misbehaved anywhere, your parents would know about it before you got home. Any responsible adult who saw a youngster up to no good in our rural area had licence to hand out a clip round the ear. No parent would complain about someone else disciplining a child; it was just accepted that kids must be disciplined if they stepped out of line. That approach might cause a few problems in England, I suppose!

Once I got to high school, cricket began to interest me more. The schools standard was very competitive, and I was proud when I won a school scholarship. It seemed the most natural thing to me that I should be a fast bowler. I was tall for my age – my mother was six feet! – and I had wide shoulders. It was just a matter of picking up the ball and bowling it as fast as I could. During the class breaks, I'd play cricket with the older, bigger boys and that helped toughen me up. I never seemed to get a bat – all I did was field and bowl, so I suppose nothing has changed over the years! There was a strong cricketing tradition at my school, and our first XI won the Sir George Headley Cup three times in a row. One year the great George Headley himself came along to present the trophy and I was amazed at how tiny he was. And to think that years later, I played in the same England team as his grandson, Dean. Who writes these scripts?!

I didn't realise it at the time, but growing up in that Jamaican climate and in a rural area was a huge plus for my later cricket career. You could play cricket more or less all year and the amount of fresh fruit available was marvellous for your health. Every day I'd feast on mangoes, pears and oranges as much as I wanted, and we'd never see a burger or greasy chips. It would be a healthy diet of rice, fish, vegetables and fruit. That desire to eat nutritious food has stayed with me and I'm sure it's helped prolong my career. Everything was set up for a budding sportsman where I grew up. You would walk everywhere, because it was safe and there was no reliable transport. I would walk six miles a day to and from school, even running some of the way, and that automatically gave me strong legs. Now, when I see my kids jump into the car and get driven to school, I smile to myself and wonder how they'd have adjusted to walking so many miles.

So I was a typical, hulking West Indian fast bowler, as my body filled out and I shot up in height. All I wanted to do was knock the heads off the older boys. Yet I wasn't the fastest in the Malcolm family. My cousin Danville, who was a few months older than me, was seriously quick and between us we started to terrorise opposition schools in the games. Many a scorecard has every batsman out to D Malcolm, although I have to admit that most of the damage was done by Danville, not Devon. He also managed to bat higher up the order than me...which wasn't difficult!

By the time I was sixteen, life appeared pretty straightforward. I was doing well at school, on course for a college scholarship, and knocking over batsmen in schools cricket. There was a complication, though. My father Albert had been working in England for many years. When I was three years old, he had gone over to Sheffield because he could earn a better living in England than in a Jamaican village. He sent money back regularly, came home as often as possible, and the plan was that his family would eventually join him over there. It was a fairly typical situation for a

West Indian family, with the breadwinner either working in the United States or England, and the grandparents holding the family together back home. Yet my grandfather had died when I was twelve and with my mother passing away a few years earlier, I needed my father's influence as I went through that difficult adolescent phase. Before that period, it was something to boast about in school that your dad was working in England. There was something so cool about showing a letter or a birthday card to your classmates, saying airily, 'Oh, I got this from England.' It gave the impression that your father was in a good job over there, even though the reality for us was that my father worked shifts as a maintenance engineer, sharing a room with others and using the bed on a rota system in his early days over there, saving every penny he could to send home to us. He worked very hard for years, missing his family, struggling with the cold weather, hoping we'd all be together again one day. When my father asked me if I'd like to join him in Sheffield, it seemed an enticing prospect. Not only did I need him but it was something to drop into the conversation at school. You know what kids are like – anything to be different and have one over the others!

So I arrived in Sheffield in April 1980 and I took to the vastly different lifestyle straight away. The cold didn't bother me and I got a place at Richmond College to continue my studies. Richmond College was an exciting place to be, because it was a melting pot of different races and I enjoyed hearing about the different cultures from Japanese, Indian, European and other West Indian students. Life was good, it was interesting. My father still worked nights, but we saw a lot of each other. I didn't see any cricket grounds, though. In fact, I didn't play cricket for the first two years that I lived in Sheffield. I was a shy, quiet teenager who didn't think about pushing myself, or walking straight into a club, looking for a game. I played football in the evenings with my college friends, and that satisfied me. There was no deep-seated urge in me to play cricket in England; it appeared to be so different in atmosphere and approach to cricket in Jamaica, so I wasn't bothered.

15

My life changed after I stopped to watch a cricket match towards the end of the 1982 summer. I was in the Concorde Sports Centre, at Shire Green, near to my home in Sheffield, when I just stole a look at the game. A black guy was also watching and we got talking. His name was Milton Samuels. Milton had worked out my origins straight away, which wasn't difficult, since I still spoke with a strong West Indian accent. 'Don't you play cricket?' he asked, and when I told him I hadn't played for two years he said, 'Give me your phone number and I'll call you.' And that's how it all started. I don't believe I would have played for England if I hadn't stopped to talk to Milton. I might have taken up cricket eventually, but too late to make a real impression. Anyway, Milton rang me, invited me along to his club's winter nets – and it all clicked again. After a gap of two years. I had the batsmen ducking and diving, and the members liked what they saw. Milton's club was called Sheffield Caribbean and I qualified on both counts: I was living in Sheffield and came from the Caribbean.

It all happened so quickly from the summer of 1982 onwards. One season, I played in three different divisions in Sheffield, moving up in standard as various clubs moved in on me. The bush telegraph around Sheffield reported that this big black guy was knocking over sides regularly. I asked to play for the Richmond College team, and after taking twelve wickets in my first two games for them, I had my first write-up. It was in the *Green 'Un*, the Sheffield sports paper, and I kept that press cutting in my folder at college. The Sheffield Caribbean boys were delighted at their new capture. They all said I was far quicker than anyone else in their league and I got used to splattering the stumps. After a season, I moved on to play for Sheffield United, after the Caribbean side sold me on the notion that it was now too easy for me in their team, and that I needed to move up another league, to stretch myself against better players. That appealed to my ego, but I'll always be grateful to Sheffield Caribbean for their support and kindness. I still keep in touch with the club and have very fond memories of those early days as a raw tearaway.

In one game, I took six for 0 and my college recommended me for the Yorkshire Senior Schools side. My father took me to St Peter's School, York for the Schools game, and he gave me the best possible advice before I went on the field. 'Devon, just do it – just bowl fast,' he said, and that's all I wanted to do. It was simply a matter of getting the ball down the other end as fast as I could. I now realise I had the raw material, that I was fit and strong, with the typical Caribbean fast bowler's philosophy. It's a relief that nobody tried to 'streamline' my action or technique when I was eighteen and playing for Yorkshire Schools. That came later, at the age of 32, after I'd taken over a hundred wickets for England!

TWO

'THANKS, BOYCS!'

Geoffrey Boycott has never topped any popularity polls among cricketers of my time – but I won't hear a word said against him. He was instrumental in me getting a trial for Derbyshire, even though he didn't realise it at the time. When I look back at the defining moments of my career, I think about that chance encounter with Milton Samuels in Sheffield that brought me back to cricket, about my first Test against the West Indies in Jamaica in 1990, and my nine for 57 against South Africa in 1994 at the Oval. But an April day at Castleford in Yorkshire back in 1984 also looms large. That was the day I clean bowled Geoffrey Boycott with a yorker. I was playing for the Yorkshire League XI against the might of Yorkshire CCC in a pre-season game. Now anyone who has followed Boycott's career will know he was never the type to give away his wicket, not even in a pre-season friendly, and this day was no exception. He was looking to spend time out in the middle, get his feet moving and just ease himself into the season ahead. A few hours' batting, ending with a not out, would be ideal preparation for our Geoffrey. Unfortunately for him, I had other ideas.

It was a fantastic thrill even to bowl at Boycott that day. Having grown up in the Caribbean, listening to the Tests on the radio, I knew how highly respected he was among West Indies fans and players. The duels between the fast bowlers and Boycott and his opening partner, Graham Gooch were fresh in my memory, and I remembered the roar of acclaim whenever one of those two great

18

players got out. They were wickets to prize, and here I was, bowling at Boycott just a few years later on. I was determined to give it my best shot, to see if I could ruffle him, yet fully aware that he'd probably just pick me off, using the pace of the ball. He wasn't prepared for the yorker that pinged out his middle stump, though. I bowled it from the extremity of the crease, angled in at him, and he was done for pace. Years later, Boycott admitted that he was rarely bowled by the yorker in his career, his defence was too sound, and I treasured the fact that a greenhorn like me got through him. He only made twelve runs and just to round off the perfect day for me, I clean bowled his opening partner, Martyn Moxon for four with a similar delivery. Amazing. I was brought down to earth, though, by another Yorkshire batsman, Jim Love. He tried to knock the cover off the ball but nicked it and was caught by the wicket-keeper. Love just stood there, brazening it out – and he got away with it, too, and was given not out. So I should have been celebrating three notable scalps in my opening burst.

We beat Yorkshire that day, which was unprecedented in recent memory. Yorkshire county pros don't know the meaning of the word 'friendly' and we were all chuffed to bits afterwards in the bar. I was grinning from ear to ear and when Boycott saw me, he said, 'Well bowled, young man.' I was floating. One of their officials asked me where I came from and I told him 'Sheffield via Jamaica' and realised they were actually sounding me out. All on the strength of two yorkers. It was a non-starter anyway, because in those days, you had to be born in Yorkshire to play for them, but I was still hugely flattered that anybody from their club would be interested in a guy like me, who just ran up and bowled as fast as possible, without much craft or thought involved. The headline in the *Yorkshire Post* read 'YORKS BEEN DEVON CREAMED' – the first but not the last time that particular pun was wheeled out – and all of a sudden people were sitting up and taking notice of me. Enter Phil Russell.

Phil was Derbyshire's coach at the time and he soon got word of my bowling at Castleford. He invited me down to Derby in April

1984 for a trial in the nets and I enjoyed myself, making the batsmen hop around and bruising one of Kim Barnett's thumbs. Kim was the new captain of Derbyshire, so I suppose it was a good idea to work over my potential boss!

I had no thought of actually getting taken on by Derbyshire. It was just terrific to have a bowl at professionals in good conditions and to realise that my pace was causing a problem or two. But then Phil Russell sat me down and talked seriously to me about my prospects. He amazed me by saying that in his opinion, I could play for England in five years' time. I was 21 then, lacking the finesse of other bowlers at the same age who were already on a county staff, getting good coaching. I was just raw and naive, unable to take in what Phil was telling me. He insisted he wasn't joking, told me that I had something different – sheer speed — and that he would ensure that I'd be able to give it my best shot and not be side-tracked by the need to bowl line and length, to conform. There was one major problem to him: my birthplace. I'd have to be taken on as an overseas player, and then he'd hope to get my registration altered over the next few years so that I'd be judged England-qualified. Derbyshire already had Michael Holding and the New Zealand batsman, John Wright, on their books and the two would alternate games, depending on the wicket. So I couldn't expect to stand in for them; I'd just be learning the ropes, playing some second XI cricket. That would do for me! I told Phil I'd be happy to play for nothing and he was amused at my naive enthusiasm. In the Caribbean, I knew that you just played for fun, that hardly any of the guys who played Shell Shield for their islands got anything for their expenses, so I thought why should it be any different at Derbyshire? When Phil told me I'd have a contract worth £3,000 a year, I was flabbergasted. I told him I was thrilled and honoured just to get a chance of playing in the second team, but to be paid as well was just mind-boggling.

Within a couple of weeks of bowling Boycott, I was watching first-class cricket for the first time – Derbyshire against Leicestershire at Chesterfield. Things seemed to be developing a momentum all of their own. The quality of coaching and advice I got in that first season with Derbyshire was fantastic. I'd look around the dressing-room and see top players only too willing to go out of their way to help me. To be coached by my boyhood hero Michael Holding was just amazing – and he was supportive of this raw kid. He'd talk about the basics and suggest one or two refinements, but hammered home to me that I must just bowl fast and not settle for conformity. He said, 'Follow through straight after delivering the ball, follow the ball.' He told me that if I veered away too soon in my follow-through, I'd put extra strain on my body and also lose direction. That advice still holds true for me and if I have a bad day, that often stems from this fault. Michael didn't believe in chopping and changing a young player's technique; he liked to keep it simple, develop the raw material and, above all, to encourage. He was very professional in his approach to fitness and diet and I simply drank in everything that he told me.

I kept imagining what my family and friends in Jamaica would say about being taken under the wing of the great Michael Holding. To me, he was as great a person as he was a fast bowler. I travelled round the country with him, picking his brains and absorbing his words of wisdom. During our innings, I'd sit with him, asking what the opposition fast bowlers were trying to do. He would stress the importance of the new ball, hammering home the point that a minimum of two wickets were needed with it, that the extra bounce and the possibility of swing were vital assets to the fast bowler. Above all, Michael preached self-discipline to me. Listen and learn, take responsibility and don't look for excuses.

Derbyshire's other overseas player was a great help in assessing the minds of batsmen. John Wright was not only a very fine cricketer, he was a charming, intelligent man who would give a young player all the time in the world. He would often get in the side ahead of Holding for away matches, where the wickets would be flatter to negate Holding's pace, and John would really fill his boots when conditions favoured the batters. I remember seeing him score a big, unbeaten hundred at Edgbaston in those early days, and the manner of that innings was very instructive. We'd lost early wickets, but as the conditions eased John just expanded his range and scored more rapidly the longer he was at the crease. He told me about the mental steel necessary for the successful opening batsman, the one who can withstand the early onslaught from the quicks, then capitalise. John was very interesting on what a batsman doesn't like when up against a fast bowler – short-pitched, 'at the throat' bowling. It was an eye-opener to me to realise just how much thought went into being a top player. It wasn't just a matter of sheer natural ability – that needed to be harnessed by clear thinking.

Bob Taylor was another to share his thoughts generously. Bob was in his final year in the game when I joined Derbyshire and I was hugely impressed by his continuing dedication to his craft, at his generosity with his advice, and the fact that he had time for everybody. He never raised his voice in the dressing-room, always had constructive things to say, and never stinted on his technical tips as to how to prepare for the game. And he had still been good enough to keep wicket for England just a few months earlier, at the age of 43! That seems even more astounding today than in 1984, but I can confirm that he was a remarkable keeper, still, in his final season. Bob made it look so easy; he had the footwork of a squash or badminton player. When he kept wicket to me, my raw speed led to many wild offerings down the legside and I'd stand there, open-mouthed in admiration at just how far he could go to the legside and haul back the ball. At his age!

John Hampshire was also in his final season of first-class cricket and his advice was generously given and simple. Stop messing about and just bowl it fast – that was the gist of his message. John had batted with distinction for England, Yorkshire and Derbyshire for more than twenty years, and he knew all about the little weaknesses of bowlers. He told me that he could tell from my tensed-up facial expression where I was going to put the ball, and so he could react accordingly. He said I had to develop a mask, to appear inscrutable

22

so that I gave away no visible clues. That would all come with experience, and although I was a little baffled initially by John's words, I could see what he meant after a time. I had some good advice along similar lines from the veteran batsman Harry Pilling, after he'd hit me all over the place during a match against Lancashire Seconds. 'You were bowling well, but I could see where you were going to pitch the ball,' he said. I was feeding his strong stroke, the square cut, by dropping it short, and my facial expression was the giveaway.

So the fires of ambition really started to burn at Derby after a few weeks. I couldn't fail to be inspired by the prospect of a career as a professional, even though I didn't rate myself all that highly. My house back home in Sheffield was bulging with trophies, but that didn't mean a thing when you looked closely at the quality of players both in my Derbyshire side and the rest of county cricket. Yet Phil Russell was a wonderfully positive coach. He kept drumming into me that I had something many others would never have. I was a big, strong lad who got the ball through quickly because of my natural strength, and Phil's advice to me was that I shouldn't complicate things unduly. He was excellent at one-on-ones; he'd go into fine detail with you, never talking down to you, always looking for the encouraging areas. He said he could live with me bowling erratically as long as I didn't compromise. His advice was to try to pitch four balls out of six in the right area, and then my sheer pace would take care of the rest. Phil was the kind of mentor for whom you really wanted to do well, to reward his faith in you.

At times during that season, things did come together encouragingly. Because of injuries to Wright and Holding, I played six championship matches as an overseas player, taking just a handful of wickets but enjoying one game in particular. On a fast, bouncy pitch at Chesterfield, I had a good contest with that great West Indian batsman, Alvin Kallicharran. He had been another hero from my youth; the runs were still flowing from his bat now he was playing for Warwickshire after being overlooked by the West Indies.

I got Kallicharran twice in this game, including clean-bowling him for 87 in the second innings. So in the space of a couple of months, I had graduated from club cricket in Sheffield to scattering the stumps of Boycott and Kallicharran. Perhaps I did have something after all.

If my team-mates and Phil Russell were hugely influential in that first summer, my captain was massively important. My relationship with Kim Barnett sadly deteriorated towards the end of my time at Derbyshire, but I won't let that cloud my assessment of his contribution in the early part of my career. Kim prolonged my time in the game by insisting that his fast bowlers should operate on a rota basis, giving them time for rest and recuperation. He had seen how the West Indies had been dominating world cricket by the use of fresh, fit, motivated fast bowlers and Kim set out to do that at county level. For most of the time, the home pitches favoured the quicker bowlers – although, in some seasons, they were mystifyingly flat – and we lacked a high-class spinner to get enough wickets consistently. So Kim was determined to look after his quicks and his method worked. He didn't believe in cortisone injections to get you through a match. That just delayed recovery and caused complications. Far better to rest an injury and return with all guns blazing. If the fast bowler fancied carrying on through to the next match, that was fine by Kim, as long as he was fresh and ready when he needed to bowl. If it was a case of missing out on the Sunday League match, and being keen and up for the championship game, all well and good. Flexibility was the key and all the quick bowlers at Derby benefited from Kim's enlightened attitude. He was convinced that fast bowlers win you matches when handled correctly, and without his common sense I would not have lasted so long in professional cricket.

So my coach and captain were very supportive about my bowling as soon as I joined the staff – but they quickly realised that my batting and fielding were more of a long-term problem. I don't think it's all that surprising that I struggled with the bat and in the field when I came into the professional game, because you have to consider where I came from. Playing in parks and club cricket in Sheffield didn't exactly equip me with the all-round finesse you see in young players who come onto a county's books after graduating through the usual channels, learning about all the game's disciplines. I was just an untutored fast bowler, aged 21, lagging behind other young county players in my cricketing development and knowledge. For two years in my teens, I hadn't even played the game. That's my excuse anyway!

I know my frailties in batting and fielding have given a lot of amusement to people and players throughout my career, but some tales have been embroidered very imaginatively. I've even heard them myself in after-dinner speeches and in articles written in my 1997 benefit brochure. For the record, it's not true that I once stood on my glasses in the outfield when they slipped off after I was about to take a catch, and that in the confusion afterwards, the batsmen ran five runs. A great story, but not true. I admit I was pretty hopeless in the field when I came to Derby, though. I never had any fielding tuition, and all I had to offer was my strong throwing arm, which has never left me, thankfully. I was uncoordinated and negative, dreading that the ball would come to me and I'd make a hash of it. For the first few years at Derby, I'd bowl and field in thick glasses. I'd have them tight against my head with a piece of elastic, but at times in the field they'd slip off or sideways, with results that must have looked pretty comical. It took me two years to get used to wearing contact lenses, by which time the legends about my fielding inadequacies were starting to grow. I have got better over the years – not many batsmen take me on for a quick run when the ball's in my hand – but I can't complain if crowds have had a few laughs at my expense. I'm sure I've deserved some of the scoffing, but I've always tried my hardest in the field.

My batting's caused a lot of merriment, too, but again I offer the fact that I started late in the professional game. Yet the spectators don't seem to mind that I just love hitting sixes. My batting technique sometimes lets me down when I'm trying to react quickly, and

I admit that my footwork leaves a lot to be desired, but when I get hold of the ball, it does go a long way! I never had a chance to get to grips with the mechanics of batting in my career. On England tours, the tail-ender forfeits the chance to bat in the nets in favour of the established batters and no one takes you all that seriously. I replace my old bat with a new one every three years, so I must be using it properly at some stage!

How many people know that I've actually opened the batting for Derbyshire? It was in a match against Gloucestershire, when Chris Marples and I walked out to open when the game was ambling towards a draw. No one told that to Courtney Walsh and David Lawrence, though, and they tore in at us for three overs before the more undemanding bowlers were brought on. Malcolm 29 not out, in case you were wondering. Then there was the ten-wicket victory I sealed for us when we beat the Indian tourists. We only needed thirteen to win, so after taking eight wickets in the game, I was deputed to go in and knock off the runs. Another not out: a handsome 12! But the one innings I feel I ought to focus on was my only first-class fifty. Against Surrey in 1989, I hit 51 off 26 balls, including three sixes and six fours. Ian Bishop was batting with me at the time and we went from looking for a third batting point to going for the maximum four. No problem! The ball went so sweetly off the bat that day, there were some serious shots. Ian Bishop just leaned on his bat at the other end, laughing and shouting 'Shot, Dev!' and we had great fun. I even got the hook shot out of the bag! My innings ended in the grand manner, caught on the long-on boundary, when a couple more feet would have brought me another six. That's the way the crowd like to see tail-enders bat. My sixes linger longer in my memory than my wickets, especially the time I hit Shane Warne for several sixes in the 1994–95 series in Australia. So when team-mates rib me about my batting, I just ask casually, 'So how many Test sixes have you hit, then?'

So those early years at Derby didn't see much batting fireworks from me, as I came to terms with the sheer hard work of bowling in the professional game. I played just fifteen championship matches in my first three years on the staff, due in part to restrictions on me as an overseas player, but also because of a series of injuries. I had the usual amount of teething problems any fast bowler faces as he comes to terms with wear and tear on the body, and for a couple of seasons I suffered painfully from shin soreness, due to the pounding I gave them as I banged my left foot down in the delivery stride. Playing at the weekends in Sheffield hadn't equipped me for this. It was only after the shin problem had dragged on for a second season that I decided to get myself some proper bowling boots. Mine were clearly inadequate, with soles that didn't give me enough support. The indoor nets at Derby were so hard that my back, shins and ankles were really feeling the strain of running up and bowling fast, so I sought advice about boots. I heard about a cobbler from Sutton Coldfield called Ian Mason who specialised in handmade boots. After negotiating a deal with the club, whereby they'd take so much a month out of my wage to pay for the boots, I found myself with new trainers and bowling boots that felt so much more comfortable and secure. Soon my vulnerable areas in the body were stronger and I came to understand what Michael Holding meant when he talked about the need for preventative training.

I picked up some valuable experience by playing club cricket in New Zealand, with the Ellesley club in Auckland. There was a strong Derbyshire connection there with many of our players enjoying the change in environment, and after being the league's top wicket-taker in my first season, I was invited back the following year. I still enjoyed it, but I had to cut short my second season for personal reasons that I hope they understood. I had met Jenny, who was to become my wife, the mother of my three lovely daughters and my rock at all times. Jenny was studying for her degree in social sciences at Sheffield University when we met, and when she graduated, both myself and her ill mother couldn't attend the ceremony. Jenny has been such a wonderful support to me, both as wife, mother of my children and adviser. After my first season in

New Zealand, she gave me an excellent piece of advice. I'd enjoyed the man-sized portions of food out there, and because I wasn't playing as much cricket as back home, I was a touch overweight – about half a stone, but enough. I'd always been careful what I ate, but I wasn't quite right for the forthcoming season. Well, Jenny took one look at me when I came home, squeezed my hips and said, 'Devon, there's only one fatty in this house, and it's not going to be *you*.' It was just a matter of fine tuning, of tapering me down, but it was needed. Having a balanced, nutritious diet has been important in prolonging my career.

After three years at Derby, Phil Russell and Kim Barnett remained convinced that I could play for England despite playing inter-mittently and, even then, impressing only in bursts. Kim had told me that only one spell in three of mine was up to standard, but he kept the faith. I know that around this time, one Derbyshire committee member was very sceptical about me and didn't think I should be kept on, but Kim stuck to his guns and won the day. He used to tell the doubters, 'Five for a hundred off twenty overs beats one for sixty off thirty any day,' and I'll never forget Kim's support and conviction that this rough diamond could be polished up. He and Phil then set about trying to get me qualified for England, so that I wouldn't have to kick my heels if the star overseas player was available. There was no question of me going back to the West Indies and trying to qualify for them by playing in Shell Shield cricket. There was too much competition among budding fast bowlers over there and anyway, I felt a great loyalty to Derbyshire and, having spent eight years in England, felt my case could be viewed sympathetically. Despite playing schools cricket in Jamaica, it could be said that I'd learned the bulk of my cricket in Sheffield and Derby, and therefore couldn't be judged a typical overseas player, who is signed as the finished product. The club enlisted the support of my local MP Margaret Beckett and she worked wonders with the Home Office. Mrs Beckett has gone on to great things as a Cabinet Minister, but she graciously agreed to be one of the patrons in my benefit year. She's one of many who have intervened significantly in the progress of my career. Bob Taylor also helped out. He wrote a reference, in which he forecast that I'd play for England if the application succeeded. All these good judges seemed convinced I had it in me. I was astonished at their confidence in me!

So, after four years with Derbyshire, I was de-registered as an overseas player and qualified for England. It was still slow progress from me, though: so much still to learn, such a lot of time to make up for. My studies at Richmond College had to go by the board after Derbyshire signed me up, but later I enrolled at the Derby College of Higher Education as a mature student, doing an HNC in business studies. That, too, had to be aborted after England called me up for my first tour. I seemed to be fated to fall at the final hurdle whenever I got near to some academic qualifications. The idea of playing cricket for a living had never entered my mind until Phil Russell had sat me down and talked so persuasively. I was then 21 and knew that I couldn't delay much longer if I wanted to carve out a professional career. But cricket took over. Later on, I was privileged to be awarded an Honorary Masters degree by Derby University's School of Business Studies, but I'm the first to admit that Jenny's the one in our family with the hard-earned, genuine degree.

The 1988 season was the breakthrough for me. I was fit, over my shin problems and beginning to get the hang of bowling fast consistently. I was an ever-present in the first team, enjoying the responsibility of trying to knock the batters over with the new ball. Some things need to be experienced, though – like playing in front of a big crowd for the first time. That had come in the 1987 season, when we played against Nottinghamshire in a local derby on our ground. It was the quarter-finals of the NatWest Trophy and they drafted me in at the last minute because Paul Newman and Alan Warner were injured. It was the biggest crowd seen at Derby for eighteen years, the first time I'd been on television and although I bowled quite well, I felt in a state of shock for a month afterwards. It was such a novel experience to have crowds cramming in alongside you on the boundary edge, distracting your attention. We lost the game, and I was left wondering what it would be like to play in a final at Lord's, because this had been a massive experience for me. A year later, I found out. We got to the Benson & Hedges Final at Lord's. I was so nervous the night before, because I knew that we might field first, and that meant I'd be opening the bowling in the biggest game of my life so far. Unfortunately the tension got to all of us and Hampshire ran out easy winners by seven wickets. We batted first and lost crucial wickets too early. The tension even got to Michael Holding, as he got himself caught at long-off from a rash shot, just before lunch, when we needed wickets in hand to try for some sort of total to bowl at. So when it was our turn to bowl, we really weren't under any pressure, because we didn't have much of a score to defend. Perhaps that's why I bowled so well. I managed to get the ball to swing and got it down the other end at a good pace. I know I made a favourable impression that day in front of such a big audience, both at the ground and on television. It was the start of two careers in the big time because Hampshire's Robin Smith also impressed with some clean hitting. Within a year, we were England team-mates.

It was good for Derbyshire that we had got to Lord's again, even though we lost so disappointingly. We hadn't been in a Lord's final since winning the NatWest Trophy in 1981, and there were clear signs that under Kim Barnett, we were beginning to build another good side. As for me, Phil Russell's crazy forecast from 1984 about my England credentials was still swirling around in my mind, and I kept discounting it. Yet there had been a vacancy for a genuine fast bowler in the England team ever since Bob Willis retired in 1984. Greg Thomas was quick in bursts and had played a few times, Graham Dilley had become a swing bowler, while Gladstone Small and Norman Cowans had found the burden of bowling fast a bit of a physical burden, and had altered their styles to become fine bowlers, but no longer strike bowlers, capable of putting the wind up the openers. I knew I was still maddeningly inconsistent, needing careful handling and nursing, and I still hadn't mastered the art of bowling four balls out of six bang on the spot – the standard that Holding, Marshall, Roberts and Ambrose all reached and often exceeded. And yet England needed a fast bowler, even if not in the class of those great West Indians. To my amazement, Phil Russell was about to prove himself a very good forecaster.

THREE

ENGLAND CALLING

I was lucky to get picked by England with so little experience under my belt. Basically I was chosen on potential, the necessity to have a genuine fast bowler on hand, and because I filled a vacuum. By the time I made it into the England team for the fifth Test against Australia in 1989, everything was coming apart at the seams under David Gower's captaincy. Not only were the Aussies 3–0 up in the series, but several of our players had decided to go to South Africa that winter, with Mike Gatting as captain. They knew they'd be banned from international cricket for a few years and so their enforced absence for the rest of the series opened the door for the younger ones, including myself. This is not to minimise the huge pleasure I got from being picked by England, but with pace bowlers such as Graham Dilley, Paul Jarvis and Neil Foster signing up for South Africa – soon to be followed by Greg Thomas – there was a golden opportunity there for someone like me. With the 1990 West Indies tour coming up and so many other contenders ruled out, I had hoped in my heart of hearts that I'd make that trip, as the new boy brought along for the experience. Instead I got the call even earlier, against the super-confident, dynamic Australians. It was a chastening experience, both for me and the England side, as we slid to another crushing defeat at Trent Bridge. I ended up bowling 44 overs (the most of my career in an innings), took the third new ball for the first time, and turned in an analysis of one for 166. When I got back to Derbyshire after that nightmare, Michael Holding cheered me up when he said, 'Dev, it can only get better after that, the only way is up.' I hoped he was right. After such an experience, I had no real confidence that I'd get picked again.

I'd had a little time to come to terms with the prospect of playing for England for the first time. My county captain Kim Barnett told me to take the previous match off to get some rest, and then the England coach, Micky Stewart rang to congratulate me before the squad was officially announced. So I was reasonably ready for the barrage of press attention. It must have been a good story – having only played around fifty championship games, I was very rough around the edges, even if I had pace. The nearest equivalent in modern times for England was Bob Willis, who was flown out to Australia after just a handful of matches for Surrey, and ended up taking more than 300 Test wickets. I was under no illusions about the tenuous nature of the comparison, though. Bob had proved himself to be a great fast bowler for England, and I was starting at the basement, with so much still to learn. All I could offer was raw speed and a determination never to lose heart. It amazed me that Phil Russell had been so certain that I'd play for England five years earlier, and I was almost as pleased for him as I was for myself, but I didn't for one moment believe that I'd take to Test cricket instantly. In fact, since that first day at Trent Bridge, I've felt on trial with England for all but a handful of Tests. That's partly due to my own bowling defects, but also an insecurity bred by unsympathetic captaincy.

I wish I could say that I loved my introduction to Test cricket, but that would be a lie. Forget the result – we were on a hiding to nothing, in complete disarray, with players coming and going all summer and the Aussies just running away with the series, awash with cockiness. Our captain David Gower kept having to get the sticking plaster out and I felt very sorry for him. I admired David hugely as a great guy and loyal servant of England. He could easily have gone to South Africa for a fortune, but chose not to, unlike some of the other England players that summer. It's fair to say that David liked the celebrity status and money that flowed from being England captain, but good luck to him. He was always one of my favourite cricketers, a brilliant player of fast bowling and an enjoyable companion. I respected him for not going to South Africa, feeling that those players who did had let him down, leaving England at rock bottom. It's all very well to say that you have to look after yourself and get some security for your family, but no one should turn down the chance of playing for England. A lot of the rebel players had gripes about the way they'd been treated in the England set-up and one of them – Kim Barnett – had been dropped during this 1989 Ashes series. He asked my opinion about the whole issue when the news finally leaked out that he and the rest were going to South Africa, and I just said it was up to him, although making it clear that it was something I would never have done at any stage in my career. We never talked about it again. It was clear to me that those guys saw it as a big pay-day, and to talk about helping to do their bit to eradicate apartheid was rubbish, just an attempt to ease their consciences.

So David Gower had a nightmare job on his hands when we assembled in Nottingham for the fifth Test, just a fortnight after Gatting and the rest had shown their hand. Our captain must have looked around the dressing-room and wondered what he had been given. There were Jack Russell and Robin Smith in their first full series, Angus Fraser playing only his third Test, Martyn Moxon still a rookie at that level, and two newcomers – Mike Atherton and me. Graham Gooch had opted out of Trent Bridge because he wasn't happy with his form in that series so far – which hardly helped his captain – and we were without the injured Allan Lamb. Ian Botham was still in the side, but he wasn't in great nick, even though it was a great thrill to be in the same side as one of my heroes. The sands of time were beginning to run out for Beefy, and he had a poor series. It all added up to an unpromising situation for David Gower, especially against an Australian team who had surprised everyone with their intelligent seam and swing bowling, and confident batsmen who kept racking up huge totals.

Yet even with so much going against England, I was still shocked at the amateurish way we prepared for my first Test. I honestly believed afterwards that Derbyshire prepared better for games than we did under David Gower. We were allowed to pitch up on Wednesday lunchtime, on the eve of the game, turn the arm over in the nets, let the batsmen have a bit of a hit, try to take a few catches, jog around the outfield, then have a soak in the bath. That was it. A decade later, the England squad for home Tests assembles on the Monday night, practises hard on the skills, works conscientiously on fitness programmes, looks at videos of opposition players and of ourselves, and talks about our strategy. There was none of that in 1989. The eve-of-Test dinner was an ordeal for me in particular. I sat beside the chairman of selectors, Ted Dexter, feeling very nervous. We were all in blazers and ties, feeling very formal, and we talked out of the corners of our mouths, trying to place who all the other officials were. I knew all the players, but there were a lot more besides them at the dinner. I just opted to lie low, speaking when I was spoken to and contenting myself with a 'yes' or a 'no'. It was hard work and did nothing to relax me. Ted Dexter and David Gower both said a few words, wished us luck and that was it. I was really disappointed; I expected some discussion on strategy, about how we would actually get the opposition out or combat their bowling. Nothing. Just good luck. That night, I tossed and turned, my mind in turmoil, expecting the worst because nobody had prepared me for what was ahead. I knew I was going to play, and dreaded having to bowl first thing in the morning if they decided to bat first. It didn't matter that I was bowling well for Derbyshire – this was the big time, and I just wasn't properly prepared.

All my chickens came home to roost that first day. I'll never forget walking off the field that night, looking at the scoreboard, which said 'AUSTRALIA 301–0', with centuries to both Mark Taylor and Geoff Marsh. It was a demoralising experience. There was no way back in the game after a first day like that. I was particularly down. Early on, I was sure I had Marsh plumb lbw, straight in front. The umpire, Nigel Plews, disagreed unfortunately. I just couldn't believe that decision and I suddenly thought: 'So this is Test cricket. If that wasn't out, then nothing is. I'll just have to rely on getting them bowled or caught!' I watched the incident again on television that night and it was still out. I agree the ball was missing off stump, and indeed leg stump – but not the middle stump. That would have been a great start for both me and the team, but the Aussies just batted us out of the game over the next two days. I thought I bowled with genuine pace and hostility, even surprising Allan Border with a couple of rapid beamers, which were completely unintentional, simply ill-directed yorkers. I kept going on a good batting wicket that lacked pace. Angus Fraser and I were both so new to this standard, though, and I'm sure that if either of us had enjoyed the benefit of an old hand bowling from the other end, we might have got some joy with the new ball before the pitch flattened out.

Finally, I got my first wicket for England, when I had Steve Waugh caught at square leg by David Gower. My captain shook my hand, and it was nice to get such a top player out for nought, after he'd filled his boots earlier in the series, but then I looked at the scoreboard – Australia 553 for five. We were being run ragged. Earlier Dean Jones came in at 502 for three and absolutely terrorised us for a short period. He really upped the tempo by treating it like a one-day game, running two to third man, taking on the fielders on the throw. I found myself bowling, then having to rush back to the stumps at my end, as Jones pressurised the fielders for quick singles. We were all very tired in the field by now and he demoralised us, putting the boot in like a typical Australian. That extra period of dominance by Jones pushed us past the physical and mental limit and so when we batted, it was inevitable that we'd fold.

We made just 255 and 167 and lost comfortably by an innings and plenty. At that stage, the Aussies were so far ahead of us in terms of training, attitude and forward planning. In our second innings,

David Gower opened the batting because it was felt that a left-hander at the top of the order would be as valuable at disrupting the bowlers' line. But why wasn't that sorted out when the Test team was picked? Why not pick a left-handed opener, rather than bat Gower out of position? It appeared that we were lurching from crisis to crisis, with no real strategy, no plan of coping. Even I, a virtual novice, could see that, so why couldn't the England think-tank?

I was really taken aback also by the Aussies' hard-nosed attitude towards us. When Terry Alderman took five wickets in our first innings, I was walking back to the pavilion and said to him, 'Well bowled.' I was astonished when he snarled and swore at me. And Alderman had the reputation of being a nice guy! Yet he was so intimidating. There was I, congratulating a fellow fast bowler on a fine performance as I had always done, and he bit my head off. I said to myself, 'Lace your boots up, Dev, this is the big time!' Since then, I've never gone out of my way to congratulate an opponent. It was bad enough getting the expected abuse from fast bowlers like Geoff Lawson and Merv Hughes, but it was a shock to cop flak from Alderman. I ought to have learned my lesson earlier that summer, when Derbyshire lost by eleven runs to the Aussies, and I got cheated out as the last man. We were all pumped up to beat them, and Reg Sharma and I were inching closer and closer to a one-wicket victory when Carl Rackemann brushed my pad with his last ball of the over. When he appealed I thought it was a joke, but when umpire John Hampshire gave me out, caught behind, I was aghast. I dropped my bat, shouted 'No, no!' and had to be sent on my way. I was called into the office afterwards, given a ticking-off and fined. That was the only time in my career that I have been guilty of such dissent and I regretted it, especially as my old team-mate John Hampshire was involved. Significantly, though, Rackemann admitted to me afterwards that I wasn't out, but he had to appeal for everything because we were close to beating them. Aussies don't like losing any games of cricket, and that's why I've loved it so much on the rare occasions we've beaten them in my time with England.

Everything went wrong for us in that Trent Bridge Test. Ian Botham dropped a catch off me in the slips, dislocated a finger and couldn't bat in the second innings. It was sad that his injury quenched his competitive abilities, because I could see from his attitude and words earlier in the match that he was desperate to see England salvage some pride. Instead, we had the young lads facing a tough opposition and we were slaughtered. Mike Atherton got nought in his first England innings and I have to admit he didn't look all that impressive on his debut. At the time, I believed Martyn Moxon to be the better player, because he could play a wider range of shots. Atherton was being pushed very hard already at the age of 21 by the broadsheets. Obviously going to Cambridge University was no barrier to progress in the eyes of influential people, and even at that stage, he was being talked of as a future England captain. I found that unbelievable. You have to be a good enough player first and when I'd bowled at him, I'd softened him up a few times. Like me, he had been thrown in at the deep end, and to his great credit, he swam rather than sank. Athers became a highly skilled opening batsman, full of bravery and good judgement, and the genuine article as a Test player – but you wouldn't have thought that possible in 1989.

So we lost badly in my first Test, but the embarrassment didn't end on the field. At the press conference after the match, Ted Dexter was asked for some straws of consolation, and he came up with this gem: 'Who could forget Malcolm Devon?' Well, Ted's had to live with that one for years, but it didn't bother me too much, it's more important that your captain remembers your name. Ted was always vague about such things. When John Morris got into the England side a year later, he kept mistaking him for the physiotherapist! I was more concerned after the match ended that we didn't have a debriefing and hear from Gower, Dexter and Stewart. Instead they settled for the old standby of 'naughty boy nets'. That sometimes happens when the team has done badly and the management aren't sure about the best way to get them back to form and renewed confidence. So the easy option is sometimes taken to stick the players in the nets for a couple of hours. It rarely works, it's just cosmetic. That's what happened at Trent Bridge. We all stayed over after losing on the fourth day, and practised on the scheduled fifth morning, before rain drove us back into the pavilion. I'm sure one of the motives for this nets session was to toss a bone to the press, but it was a waste of time. We were shell-shocked and it would have been far more beneficial for us raw recruits to hear some experienced advice from Gower and Botham, for Dexter and Stewart to get out the video machine and go through the key periods of the match. It was all so haphazard. There had to be a better way of playing Test cricket than this. During the Australian innings there was never a concerted effort to analyse what we had done and get some constructive advice about the session to come. It was a case of sitting down, change your shirt, slurp a drink and 'Let's see how it goes, boys.' There were no discussions in the dressing-room at close of play, no dossiers on where the Aussies like to bowl or get their runs, or an assessment of their field placings. David was never a great fan of such tools, believing that a Test player should take responsibility himself – but I had no chance of that with so little experience, with my confidence ebbing away from me, session after session. I was very surprised and sad at the whole amateurish set-up of the England Test team.

Although a fantastic player, David had to be replaced as England captain. He lasted just one more Test that summer, at the Oval. I was sorry to see him lose the job, but it was inevitable. It wasn't his fault that he had lost so many good players to South Africa and that Graham Gooch was brooding about his trough of low scores, but we did need a change of direction, greater professionalism. Turning up the day before a Test match and expecting to switch on the tap may well have worked for a brilliant batsman like David, but it was no way to prepare the majority of players for representing their country. It made sense to bring in Graham Gooch as captain at that time, because we had to have some forward planning and we needed to be fitter. Test cricket was moving on fast.

I didn't know for a time whether I'd be part of that international scene after my disastrous debut. I strained my intercostal muscle during a county match after Trent Bridge and that finished me for the season. For a time, breathing was very painful and I wasn't even considered for the Oval Test. The medical opinion was that I wouldn't be fit for at least six weeks, and I started to get worried about the West Indies tour. The party would be picked early in September, so would they pass me over, especially as the rumours were that the new captain was insisting on a detailed fitness regime? After all, I hadn't exactly staked my claim in my only Test! Eventually, I got a reassuring call from Micky Stewart who said I'd be in for the Caribbean tour, as long as I could prove my fitness. By the middle of September, after a lot of swimming, I started to bowl a tennis ball, then graduated to a cricket ball – and all of a sudden I was fine. So I made the tour, to my intense relief and pleasure. Everyone said I was going as a wild card selection, to pick up experience and possibly play a Test or two, but no way was I an automatic choice. I had other ideas. Those horrendous Trent Bridge figures weren't going to be the last against my name if I could help it, and I was determined to give myself every chance to make an early impression when the tour started in January. Returning to Jamaica for the first time as a professional cricketer was a fantastic prospect, but going back to play in a Test match was really my aim.

I was very impressed by the way we prepared for that tour, heartened by the standards that Graham Gooch expected of us, and delighted that there would always be the chance to discuss our aims with a strong back-up team. I could see what Gooch was trying to do. It did go from one extreme to another, the hard work and detailed planning replacing the laid-back nature of Gower's captaincy, but it needed to be done. More knowledgeable guys than me in the England set-up knew that the Caribbean tour was the toughest one of all, and the massive fitness programme we undertook in the autumn and early winter of 1989 was essential. By the time we got to the Caribbean, we were bursting with confidence, feeling we could take on the West Indies. We were set our own individual training routines, then group programmes at the National Sports Centre at Lilleshall, and those weeks spent there really moulded us into a unit, and fostered a tremendous team spirit. The players were also sectioned off into regional areas where we worked on our cricketing skills, and here I was very lucky to be sent to Leeds. Geoffrey Boycott was in charge of the batsmen at Leeds, but he soon turned his attention to the bowlers as well. After the obligatory stuff about helping to launch my career five years earlier by missing a straight one – yes, yes Geoffrey, if you say so – he was tremendously useful. He was certainly vocal. He'd shout, 'That's crap – if you bowled that at me, I'd score a lot of roons. Get it oop his nose,' and when I did just that, he'd say, 'That's better – now that would worry me.' I didn't mind his mickey-taking, that was just his way. You could learn such a lot from Boycott; he could spot things so quickly. Michael Holding respected his technique. He used to tell me, 'I don't like bowling at Boycott, he gives you nothing,' and he certainly had that huge self-confidence and style of speaking which indicated he knew his own worth. He used to slaughter the batsmen vocally in the nets if they played a bad shot and I agree that he would have probably been too abrasive if he had been given the job of England supremo, and would have had little credibility in the dressing-room, but he was good for me in the build-up to my first England tour. Boycott was a lot more constructive with me than another tough-talking Yorkshireman a few years later. It was music to my ears to hear Boycott telling me to run in hard to the crease, not to bother about the risk of no-balls and to try knocking the batters' heads off. That's what we would face in the West Indies and he knew that because he'd been on the sharp end of it out there.

Our build-up to that West Indies tour was absolutely spot-on. Micky Stewart was in his element as coach, now that Gower had gone, and he was a lot more vocal with his ideas and fondness for detailed planning. Gooch was setting a very high standard as captain in fitness and consultation, and his top-quality batting was bound to return after his setbacks against Australia. He was just too good a player to miss out again. Mentally, we were very positive, revelling in our fitness, convinced we could make an impression early on and catch the West Indies cold. Nobody gave us a chance, which suited us. There was such a lot of media attention about the dropping from the tour of Botham and Gower that we felt the West Indies would be complacent against us at the start.

Not until the season had finished and I was certain of my place in the tour party and my fitness did the implications of that 1989 summer sink in. I had come from nowhere and endured a very harsh introduction to Test cricket, but that only made me even more determined. It was a wonderfully fulfilling feeling to look back on a five-year period that saw me go from league cricket in Sheffield to qualifying for England, then actually getting on a tour to the island where I was born, returning as an international. Now my loyalties were totally with England, and I wanted to make it not just for myself, but for all those who had shown such faith in me. I couldn't wait to get to the Caribbean.

FOUR

BREAKTHROUGH IN THE CARIBBEAN

The first few months of 1990 were the most significant so far in my short career. On my debut tour with England, I went to the West Indies as an untried fast bowler, distinctly raw around the edges, labouring under the shadow of my only, disastrous Test. I wasn't expected to be more than a back-up bowler and the best scenario would be to get into the Test series later on, accumulating some valuable practical experience of bowling against top-class batsmen and trying to put in some hostile spells that weren't too expensive. Instead I forced my way into the first Test, bowled rapidly and was then named Man of the Match in the third Test. When you consider that the first match of the series was on my home island of Jamaica, that we won it against all odds and I dismissed the great Viv Richards both times – all that was just schoolboy fantasy stuff. Within just a few days, I had gained the respect of the home supporters and the West Indies batsmen, and I didn't feel any of the inferiority experienced against the Australians the previous summer. This time, I was looking to kick the door down, I was itching to make an early, favourable impression.

Right from the start of the tour, things went well for me. The team spirit was tremendous, with all the boys rooting for each other, eating out as a group at night, talking about our aims and our tactics for the coming series. The atmosphere was supportive and professional, with the chemistry in the squad perfect. I thrived on it, and getting to bowl so soon in Jamaica meant a lot to me. We played

43

against the island in a warm-up match before the first Test at Sabina Park, and I was a little wary of the sort of welcome I was likely to get from the locals. Yet I was treated well by them in the Jamaican game, simply because I bowled very quickly in the first innings and they loved that. I bowled 24 overs of high pace, taking two for 24 and one of the locals came up to me and said, 'Hey, man, you're faster than Patterson!' Now Patrick Patterson was an occasional quickie who played for the West Indies around that time and he had been dangerously fast at Sabina Park against England four years before, on a spiteful pitch. He was obviously a bit of a local hero, but after seeing Patterson play for Lancashire in county cricket, I considered him capable of fast spells, rather than being consistently quick. So I was more than pleased to get that compliment from the locals, because I was particularly aware of how they venerate genuine fast bowlers in Jamaica. I was never going to be a Holding, with all his finesse, athleticism and accuracy, but I could make batsmen hop around a bit. So that first game against Jamaica boosted my confidence and I felt sure I'd get into the side for the first Test after that. I was also certain that I'd get some flak then from a larger crowd about being a traitor to my homeland, and absolutely positive that scores of people would be looking for tickets from me for the game. So many people kept coming up to me during the island match, saying, 'Hey, Dev, don't you remember me, we were at school together?' and all sorts of long-lost relatives turned up, claiming they'd known me all my life. All I could do was remain friendly, tell them how my family was doing and that England were going to put one over on the hot favourites in a few days' time. And we did!

Going into that famous Test, we were in great shape. Allan Lamb and Graham Gooch were reassuring figures, guys who had batted very successfully against the West Indies in the past, and we drew a lot of confidence from their presence. We were supremely fit, convinced we'd get some payback for all those winter days spent running around the fields of Lilleshall, jumping over fences, doing endless squat thrusts in the gym and running all those shuttles.

Although massive underdogs, we were quietly confident because we basically had nothing to lose and the opposition were bound to be a little complacent. There was also a bowling plan. Our management team decided that we should try to bore them out by aiming for an area just on or outside off-stump. If we bowled too straight, they'd whip us away through legside, and if we tried to bounce them, they'd hook and pull. Our bowlers were to look for nicks to the wicket-keeper or slips, or try to frustrate the batsmen, so that they played on to balls that were around off-stump – in the words of Micky Stewart, 'Get them in the corridor of uncertainty.' There was one exception among the bowlers. They told me that I should be the wild card, the one who fights fire with fire. Go for extreme pace to rattle them, and rely for accuracy and patience on Angus Fraser, Gladstone Small and David Capel. Music to my ears, just what a fast bowler needs to be told, especially when he's feeling so confident about his form and fitness. It was such a contrast to the slapdash strategy of my Test debut: this was what I imagined went on in team meetings before a Test match.

That first day of the Sabina Park Test is still so fresh in my mind. The West Indies batted first and their great opening partners, Gordon Greenidge and Desmond Haynes, went off like a train. We were getting some stick from them, and so was I down on the boundary edge. Some of the crowd were telling me in no uncertain terms that I was a traitor, that I wasn't good enough to get into the West Indies side, so I had slipped off to England to play for them instead. My understanding of the Jamaican dialect wasn't exactly an advantage then, because I knew what they were saying, and some of it was a little unpleasant. It was definitely putting me off in that first hour, but then I got lucky. I had already gifted Gordon Greenidge three runs with one of my characteristic misfields – looking at the batsmen from fine leg, as they debated a second run, taking my eye off the ball, and letting it run through my legs over the boundary. Not very clever, and my hecklers in the crowd loved that! A couple of overs later, Greenidge did it again, putting pressure on me for the second run, as I fielded the ball at long leg. I thought, 'Oh no, not again,' and I was absolutely determined that I'd get some part of my body behind the ball, to prevent another boundary. The ball banged me on the knee and rebounded two yards in front of me. They decided to take the second run at the same time as Micky Stewart shouted, 'Oh no!' A few seconds later and Micky was cheering. I sent in an Exocet of a throw to Jack Russell behind the stumps, and Greenidge was run out by a good two yards. So the secret was out at last about my fielding – I may be clumsy at times when the ball is bobbling along towards me, and I may miss a few catches, but I've always had a very strong throw. Gordon Greenidge was the first to suffer from that in a big game, but he wouldn't be the last.

After that, the West Indies went from 62 for nought to 164 all out, cracking under the pressure exerted by Angus Fraser in particular. And I got Viv Richards! The greatest batsman in my time was done by speed and some valuable advice from a former West Indies fast bowler. Earlier in the tour, I had been talking to Wes Hall, and he had suggested that if I held the ball across the seam and tried for a fast delivery, the ball wouldn't bounce but would keep low. He said it was now a myth that Caribbean wickets were full of bounce; it was more a case of unevenness and the odd ball scuttling through low. That's how I got Viv in the first innings: a bouncer with the ball held across the seam, which shot through low, leaving him plumb in front, lbw. Clearly the faster I bowled it on these uneven wickets, the more chance I had of getting one to kick off a length or scuttle through. That's why it made sense for Gooch and Stewart to give me my head and tell me just to bowl fast.

That first day couldn't really have gone better for us, and then Allan Lamb's hundred and a gutsy fifty from Robin Smith gave us a big lead to put the West Indies under real pressure. When we bowled again, it all fell in to place and I got the demon yorker working, the one that did for Boycott all those years ago. Two balls after Haynes had clipped a straight yorker away to leg for four, I got one through him and yorked him leg stump. Then I had Greenidge caught at deep cover by Nasser Hussain to leave them 87 for three and in trouble. So in walks the emperor, I V A Richards, looking as majestic and arrogant as usual. His presence alone was enough to demoralise some bowlers, but I saw it as the ultimate challenge. I was going to bowl some quick deliveries down his end, and we'd see if he regretted not wearing a helmet. Viv looked awesome as he strolled out to the wicket, as if he was going to murder someone. Afterwards, my county colleague, Ian Bishop, who was in the West Indies team, told me that no one could speak to Viv in their dressing-room that day, as he was waiting to go in to bat. He was striding up and down, chewing gum, looking fired up and ready to take the England attack apart. Bish was convinced that Viv was lining me up, that he was going to settle with this new young upstart. It was to be him or me.

Right from the off, Viv played magnificently that day. The plan of bowling on or around off-stump didn't work, because he just played some unbelievable shots, flicking good deliveries through mid-wicket. If it was bowled straighter, he would cream the ball through offside or between square leg and mid-wicket. He was starting to run away with the game, adding a rapid eighty with Carlisle Best. A couple more hours of this and we'd be in deep trouble. I came on to bowl and immediately he raised his game even further, flicking me off his toes then crashing me like a rocket to the third man boundary. I dragged one down legside and that disappeared through mid-wicket for another four. Then I pulled the yorker out of the bag, and it worked. It was quicker, it swung in a fraction, and it squeezed through bat and pad, taking the leg-stump. I couldn't believe it as the boys clambered all over me.

I was so shy and inexperienced that I didn't know how to celebrate, so I just kept my head down and smiled broadly as the rest of the team went wild. Meanwhile, up in the stand, my wife Jenny was going crazy. She had been watching the Test with two of my cousins and in the first innings, the banter had been terrific. One of the locals turned to her, noticed she was as black as him, and said, 'What you doin' supporting them, what you sittin' here for? You just wait till de Master Blaster comes out to bat!' Well, when I got Viv in the first innings and the crowd around Jenny discovered she was Mrs Malcolm, she got a lot of good-natured stick. After I got Viv again later in the match, that guy who joked with her first time around smiled at her, shook her hand and said, 'OK, mam.' It was almost an initiation ceremony, a case of 'Nuff Respect, man' and Jenny loved it. The West Indies crowd are in general the fairest and best-educated in world cricket. They want their side to win, no question, but they'll appreciate good skills from either team. You can sit in the stand among all races and have great banter with them. If an opposition player plays a good shot or bowls well, they'll applaud heartily. They love challenging cricket and if you're a fast bowler who makes their own batsmen hop around, then you get big support – as I was to learn during this Jamaica Test.

After Viv's crucial dismissal, the West Indies collapsed. I bowled Jeff Dujon when he was a little late on the back foot drive. He got an inside edge onto middle and leg stumps, and it was a great sight to see that fine player on his way. I ended up with four for 77 – the useful quartet of Haynes, Greenidge, Richards and Dujon – and we needed just 41 to win. Only the weather could stop us now, and for a time it threatened to do so. On that third night of the match, I just couldn't sleep. It was raining. Every hour, I'd go out onto the balcony, looking for the stars, but they were obscured by rain clouds. The next day, there was no play. There was now a distinct possibility that the final day would be affected by rain. We were now very concerned. On that fifth morning, Micky Stewart played a blinder for us by getting down to the ground four hours before the scheduled start. He had suspected that perhaps the groundstaff might not be particularly keen to get things mopped up, because that would ensure a defeat for the West Indies. Micky was chivvying them along, suggesting they should start mopping-up operations as soon as possible, and basically standing over them till they set to work. In the end, we started on time and, with sawdust around some parts of the square, we won a famous victory by nine wickets just before lunch.

That was the cue for the best party of my life. Allan Lamb had been appointed our entertainments manager for the tour and he set up a brilliant celebration at our hotel, a mile away from the ground. Amid all the telephone calls and faxes, a lot of drink was consumed, music blared out for hours and our wives and girlfriends joined us in the team room for a long party. I've got a photo of Jenny dancing on the table with Rob Bailey, who had the cheek to tell me afterwards that she was a far better mover than me! It's such a great feeling when the team does well, but the extra pleasure also comes if you do well personally. Only, though, if you win; it can be hollow to reflect on individual achievement when you haven't won the match. That's why Jamaica 1990 will always be so special for me. I'd gone back to Jamaica to play for my adopted country, won the knockers over by some hostile fast bowling, dismissed Viv Richards twice, and in front of my family and so many Jamaican friends, we had beaten the West Indies. One of my old school cricket coaches, Dr Bennett, had come up to me during the game and said I was the first from St Elizabeth Technical School to play Test cricket and I was very touched that he was so proud about that. It had been a memorable few days in Jamaica.

After that, it was a huge anti-climax when we flew to Guyana. Not a ball was bowled in the five days scheduled for the Georgetown Test, even though it was bright and sunny during the day. The problem was the deluge of rain every night! It was very frustrating, because we were very keen to get at the West Indies as soon as possible, before they regrouped and came back strongly at us. Yet we did work constructively at our fitness in Guyana, topping up our training and working on our stamina instead of hitting catches. It helped stave off boredom, and gave us a second wind. By the time we came to the third Test in Trinidad, I was raring to go again, with extra fuel in the tank.

I bowled 46 overs in that third Test, in some of the most sapping heat I can ever remember. One day I sent down 24 overs, guzzling down bottles of water to combat the dehydration from the heat. The

49

fitness work in Guyana certainly stood me in good stead as I took ten wickets in the match. I was named Man of the Match and I relished being given the responsibility of being the strike bowler, but it wasn't the same as Jamaica because we didn't win. We deserved to, and would have done so had it not been for the rain that held us up when we were easing comfortably on the last day to a target of 151. We'd got a great start, at four an over, when Gooch had his hand broken by Ezra Moseley, which not only put him out of the innings, but also the rest of the tour. Yet only Micky Stewart and our physio, Lawrie Brown knew that during the tense final day. When Goochie came back from hospital, he put his pads on, apparently ready to bat again if needed. We found out later that he'd decided to do that to help keep our morale up, and to make the opposition think he wasn't so hurt after all. It was obvious that the West Indies rightly rated him highly, and they kept looking over to our viewing area in the dressing-room to check that our captain was still in his whites and if he was padded up or not. It was only after we got back to the hotel that the rest of us found out just how serious that injury was.

In the end, we fell short of the target because the rain had lopped off precious hours on the final day. It got too dark and Desmond Haynes did his best to thwart us with some blatant gamesmanship. Dessie was stand-in captain at Port-of-Spain because Viv Richards was ill, and he certainly had no intention of harming his long-term ambitions for the job by losing to us. The groundstaff did exceptionally well to get the ground playable after all that rain, and certainly conditions weren't good for the fielding side when we went out again. There could only be one winner, so Dessie did his best to slow things down. At one stage, they bowled just nine overs in an hour, which was ridiculous – although to be fair, it was still very wet in the area where the fast bowlers were running. They, of course, made it look impossibly wet, and kept stopping to check their spikes and how much sawdust had been sprinkled. It got very frustrating. They escaped with a draw as the light closed in, but I honestly don't blame Haynes all that much. He captained within the rules, if not the spirit of the game and if the positions had been reversed, we'd have probably done the same. We might have forced ourselves to bowl maybe another two overs per hour more than them, but that's all.

The biggest frustration, though, stemmed from the fact that we ought to have wrapped up the game before that final day. On the first morning, we had them 29 for five, then 103 for eight, but they rallied to 198. Gus Logie ended up making 98, but just after he came in, he nicked me outside the off-stump, a regulation catch to Wayne Larkins at first slip. But Jack Russell moved across him and somehow dropped it. Jack was as astonished as everyone else, but it was a vital miss. On the second day, we took too long to score our runs – just 146 in the day – and although we weren't to know it was going to rain later, we did use up valuable time in building up our lead. Even then, it was only a lead of 89 and Greenidge and Haynes soon wiped that out, putting on 98 for the first wicket. Then I suddenly found the range and fired out three batsmen in four balls in the same over. Haynes was caught in the gully, Carlisle Best lbw and Jeff Dujon bowled, both to ones that scuttled through low. With Greenidge going lbw to Gus Fraser, they were now, in effect, 11 for four. That was a furiously fast over from me, the rhythm was perfect and the tip from Wes Hall about putting the fingers across the seam had claimed Best and Dujon.

Their middle order did well to stick it out after that, chiselling out precious runs to set us some sort of a target, but we were very confident before the rains came. A genuine hard-luck story, Trinidad. We were so disappointed not to have won that the reaction was muted when I was named Man of the Match soon after the close. There wasn't a smile from any of the boys, nor from me, because that was an opportunity missed. We would then have been 2–0 up, with two to play and all the psychological bonuses coming our way. The order from our entertainments manager Allan Lamb would have been 'Crack on boys, party, party, party!' Instead, they had got away with it, and we had lost our captain and best player for the series. Amid all the disappointment, I was obviously chuffed to have taken fifteen wickets in two Tests. I felt I'd justified England's faith in me after the horrors of Trent Bridge, and my confidence was soaring. Inspired by the Caribbean atmosphere and the love of bouncers, I could sense a buzz of positive encouragement for me everywhere. All of a sudden, the West Indian players and selectors were talking about us with respect. They had treated us to two successive 5–0 thrashings a few years earlier and a 4–0 hiding the previous time in 1988. This series, there would be no 'Blackwash' as their supporters called it, and we could still win the series.

In the end, we just ran out of luck at Barbados and fatigue had got to us by the time we were easily rolled over in Antigua. So we lost the series 2–1, but not before we made a great fight of it in Barbados. We were without Graham Gooch, and Angus Fraser's damaged rib also kept him out, while they had Viv Richards back in the fray, snorting defiance and looking for revenge against me in particular. He got that, but not before one of those maddening captaincy decisions that I came to experience far too often. It happened on the first day, when Viv came in at 108 for three. It's no exaggeration to say that the series was now in the balance. If we could get him out quickly, the psychological impetus would be massively tilted our way, but if the great man stayed in for any length of time, his rapid rate of scoring and massive influence on the rest of his team would count against us. Viv was undoubtedly under pressure at this stage. He had been the losing captain at Sabina Park, and now he was back in the side at last after illness, needing to lead from the front. Losing this series to England was unthinkable to home supporters, and to Viv Richards. So when Viv and I squared up to each other on that first afternoon, it was clearly a trial of strength. There would be no draw in this personal contest. He had obviously been pumped up by the feeling that I had so far had the upper hand against him, getting him twice in Jamaica. One placard at the ground had said 'Doctor Malcolm – he has de formula against Viv', not something I'd ever agree with, but just another little way to get the great man fired up.

Almost as soon as he came in, Viv hit me for eighteen in one over.

Sounds a one-sided contest, except he could have easily been out three times in that over. I knew he'd take me on if I bounced him, and he went for it with a top-edged hook that just plopped over the boundary for six, with Alec Stewart stranded on the edge, the ball just clearing his head. He then mistimed another hook, and it went over the head of our wicket-keeper Jack Russell. It would have been an easy catch for anyone in the long-stop position, but Jack, running back with his pads on, couldn't quite get to it. Then a carbon copy of the top edge to Stewart out at deep square leg, and again the ball just cleared him. If the wicket had been pitched one strip further towards the Kensington Stand, Viv would have been caught the first time by Alec. I could have had Viv at any time in that over, because he was playing rashly, overdosing on adrenalin. We needed to get him before he settled down, took fresh guard and picked us off. Instead, my captain Allan Lamb took me off immediately. I was dismayed. He'd taken too much notice of eighteen runs being conceded in that over, rather than the lucky way those runs had been made. Viv was still vulnerable, but Lamby didn't understand that. Another eighteen runs in my next over wouldn't have mattered all that much, and then he'd be perfectly entitled to take me off. The important thing was to get Viv out cheaply, and at that time I had the best chance because I had got under his skin. We both recognised the pride involved in that personal duel and it was nipped in the bud through unimaginative captaincy. It was a scenario that was to become depressingly familiar to me during my England career.

So Viv settled in, made 70, Carlisle Best got a big hundred and they made 446. I didn't bowl at all well in my later spells, ending up with nought for 142, going for four an over. Even then we could have saved the Test, because we were only 88 behind on first innings. Then Dessie Haynes got a hundred and set up a bad final hour for us on the fourth evening. From his position in the slips, Viv Richards was convinced that Rob Bailey had been caught down the legside off a short ball by Curtly Ambrose which had brushed the batsman's hip. The West Indies captain appealed vociferously to umpire Lloyd

Barker, who gave the batsman out. It was a poor decision, especially as the umpire was heading off to square leg after the ball had been delivered – and then turned round to give Rob out after Viv's excitable appeal that saw him rush up from slip. That was unsavoury, desperately hard luck for a player drafted into the England side through Gooch's injury. We ended that fourth day at 15 for three, looking down the barrel and feeling annoyed.

Again we showed our character on that final day, losing with just a few minutes to go in fading light. Robin Smith and Jack Russell almost saved us with a defiant, brave effort that saw us through to the second new ball. Enter Curtly Ambrose. Jack had batted for five hours until Ambrose bowled him with an unplayable delivery, a grubber that just shot along the ground. Ambrose had suddenly found his line on a deteriorating pitch, and the ball started to keep alarmingly low. We were simply swept aside by a great bowler who took the last five wickets in five overs. Poor Robin was left high and dry at the end, with just a couple of overs left in the gloom. So near. We didn't have the best of luck on that tour, and those Trinidad and Barbados experiences summed that up.

Then it was back to the hotel in Barbados, to pack up everything and fly off with our families that night to Antigua for the last Test, which was due to start in 36 hours' time. That was no way to prepare for an international sporting encounter at the end of a long and tiring tour. We only managed a quick look at the wicket the next day before dragging ourselves away for some rest. The force was with the West Indies now. They'd hauled themselves back in the series, while we were shell-shocked after coming so close to saving the Barbados Test. We were missing the injured Fraser and Gooch, and the minds as well as bodies were tired. The writing was on the wall, and after being bowled out cheaply, we had to watch Greenidge and Haynes put on a little matter of 298 for the first wicket. I had the consolation of getting Viv for the third time in six innings. I charged in, letting him believe I was going to let him have the bouncer, but pitched it up instead. It was a case of banking that he'd be on the back foot, waiting for the bouncer and he was. Viv adjusted just a little late and he pushed the ball in the air to mid-off for a pleasing dismissal. Not all of my wickets have come through brute force!

When we batted again, we were put through the mincer by Ambrose and Bishop. Robin Smith had his right forefinger broken, Allan Lamb chipped a bone in his elbow, and we just couldn't withstand the onslaught. As a fast bowler, there were no complaints from me about their hostility, we would have done the same if we could have raised the gallop. Quite simply, we had hit the wall and the innings defeat was a formality. There was no disgrace in losing the series, it was simply a case of running out of luck at key times. At least we had competed hard with them in all but the last Test, and that hadn't been the case for more than a decade. We had given them a fright.

We'd also had a lot of laughs along the way. Graham Gooch and Micky Stewart were very positive about developing a good team spirit – you'd call it 'bonding' nowadays – and we all laughed at, as well as with each other. My batting and fielding lapses kept the boys amused. Just before the Jamaica Test, Micky was taking fielding practice and I wasn't acquitting myself all that well, much to the coach's exasperation. He was hitting the ball up into the clear blue sky and I wasn't shaping up too confidently. The old co-ordination wasn't at its smoothest, and all the other guys would stop to watch my efforts, waiting for a good laugh. Then I pulled out of one high catch because the sun was in my eyes and Micky shouted: 'Dev, get the other side of the sun!' I shouted back, 'How can I do that – it's fifty million miles away!' That floored everybody, including a gobsmacked Micky, and he called a halt to that particular fielding session. I gave the boys another good laugh when we got to Trinidad and I compiled one of my major innings. We were playing the President's XI, and when I went in as last man, Robin Smith was in the seventies. I was absolutely determined to see Robin to his hundred that day, and it went well for a time. Robin kept saying, 'OK, Dev, just face one or two balls an over and we'll be fine.' I was rather enjoying this batting lark, playing cat and mouse with the fielders until Robin chipped one away to get the strike at the end of the over. Unfortunately, he hit it just with enough force to get to the boundary, and the fielder escorted the ball over the ropes. So Robin got another four, but not the strike. The next over to be bowled to me was from Patrick Patterson, the Jamaican known for some rather rapid spells. But I was feeling fairly confident by now – after all we'd added 24, and I'd got Robin to 99 not out. Just play out this over and he'll get his hundred, no problem. I blocked the first ball and Robin was clearly very pleased with that. 'You can rely on me, mate,' I reassured him. The next one I missed, but survived. The third was steered with some confidence by me to the third man boundary and Robin was very reassured. 'Rely on me, mate, I'll get you there.' The fifth delivery was met by an immaculate defensive stroke, and I could see my partner heave a sigh of relief. Just one ball to go. For some reason, I took a huge swing and my middle peg was knocked out of the ground. I have absolutely no idea why I did such a stupid thing and I couldn't apologise enough to my partner as he walked back, stranded on 99. I told him I'd carry his bags for the rest of the tour, and that one day, I'd make amends when it was more important. Six months later, I did just that. We put on sixty for the last wicket at Old Trafford against India and Robin ended up 121 not out, with strong support from my 13. I kept saying, 'This time, mate, I won't let you down – this is a Test hundred, and it'll mean much more to you.' One of the game's great gentlemen, Robin Smith and he didn't even complain when I had a few daft wafts before he reached the landmark.

Anyway, England were more interested in my fast bowling in 1990 and I was very happy with my performance in the Caribbean. I came home with my confidence very high, although I was tired. On the tour, I'd bowled more first-class overs than anyone else and more in the Test series than any bowler on either side, with the exception of Ian Bishop, who managed one extra over. Our management seemed happy to have a strike bowler with a heavy workload and I wasn't complaining, because I've always wanted to bowl. I've never tossed the ball back to the captain, saying I had a little twinge. That's a matter of pride to me, you just have to keep going. The batsman doesn't step on his wicket when he's just reached a hundred in a Test, so the bowler shouldn't pull the ladder up at any time. At Sabina Park and Port-of-Spain, I bowled quicker than any of the West Indies boys, and I remember the reaction from Desmond Haynes in Trinidad when I was into a particularly rapid spell. Richie Richardson was getting some fierce deliveries from me, and as I walked past Haynes at the non-striker's end, I saw him gesture to Richardson as if to say 'You can't do anything about this, just hang on in there.' That gave me a great boost, I knew then that they had been rattled by me. It was also tremendous to have Gus Fraser at the other end to me in Jamaica and Trinidad, and I really missed his steadiness when he didn't play in the last two Tests because of his rib injury. I've always enjoyed having Gus as the foil, because his nagging accuracy has definitely helped get me wickets from frustrated batsmen.

So, at the advanced age of 27, I'd established myself in the England side. Or had I? Many experts were predicting that Fraser's control and my pace would be the bedrock of our attack for a few years to come after that 1990 Caribbean tour, but it wasn't to be. Poor Gus suffered some serious injuries before a hugely successful return on the 1998 West Indies tour, while I came to be categorised as a high-risk case, dangerous some days but too erratic at other times. I didn't know it, of course, but my first England tour was to prove the most fulfilling and happy of them all.

FIVE

DOUBTS CREEP IN

Within a week of returning from the Caribbean, I was playing a Sunday League game for Derbyshire. I didn't mind, hard work was no problem to me, and I felt that I was on a hot streak, very keen to build on my good tour. Having taken 19 wickets in four Tests, at a strike rate of one every seven overs, I was being hailed as the new star bowler. England had been desperate for a consistent fast bowler since Bob Willis retired and the general feeling in 1990 was that I was the best bet. The word was that I was going to make a lot of money through endorsements as the latest big name in English cricket, but that never materialised. It might have been so if we had actually won that West Indies series, but I wasn't bothered about all the fringe benefits in any case. I never had an agent and the only endorsement I've had over the years has been for ankle supports – hardly glamorous! My aim was not to make pots of money, but to stay in the England side. After just one good series, there was no way I was likely to forget the traumas of my England debut, and think I'd finally arrived in the big time, there to stay for years. Subsequent events proved my scepticism to be correct. I played in all six Tests for England in the 1990 summer, taking 22 wickets against New Zealand and India, but that proved to be a flattering summer for my Test career. After that, I never played an entire Test series at home. Within a year, I was out of the England side and the practice of wheeling me out for particular grounds had started. By then, I was having misgivings about the way my captain, Graham Gooch, was handling me.

It was exciting to play on all the Test grounds in 1990 for the first time. Of course, I had practical experience of them from county cricket, but the big occasion and the large crowds made it a totally different challenge. Yet I was strangely disappointed with Lord's when I made my Test debut there, against New Zealand. It was a magnificent feeling to walk through the Long Room, past the members, and then onto the pitch. The feeling of cricket history was certainly inspiring, but the atmosphere when we got out into the middle was anti-climactic. It was muted, the spectators were too disciplined, almost as if the game's history was weighing too heavily on everyone at the ground. It was all too gentlemanly, too restrained, in contrast to the buzz I had experienced on the Caribbean grounds. I also played at the Oval that year for England, and that quickly became my favourite home ground – for the lively atmosphere and the bouncy wickets that favour strokeplayers and attacking bowlers. It's significant that my best performances for England have come at the Oval, because that's where I feel most comfortable as a fast bowler. You get what you put in on those pitches, it's a fair contest between bat and ball. And it's more uninhibited, the crowd tends to get behind you more spontaneously. It's too genteel at Lord's for me, even though I respect it as the home of cricket. It counts against England, though. I'm sure that one of the reasons why we have such a poor record there is because overseas sides raise their game at Lord's and we lack vociferous support.

In the New Zealand series at the start of the summer, I did well, taking fifteen wickets at seventeen apiece, bowling with hostility on slow pitches. At Lord's, I sent down 43 overs, more than anyone else in the innings, took five for 94 and in the process, cracked Trevor Franklin so hard on the head that he ended up bleeding. I was pleased by that delivery, because I was proving that I could get more bounce than anyone else, even on slow wickets. There was never any intention on my part to hurt Franklin, but I had no worries about seeing the blood; he had a helmet and all the appropriate protective equipment, so why should a fast bowler be inhibited about trying to get one past his nose? The opposition fast bowlers I'd watched since my entry into Test cricket didn't stand on ceremony. It's a hard game and I wasn't concerned about hitting someone with a legitimate delivery. I'm certain Graham Gooch was very happy to see one of his fast bowlers dishing out the treatment for a change.

In the Edgbaston Test, I bowled 49 overs in the game, including a spell when I bowled all but one over from one end through an entire session. I wasn't bothered about the hard work, and taking eight wickets in that Test was the justification for all those overs. I also collected a 'pair', but the second nought was a special one. I was the last victim in Test cricket of Sir Richard Hadlee, who retired straight afterwards. I can honestly say that it was an honour to be dismissed by one of my favourite bowlers, a gentleman and a consistently superb performer. Sir Richard was taken aback, though, when I approached him with my pen and a run chart afterwards. Some fan had sent me a scoring chart of my two innings, even though I hadn't troubled the scorers either time, and Sir Richard was highly amused to sign the second innings details. I've got it hanging up on a wall at home, a treasured item because of the Hadlee connection. You've got to laugh at yourself, haven't you?

Not that I found the Indian series a laughing matter later that summer. The wickets were ridiculously flat, with the batsmen on both sides cashing in. In just three Tests, fifteen hundreds were scored, including that amazing 333 at Lord's by Graham Gooch. In that Test, I didn't bowl till the final hour on the second day, and the fantastic food laid on in the players' dining-room by the legendary Nancy Doyle was greatly appreciated by the England bowlers after we had seen the placid nature of the pitch. The cry went up 'I'll have the Spotted Dick, Nancy – with custard – and some ice cream as well, please!' It was a case of checking with Micky Stewart when we were going to declare, because I needed at least an hour's notice after the indulgences at Nancy's dining table. No wonder Mike Gatting never left Middlesex – if he hadn't played county cricket at Lord's, and enjoyed Nancy's cooking for so long, he would have been two stones lighter! Seriously, though, that Indian series wasn't a fair contest between bowlers and batsmen. It was one of the hardest I've experienced, because the pitches were so dead. It was like playing abroad. I couldn't work out why they were prepared so much in the batsmen's favour. The Indians must have thought they were playing at home; they didn't have a fast bowler, so why didn't we green them up to favour our seamers? When we play Tests abroad, the pitches are never made to suit us, it's always slanted in favour of the home side. That doesn't seem to be the case in England. Are we perhaps too gentlemanly about such matters?

That summer, Graham Gooch was head and shoulders above any other batsman, and he was now installed as the obvious man to lead England to Australia later that year. To my mind, he hadn't put a foot wrong in the Caribbean, getting the preparations absolutely right, delegating certain matters to Micky Stewart and Allan Lamb, fostering an excellent team spirit, leading by personal example until that cruel hand injury in Trinidad. By the end of the 1990 summer, he had solidified his power base, and the doubts about his captaincy credentials in the wake of David Gower's sacking had faded inside a year. Yet I was starting to have my own doubts about him. It all started at the Oval, straight after the one-day international when we beat New Zealand comfortably. I had picked up the Man of the Match award, taking two for 19 off eleven overs, bowling with lot of fire and pace on a bouncy, even wicket that I would have loved to carry around with me for the rest of my international career. Everything went right for me that day, as I peppered my old Derbyshire colleague, John Wright, and the rest of the batsmen decided simply to block me out. If they tried to play forcing shots, they couldn't lay a bat on me. The other bowlers went for a few in their allotted overs – Chris Lewis for 51, Gladstone Small for 59, Phil DeFreitas for 47 – while I conceded just 19 runs. Afterwards, when he was interviewed on television, Gooch was asked about my bowling and he answered 'Dev had the radar in the right place today.' Nothing else. I expected more from my captain than just grudging praise. He should have been more positive, more publicly supportive, rather than trotting out the 'radar' line that was to become a millstone around my neck whenever I bowled badly or expensively. If he had reservations about me as a one-day bowler, he ought to have expressed them to me privately and we could have talked as constructively as we all did in the Caribbean just a few months earlier. I started to get the feeling that Goochie didn't trust me as a bowler, and over the next three years I was proved right. I resented being categorised as someone who was too risky to play in one-dayers. Derbyshire had started to play me more often in such games, because they realised that a strike bowler's ability to knock over the dangerous early batsmen can be invaluable. If you get ten batsmen out cheaply in a one-day game, you're probably going to win. Although Kim Barnett understood that, Graham Gooch appeared dubious about my value in one-day games. So the cliché about 'Devon's radar' was born and I've never been able to shake it off.

By the time we had come back from Australia and New Zealand in the spring of '91, I had lost a little more respect for Graham Gooch, and I wasn't the only one in the squad. We were badly beaten by the Aussies in the Tests, played poorly in the one-dayers against the New Zealanders, and at the end of the tour, Goochie looked to be at the end of his tether. His philosophy of hard work and then more hard work hadn't paid off this time. He was right about that approach in the Caribbean, but got it all out of perspective in Australia. It was the most gruelling of all my England tours, lasting four months, with an amazing amount of travelling across a vast continent. We had a crowded itinerary, a prolonged heatwave – and we weren't playing well. We'd be carted from Perth to Tasmania to Brisbane, sometimes suffering a drop in temperature of around forty degrees, and then you're straight into a Test match. Stress and fatigue leads to injuries and it was significant that we suffered so many on that tour. We compromised on so many things, like agreeing to play in one-day internationals in between some Tests, just because it suited the Australian Board's desire to make money. We wondered just how much the Test and County Cricket Board fought that itinerary on our behalf. Take the period between the fourth Test at Adelaide and the fifth at Perth. The Adelaide Test ended on the final day after a tense run chase by us ended in a draw and that night – 29 January 1991 – we flew out to Perth. We were diverted via Alice Springs because of an airline dispute, and when we arrived at Perth, the temperature was still 35 degrees centigrade, at one o'clock in the morning. Later that day, Goochie had us practising in 45 degree heat while officials at the ground were telling us that the Test might be delayed due to the overwhelming weather conditions. I bowled three overs out in the middle that day and they killed me off. It was the hottest I ever felt and here we were, practising in a sauna. What was that about Mad Dogs and Englishmen? Two days later, the Perth Test started and predictably we got rolled over, because there was nothing left, we were out on our feet. The management had barely give us a day off on the entire tour, unaware that the cycle of fatigue leads to injuries, then to defeats and on to a demoralised squad. The psychology was all wrong. Micky Stewart should have reined in Goochie, but they were too similar in outlook, too committed to hard work as the answer to all our ills.

That tour was billed as a clash of philosophies between Gooch and David Gower, who had deservedly regained his place as a player. But it was too simplistic to see it as Roundhead versus Cavalier. Certainly David made it quite clear that he felt we were being overworked, that we needed some free, recuperative periods, but he wasn't alone in that. Many of us who had been in the Caribbean and approved of the disciplined approach and would still go through a brick wall for Goochie, nevertheless felt the captain was now guilty of over-emphasis. His philosophy was 'We're not playing well, so we'll just have to keep working even harder until we start to play better,' but that felt like 'naughty boy nets'. We needed some outside influence to break the monopoly of Stewart-Gooch wisdom. It was a case of train, travel and play with no time to take a step back and work out where we were going wrong.

We just didn't pull in the same direction, and you have to blame the management for that. Mind you, that Tiger Moth incident involving David Gower and Johnny Morris was ill-advised. It may have been David's attempt at rebellion against the hard-line regime as we entered our third month, but it could have backfired. It came between the third and fourth Tests and I'm convinced that if it had happened earlier in the tour, both players would have been sent home. We had no idea that the plane which buzzed over our ground contained two of our players. We were all sitting watching our innings, with the management alongside, and when we later discovered that David had borrowed the money for the flight from our unsuspecting manager, Peter Lush, we knew he was in trouble. At that stage of the tour, I was travelling with Johnny, my county team-mate, and after the day's play ended, I hung around the ground for ages, waiting to go back to the hotel with him. He pitched up with David Gower and apologised, saying, 'We've just been back to pose for some photos. Did you see the Tiger Moth buzz you? It was us up there!' Johnny obviously thought it a great laugh, and on the way back to the hotel I pointed out he was for the high jump. 'Think about your family if that plane had crashed, think about how the management are going to view it. They'll see it as you two taking the mickey out of them.' Johnny went quiet. He'd been gullible. As a fringe batsman, this was no way to stake his claims for a place in the side. The £1,000 fine he collected for the Tiger Moth prank could easily have been topped up by expulsion from the tour. He hadn't helped himself on tour even before that incident. Johnny was very impressionable towards David Gower, not only admiring his ability enormously but also David's fondness for a good time, some rest and recuperation. That ignored the fact that David was still a top player and naturally fit – he'd glide over the ground beautifully and beat you over a short distance in the sprints, because he was just a natural athlete. None of the other players apart from the captain begrudged David his laid-back approach, because he was so obviously a marvellous player. Johnny, on the other hand, was inclined to fleshiness and couldn't afford to be like Gower if he wanted to impress this particular management. Yet he never saw that. David's champagne image appealed to Johnny, and even on the flight over from England, he was grilling David about the best types of wine to drink. When we settled down in Australia, he used to quiz David about where he'd be eating that night, because he knew the wines would be good. David didn't lead him astray at all, Johnny did that for himself, failing to understand that the England captain deserved his lifestyle because he delivered at the highest level and was still a fantastic player.

The worst thing for Johnny Morris's career was to be picked for that Australian tour, because his gullibility led to a black spot that stayed with him. He should have been picked for the 'A' tour to Pakistan and Sri Lanka, where the social distractions would have been less plentiful and he could have knuckled down to learning about international cricket. There was absolutely no doubt that Johnny had the talent to be a genuine Test batsman. He was a brilliant batsman on his day, one of the best English players of fast bowling in my era. Time after time in the Derbyshire nets, he'd take on Holding, Bishop and myself and never flinched, giving us some real hammer. Like Gower and Gooch, he saw the ball early, so fast bowling held no terrors for him. I can't forget his double hundred at Cheltenham, when he climbed into Courtney Walsh, making him look like a club bowler, on a fast, bouncy wicket. Johnny liked to show off a little at the crease, making it clear he felt they couldn't bowl at him, but he believed that cockiness had got him where he was. At times, though, he went over the top and it rebounded on him. When he left Derbyshire for Durham in 1993, I was sad because that was his way of writing off his international chances by opting for the financial comfort zone. Yet he had done that two years earlier when he climbed into that Tiger Moth with David Gower. A pity – he was an ideal number three batsman, and one of the major losses to English cricket during my career. Johnny Morris was that good.

There were other times when we didn't help ourselves on that

Australian tour. Allan Lamb's trip to the casino during the Brisbane Test wasn't a great idea, when you consider he was one of the overnight not-out batsmen. When he was out in the first over the following morning, it looked an even worse idea. Not that Lamby was out late, or had drunk much, but you have to give yourself every chance when you're playing for England, otherwise the press will be after you, and I don't blame them for that. Lamby's crucial dismissal after his casino visit led to a collapse from 42 for one to 114 all out, after we had led by 42 in the first innings. We lost by ten wickets and Lamby's little trip was bound to make headlines, and so it did. It was typical of the daft things that have happened on England tours during my time in the game. What about Lamby missing a Test on that tour because he had torn a calf muscle in Ballarat, jogging back to the team hotel just after scoring a magnificent hundred? Crazy – hadn't he done enough physical work for the day, batting in the heat for three hours? He'd done exactly the same thing earlier in the year in the West Indies, again missing a Test. We did make things difficult for ourselves. On the field in Australia, we kept letting our guard down when we had a chance of victory. After handing the Brisbane Test over on a plate, we went to Melbourne and lost it in one session, going from 103 for one to 150 all out. We should have batted Australia out of the game, but they coasted home by eight wickets – a margin that flattered them, but flattened us.

When we had the chance to win the third Test in Sydney we blew it, and the captain was badly at fault here. On the final day, they were hanging on for dear life, with Greg Matthews gutsing it out, supported by Carl Rackemann, a tail-ender in my category. Phil Tufnell bowled over after over at them, and they were resisting quite comfortably. I was desperate for a bowl, convinced I'd blow away Rackemann so that we could get in again and knock off the required runs. I did all my exercises in the field, trying to drop heavy hints to Goochie, but he ignored me. Finally, he brought me on. I took the new ball immediately and bowled Rackemann with the sixth ball of my first over. It was too late, however, and we didn't have enough time to win. I was so frustrated: surely a strike bowler is used for the purpose of blasting away the tail when the spinners are being blocked? Gooch's delay in calling me up was to be repeated many times in subsequent Tests by both him and Mike Atherton. Neither seemed to have that killer instinct, the awareness of when to move in for the kill. You can end up losing a Test by a huge margin, but often the balance is altered in just twenty minutes or so by a decisive bowling spell. If you can keep your nerve, and don't opt for the preconceived strategy, you can shape a game your way if you have that in-built antennae telling you when you must go on the offensive. I haven't been lucky enough to enjoy such enlightened captaincy with England, so that often I have been used at the wrong times and ignored when the game was in the balance.

Our performance on that tour was summed up in the last Test at Perth when we subsided from 191 for two to 244 all out, to lose by nine wickets. We were physically shattered and they ran us off our feet in typical hard-nosed Australian fashion. Their winning stroke was a little push to square leg by David Boon that was just a single to any other batting side. They got two from it. That's why I love playing against the Australians. They try to stretch you, grind you down, then run you ragged. So when you manage to beat them, it means a lot. I don't buy this notion that they take the foot off the gas at the end of a series that they have won, leading to victories for us at the Oval in '93 and '97. They don't know any different way to play the game, they never coast. How about crediting the winners instead in those circumstances?

Immediately after we lost the Perth Test, Graham Gooch climbed into his own players in the press conference. He said that some players should be looking hard at their own performances, hinting at lack of commitment and pride. The Aussie press loved that, but our captain lost some respect from his squad for going public. We didn't need to be told how badly we had played, but there were extenuating circumstances – one of them the management's obsession with hard work to cure all our ills. It was a damaging accusation to suggest that some of the players didn't care enough. He used to say on that tour, 'Remember you're playing for England', as if we needed reminding. He was the one happy enough to go to South Africa in 1982 when he was England's regular opening batsman, so it was a bit rich to hammer the patriotic point at us. He should have saved that criticism for the team room, where we could have thrashed out our problems and shortcomings. Instead we just ran around aimlessly, with little planning or organisation. No player on that tour will ever agree that the major problem was the deteriorating relationship between Gower and Gooch. The heart of the matter was that our management's approach was ill-judged, short-sighted and unintelligent, and the captain must take overall responsibility for that.

By the time I got back home from Australia, even this willing workhorse was out on his feet. I now understood just how hard international cricket can be if you want to stay in the side. From January 1990 to February 1991, it had been almost non-stop cricket apart from a few weeks at the end of the English season and the ritual of airport-hotel-ground was becoming a familiar one. My sixteen Test wickets in the Australia series must have looked horribly expensive at 41 apiece, but with Gus Fraser suffering a serious hip injury and Gladstone Small losing his control and penetration, I had to put in a lot of overs. I averaged 25 an innings, bowled fifty overs more than any other bowler on either side and a hundred more overs than any other team-mate in first-class matches. That's not a complaint from me, because I believe you should always be there for your captain, but when my detractors look at my high average in Tests, they might consider how often I was used as a stock bowler, as well as a strike bowler.

There seemed to be some confusion about my role at the end of the Australia tour and I had definitely lost confidence compared to a year earlier. I felt that Gooch no longer thought I was the answer as his strike bowler and I was disturbed at his lack of positive support on the field when things were tough. If ever I got clattered to the boundary, he'd be looking at the ground, with his arms folded, muttering to himself and kicking the ground irritably. That's the last thing a suffering bowler wants to see, because the batsman gets a boost when he sees the captain and fast bowler at odds with each other. You need the skipper walking back with you, or strong vocal encouragement – something like 'Come on, let him have it!' – anything to lift your spirits. Goochie probably believed that some of the dross I bowled would have suited him down to the ground if he'd been the opening batsman, but you don't have to show that. It may sound cosmetic, but so much of cricket at the highest level is played in the mind and you need every scrap of support you can get.

After just two Tests against the West Indies in the 1991 summer, I was dropped for the first time in my England career, after seventeen successive Tests and sixty wickets. Since then, I have been expendable, getting wheeled out at certain grounds in England on the 'horses for courses' principle. It hurt to miss out for the first time at that Trent Bridge Test, although the papers had clearly been given a massive steer by our management. On the first morning of the Test, 95 per cent of the papers said categorically that I would be stood down in favour of David Lawrence. I wish we'd both been picked, because it would have been lovely to fight fire with fire at both ends, but sadly 'Syd' and I never played in the same England side. The following winter he picked up that horrific knee injury in New Zealand and was never the same again, poor guy. I suppose the England selectors felt that they couldn't afford two 'wild cards' with the new ball, but it would have been fun getting the batters hopping around. Of course, I felt I was faster than 'Syd', but then I would, wouldn't I?

I suppose I couldn't really complain about being dropped, because I hadn't started the series very well. A shoulder injury picked up in Australia had hampered me in the first month, and I didn't bowl well in the Leeds Test, where Viv Richards got after me with some blazing strokes. I went for five an over in that first innings; then at Lord's, where I really felt under pressure for my place, I was lacklustre on a slow pitch, going for four an over, but left frustrated in the second innings. Then all of a sudden, everything clicked into gear, my pace and rhythm returned and I got Richie Richardson straight away. I was feeling better than for some time when it began to rain. We never got back on and I was now vulnerable. So the chop didn't come as a great surprise, although the surrounding publicity about my England status did.

First of all, I got some undeserved stick for missing out on Derbyshire's match against the West Indies immediately after the Leeds Test. It came from an interesting quarter. Jonathan Agnew was the new BBC Cricket Correspondent, who also had landed a job with a tabloid newspaper in his first year with the media after retiring from playing for Leicestershire. He took me to task, saying that I should be playing for Derbyshire after the way I'd bowled in the Leeds Test. Now no one needed to tell me about the standard of my bowling at Leeds, but it was a bit rich coming from Agnew. I cast my mind back to the first game I ever saw in first-class cricket, back in 1984. Derbyshire's Bruce Roberts had hammered Leicestershire's attack which included Agnew, who proceeded to put on an amazing display of histrionics out in the middle. He sat down several times, moaned, waved his arms around, making it quite clear that he felt hard done by, that Roberts was just a lucky slogger who was fortunate to be playing on the same pitch as him. To my naive eyes, it was a unnecessary show of petulance and I couldn't understand why Leicestershire's captain didn't order him from the field. It certainly wouldn't have been tolerated in the Sheffield League where I'd just come from. So when I read Agnew taking me to task, I wished he had bothered to check the facts in his new role as journalist. My club had given me permission to miss the West Indies game because my wife Jenny was in labour with our first child. After we had won so marvellously at Leeds, I had time only to gulp half a glass of champagne before rushing off to hospital in Derby to be with Jenny. She was on her own, none of her relatives from Sheffield could get off work, and she was understandably nervous. My place was with her and the club fully understood that things like that take precedence over cricket. Jenny was in labour for twenty hours before Erica was born and I was there to witness the birth, a special moment that I'll never forget. After seeing what Jenny went through, I won't let any man talk to me about the pain barrier!

Any perception that I was unconcerned about my bowling form at that stage was totally wide of the mark, but an enquiry to Derbyshire about my absence from the tourists' game might have avoided some hostile publicity that was ill-informed. I also got dragged into another trumped-up row after that season's Trent Bridge Test, when the Derbyshire chairman fell out with Lord's, saying that Micky Stewart had no right to interfere in my bowling programme, and that he should stay away from me when I wasn't on England duty. This was handled badly and I got sucked into it innocently. It all happened because Micky wanted a one-on-one with me, a coaching session to see why I wasn't bowling very well, so he arranged to come over to Derby at the end of the Trent Bridge Test from which I'd been dropped. I was quite happy about that, because it showed that Micky cared about my cricketing welfare, and wanted to see if he could help iron out a few technical details. He was good at geeing up players and I appreciated that he was doing his best to perk me up during a difficult time. In any event, if the England coach says he wants to work with you, that's what you do if you want to get back into the England side. Micky approached my county captain Kim Barnett for permission to work with me for a day, it was readily given and all set up. Then things got a little complicated.

Our club chairman, Chris Middleton was a solicitor with a sharp tongue and a quick wit. Chris was a great guy who cared passionately for Derbyshire cricket, feeling that smaller counties like ours were barely tolerated by the big guns at cricket's HQ, and he never lost the chance to say so, in private and in public. He was God's gift to the press, always ready with a quote, and when he heard about Micky's proposed visit, he went in with all guns blazing, saying that

Micky should keep off his patch, that if I needed specialist coaching, then we had a perfectly good coach at Derby called Phil Russell. Chris loved all that 'them and us' stuff, but unfortunately, no one told him that our captain and coach were perfectly happy with Micky's visit. It was supposed to be a private session, and we weren't happy that it was now public knowledge. In the end, Chris got fined £750 by Lord's, which was rather harsh when you consider he was an unpaid chairman who did the job for the love of his county. He then resigned from the TCCB's disciplinary committee in protest at the fine, so a good man and genuine cricket-lover was lost to committee meetings at Lord's that needed a few more straight talkers like him. It was a great shame, all due to a misunderstanding. There was I, stuck in the middle of it all, respecting both of the parties involved, knowing they wanted the best for me – yet I was the fall guy. And there's no happy ending to the story, because I didn't get back into the England side for the rest of the series.

Happily, Derbyshire provided me with consolations that summer. We were becoming a good side after a rebuilding process and we finished third in the championship. The season before, we had won the Sunday League, and it was terrific to be part of a side bringing the first trophy to the club since 1981. John Morris and I were on England duty when we needed to beat Essex to secure the Sunday League trophy, but we were lucky enough to have a rest day. So we hopped into a car, drove up to Derby, saw us win by five wickets and enjoyed the celebrations before driving back to London on the Sunday night. Our team spirit was that good and it lasted through to the following season in the championship, and in 1992, when we finished fifth. The 1991 season saw the emergence of a matchwinner for Derbyshire. Dominic Cork took 55 championship wickets, including eight for 53 against Essex on his twentieth birthday and he looked a tremendous prospect. He was deservedly named Young Player of the Year by his fellow professionals in the Cricketers' Association poll. Without a shadow of a doubt, he had England potential as soon as he cemented his place in our first team. He was very brave as a batsman, ready to take on the fastest bowlers, loving the challenge. Ian Botham was his number one hero, and he had a lot of Beefy's bravado. He lacked his physique, though. He was all skin and bones when I first met him in the winter nets at Derby. He was sixteen, on a YTS contract, and I was the first player to meet him, as he stood in the bar with his father. I bought him a beer, chatted for a while and I was struck by his ambition and self-confidence. When he came on the staff, Phil Russell got on to him to change his diet, to build himself up, but he still got the ball down to the batter's end quickly. Dominic was very keen, highly strung, noisy, hyperactive and inclined to irritate team-mates with his antics. Right away, when he got into the first team, Dominic's brashness grated with some senior players, because rather than easing himself gently into the first team dressing-room, he acted as if he owned the place. But he had a massive supporter in the captain Kim Barnett, who made it clear that he saw Dominic as a major power in the team for years to come. So Dominic could afford to be insensitive sometimes with Kim's support behind him. All he wanted to do was play cricket and win everything. He certainly had something as a player, though, and I think he was unfortunate to miss out on an England cap until 1995 – and then he showed them what they had missed, with that amazing first Test against the West Indies, when he took seven wickets and the best analysis by an England player on debut. He should have gone to Australia in 1994-95 and he certainly thought so. On the day that the touring party was read out over the tannoy, Dominic dropped to the ground when he heard he wasn't in the squad. He was furious, foaming at the mouth, saying repeatedly, 'What do I have to do?' It was hard to disagree. After all, he had been blooded in one-day internationals in 1992, and he was more than ready for Test cricket by the time we went to Australia. Did I hear someone mention the words 'unfashionable county'?

That frustration was still to come for Dominic Cork at the end of the 1991 summer, because at the close of his first full season he was picked for the England 'A' tour to Bermuda and the West Indies. He would have a county team-mate with him on that trip – me. I was now relegated from the seniors to the nearly men and the promising young players. At the age of 28, I had been demoted from being a hero of the West Indies to the old sweat who was expected to pass on his knowledge to the next generation. What knowledge? In my confused state, I barely knew the length of my run-up.

SIX

ON TRIAL

For the last eighteen months of Graham Gooch's captaincy, my England appearances were intermittent and, I admit, my performances were erratic. I lost confidence in my captain and clearly he felt the same about me. Goochie obviously believed I was an enigma, that he couldn't get through to me and that I couldn't be relied on for consistency. For my part, I became very confused. Goochie wanted raw pace from me, while the various England coaches that came and went during that period would preach line and length to me, with the old 'corridor of uncertainty' phrase getting trotted out. I didn't know who I should be pleasing here, and there was a lack of continuity. When I did play for England, I missed the steadiness and control at the other end of Angus Fraser. Gus had picked up a serious hip injury that threatened his career, a severe blow to England and, of course, himself. He missed the best part of two seasons, and I certainly missed him. Whenever I've bowled at my best for England, a steady seamer at the other end has been a great foil for me, because they can tie down the batsmen, get them frustrated, so that they will be more inclined to take risks against me. The outstanding partner for me in my England career has been Gus Fraser. He is so naggingly accurate that he only goes for around two runs per over in Test cricket and that creates its own special pressure. We called him 'the toothache bowler' because he kept nagging away and I don't think people realised just how valuable he was until he was missing for such a long time. I always did, though, and between

1991 and 1993, his absence contributed to my fluctuating standards on England duty.

At the start of 1992, I had clearly moved down the pecking order, having been shunted off to the 'A' tour. They'd clearly categorised me as being too high-risk to be a one-day bowler, so that I never had a chance of making the World Cup in Australasia. I had hopes, though, of making it to New Zealand for the Test series, but Syd Lawrence got the nod ahead of me as the express bowler, with disastrous consequences for poor Sid. As one of six players kept on a retainer during the winter, to keep fit, I was hopeful of getting a late call for New Zealand but it never came, so off I went to the Caribbean on the 'A' tour. To me, I was a waste of a place. What was the point in taking someone about to celebrate his 29th birthday? Surely, an 'A' tour is designed to bring on the young players, rather than give some winter work to an older player? It felt like I'd just been tossed a consolation prize. Two years ago, I'd been running in to bowl to Viv Richards in front of packed houses in the Caribbean; now I was playing in the same places, in front of nobody, trying to tell Mark Ramprakash to cool down.

'Ramps' was unbelievably tense on that tour and whenever he got out, you had to keep out of his way. He was ridiculously disruptive when he came back to the dressing-room, throwing massive tantrums. The other guys would stir uncomfortably in their seats, waiting for the storm to blow over. Normally, a disappointed batsman rants and raves for a minute or so, but an hour later Ramps would still be at it, smashing his locker with his bat, chastising himself out loud. It wasn't the kind of thing that batsmen who are waiting to go in want to hear. In Barbados, I tried to talk to Ramps, who was fuming even though he'd scored 86. I popped into the showers to have a quiet word with him, taking a glass of water with me and he just knocked it out of my hand. Later I asked why he did things like that and he said, 'I don't know, Dev. I just hate getting out.' I told him, 'That could be a negative on you, Ramps. It could stop you progressing as a batsman,' and he agreed. Ramps is a nice bloke, such a good player, and I could just feel his frustration at missing out on the World Cup, going to New Zealand and not playing in a Test, after battling away hard against the West Indies in the previous summer. Yet I did find myself wondering why I was the one putting an arm round his shoulder, rather than our coach on that tour, Keith Fletcher. Ramps has such talent that if he had been handled more sympathetically from 1992 onwards, he would have been a major batsman for us. Instead, he was in and out of the side, playing mostly against the West Indies, missing out on the chance to build up his confidence against weaker attacks. I'm just one of many England players who felt on trial throughout the nineties. There never seemed to be any continuity of selection. Fortunately for Ramps, he became captain of Middlesex in 1997, and his increased maturity both on and off the field was reflected in a highly successful 1998 West Indies tour.

Several other young players who later made England careers were also on that 'A' tour. There was Graham Thorpe and Nasser Hussain, and, of course, Dominic Cork. Unfortunately, Dominic returned to Derby a poorer bowler after spending time with the England 'A' bowling coach, Geoff Arnold. Instead of trying to build on Cork's impressive start to his bowling career in county cricket, Arnold tried to get him to bowl quicker. That almost destroyed him and he ended up bowling short and erratically, and he lost his dangerous late swing. He wasn't getting close to the stumps anymore, one of his key attributes, and he looked bewildered by the end of the tour. It took Phil Russell and Kim Barnett some time to get him back to his usual action and style when he got back to Derby.

This meddling around with bowlers became a feature on England tours from that time onwards. It was almost as if the coaches had to justify their presence on the trip by trying to alter radically a bowler's technique. On tour is a good time for a bowling coach to offer technical advice, do some fine tuning – but not a drastic overhaul that leaves the young bowler bemused. It also wasn't done in a very pleasant way and I felt sorry for Dominic. Three years later, in South

Africa, I had the same distressing experience. For Geoff Arnold, read Peter Lever.

I didn't do much bowling on that 'A' tour, because I spent a fair amount of time flat on my back, suffering from back spasms. It happened during close fielding practice, which involved running in hard and flicking the ball at the stumps – not an area of fielding in which I'm particularly distinguished! So I could barely move for a time and that just about summed up my value to the tour. It really was a waste of a place at my age. I needed to be on the senior tour, putting pressure on the other seam bowlers. They seem to have got it right with 'A' tours at last, giving places to young guys who have barely played first-class cricket, and I'm sure that's right. You shouldn't go on an 'A' tour, as a consolation prize for just missing out on the senior trip.

When I got back into English cricket, my 1992 season started sluggishly and by the middle of June, I had only taken twelve first-class wickets. There had been a fair amount of rain and the wickets that year at Derby were very flat, but I wasn't firing properly either. Micky Stewart spent two days watching me at Harrogate and he was supportive and encouraging. I appreciated that and I'm sure he had a lot to do with my recall for the second Test against the Pakistanis, at Lord's. My confidence wasn't exactly sky-high, but at least I was back.

I remember this Test very clearly, because two incidents in it encapsulated the best and worst of Graham Gooch's captaincy. In their first innings, I was working up a fair head of steam from the Nursery End when Salim Malik played me through the covers on the up, a dismissive stroke reminiscent of Viv Richards. For a fast bowler, it was a demoralising shot, because he seemed to have so much time to play. Instead of kicking the ground and avoiding eye contact, Gooch ran up to me and said, 'Dev, that was a great shot, you couldn't do anything about that,' and patted me on the back encouragingly. I walked back to my mark a different bowler. Three balls later, I got Salim out and I felt inspired. I then nailed Asif

Mujtaba and in walked the young star, Inzamam-ul-Haq – without a helmet! Now that really got me going, and I began snorting fire and fury. After a couple of balls, when it was clear I meant business, a helmet was sent out. Then he gloved a bouncer, trying for the hook. All of a sudden we were back in the game, and I had taken three wickets in thirteen balls. We had a lead of 38 after it looked as if they'd rack up a big score and I couldn't wait to get at them again. I was inspired by my captain's public and vocal support, wondering also why he hadn't done that more often.

We didn't bat very well in our second innings, falling to Mushtaq Ahmed's legspin as the wicket turned, and they only needed 138 to win. But we got stuck into them, with Chris Lewis bowling brilliantly in a long spell. Unfortunately, Ian Botham and Phil DeFreitas couldn't bowl because of groin strains, so we were down to three fit bowlers – the legspinner, Ian Salisbury, Lewis and myself. Gooch had the difficult job of attacking to get ten wickets, exerting pressure while at the same time needing to keep it tight in the field. We had them 62 for five, 81 for seven and then 95 for eight, still 43 runs adrift and the game was ours for the taking. The last man, Aqib Javed was about as good a number eleven as me, so it was down to their ninth-wicket pair Wasim Akram and Waqar Younis. You could see how nervous they were and it was set up for the quick kill for us. I was bowling when they came together, and Goochie told me he wanted me to pepper Waqar with bouncers. I asked for a short leg straight away, because I felt Waqar wouldn't play the bouncer very well. Goochie wouldn't let me have it. My first ball to Waqar was fended off awkwardly in the air and dropped in the vacant short leg area. It was an easy catch, but there was no fielder there. I was annoyed, because I knew what I was doing and should have been given the field I wanted.

Then the captain made another error. Ian Salisbury should have been brought on early to have a bowl at Waqar who wouldn't have been able to resist having a slog at him. The ball was turning, as Mushtaq had shown earlier in the day, and Waqar usually likes to have a go at the slow bowlers. Yet by the time Salisbury came on, Waqar's eye was in and he was playing well. They knocked off the runs, winning by two wickets, and although I pay tribute to the two batsmen, I do believe that Graham Gooch's captaincy cost us that match. We were so surprised to be back in the game that Goochie didn't put the boot in and they were let off the hook. If we had been batting in similar circumstances against one of the top sides, we'd have been killed off, bounced out by their fast bowlers before they even needed to call for the spinner. I still find it hard to believe we lost that Test, but it was typical of the soft way we played our cricket in the nineties.

That Pakistan series in 1992 was a controversial one and when I came up against them on the next occasion, in the Old Trafford Test, I was involved in the nastiest incident I've ever experienced on the cricket field. The seeds were sown during the Lord's Test, when I bounced Aqib Javed and also sent a wicked one past Wasim Akram's nose, grazing his helmet peak. I wasn't bothered about getting it back because I knew I'd cop a few bouncers anyway, with the Bowlers' Union a thing of the past. What I wasn't prepared for was the sight of Aqib Javed running through the crease to bounce me. He was so far over the line that I could see from my end that he had broken a rule of cricket, never mind the spirit of the game. He had got riled up because umpire Roy Palmer said that he had exceeded his limit of bouncers at me but Aqib knew what he was doing, he was deliberately trying to hurt me while breaking a law. That's something I'd never do. Running through the crease to deliver a bouncer at shortened range is almost as inexcusable as bowling a beamer at a batsman's head. Anyway, I left it to the umpires to sort out and when Roy Palmer signalled the end of the over, I joined my partner, Tim Munton in the middle for a chat.

Suddenly, all hell broke loose. Roy Palmer had some difficulty getting Aqib's sweater out of the loop of his pocket, and when he tugged at it, the sweater came out quickly in the bowler's hand. Aqib took offence at that, thinking the umpire had thrown the sweater at him, and he started to gesticulate and shout. Their captain, Javed Miandad then waded in and it was a terrible scene. Thank goodness for a calming intervention from the vice-captain, Salim Malik. He kept pushing Javed away, stopping his gesticulations while Tim and I looked on, bemused. No wonder those guys had a poor reputation around the world at that time. It was an awful scene, totally out of proportion. Javed had poured fuel on the fire and yet he got away with it when match referee Conrad Hunte fined Aqib Javed just £300. Javed wasn't fined a penny, and to make matters worse, Graham Gooch was dragged into the referee's statement which called on both captains to play to the spirit of the game. That was an accusation you could never level at Gooch, and he was rightly annoyed at being named in the statement as he and his players were totally innocent. My respect for Javed Miandad really dipped after that incident.

So by the time we got to the Oval for the final Test, both sides were sick of the sight of each other. In our dressing-room, all the talk was about the amount of prodigious late swing they were getting from the ball when it was about sixty overs old. Goochie joked that the best time to bat against Waqar and Wasim was right at the start, against the new ball, which somehow didn't swing all that much – so why not reverse the batting order? No thanks, captain! He believed that once the ball starts to swing late, the batsmen had no price if they tried to drive, because they'd get bowled or lbw. That left the problem of where to get your runs – deflecting the inswinger to fine leg? We kept asking 'How do these guys do it?' and, of course, there were all sorts of rumours about ball-tampering. Later that month, Allan Lamb went public, alleging that the Pakistanis had in fact altered the shape of the ball in the one-day international at Lord's, and that was a brave thing to say. Inevitably, the matter was brushed under the carpet, yet the suspicions remain.

I have to say I never saw any evidence of ball tampering, and I wouldn't want to take anything away from two fantastic bowlers. Wasim appeared to be using a different ball at times and Waqar could be seriously quick. I once saw him blast out John Morris' middle stump with such a rapid delivery that Johnny was about a week late on the shot – and he could play fast bowling. Wasim had this lightning fast arm, the ball was on you in a trice. When a player of David Gower's class and experience gets bowled off stump in that Oval Test, shouldering arms to a wicked inswinger, then you know that something different is going on. No batsman in the world could have coped comfortably with Wasim and Waqar in 1992, and that's not meant as an excuse for our ten-wicket defeat at the Oval. These two bowlers were just different, devastating and I had no idea how they managed it.

Before I left the Oval after our chastening defeat, I'd had another indication from Graham Gooch that he had put me in a particular category. I was working up some good pace, clean bowling Salim Malik with a beauty and I was looking forward to getting stuck in with the second new ball. But then Goochie told me I wasn't going to get the new ball, that Neil Mallender and Chris Lewis would be ahead of me. When I asked the reason, he told me that I wasn't a swing bowler. Setting aside for a moment the fact that I could swing the ball – mostly away from the right-hander when I was in rhythm – that was a daft comment. A fast bowler like me needs the new ball to get extra bounce from the hardness and new seam. It just didn't make sense, Goochie was moving the goalposts. In that Pakistan innings, I ended up with five for 94, enjoying the Oval conditions, but I feel I'd have done even better if my captain had trusted me with the second new ball.

Graham Gooch's last tour as England captain was a personal nightmare for him and a cricketing one for all of us. Normally, an England tour throws up a few silver linings, even in defeat, but it's hard to find anything positive to say about our efforts on the 1993 trip to India and Sri Lanka. We lost all four Tests by a wide margin, playing like chumps in village cricket. For some reason, Goochie had been given permission to leave the tour after the Indian series, missing the Sri Lankan leg, which I found unbelievable. That shouldn't have been allowed, and was unfair on his deputy, Alec Stewart. I thought Alec was the ideal man to be the new England captain, I liked his 'up and at 'em' approach, his positive ways with his players, the fact that he'd take differences of opinion like a man and not harbour any resentment.

Goochie's arrangement to miss out on Sri Lanka had been finalised when the tour party was picked in September 1992 and it was nothing to do with the news that shocked us all when we arrived in India months later. He called us together to reveal that his marriage was over, that the papers would be carrying the story and that we should just concentrate on the cricket. I was shocked and felt sorry for all the family. Graham often used to talk about his wife, Brenda and his three girls and he was always on the phone to them, wherever we were in the world. I thought that was one marriage made for life. That surprising news proved to be an omen for the tour. The personal stability of the captain was obviously affected and understandably he spent a fair amount of time in his room. He was absorbed and that was a problem, because you need to see your captain at the start of what was bound to be a difficult tour. The captain should be rallying everybody round, forging an excellent team spirit, as Goochie himself did in the Caribbean in 1990. When your best player and captain is distracted, you start off a tour on the back foot, and although I cannot tell if this was a contributory factor to his meagre total in the India series of 47 runs in four innings, his personal situation can't have helped.

There were a lot of other things to contend with on that trip. Early on, the British High Commissioner paid regular visits to reassure us about the violence which led to mosques being burned down and some grisly deaths. A strike of airline pilots meant some hair-raising flights taken by former pilots who had been grounded or retired. We'd read about some frightening mid-air collisions and wondered if it was wise to be up in the air. In the fortnight before the first Test in Calcutta, we went from Delhi to Jaipur, back to Delhi then to Chandigarh, back to Delhi, then to Bhubaneshwar, to Cuttack and finally Calcutta. It's a vast continent, and with the pilots' strike causing so much hassle, was that a wise itinerary before the first Test? At times, we had to take the train and that took hours. We'd travel overnight, sleeping on narrow benches and arrive next morning bleary-eyed. We then had our photos taken with us looking scruffy and unshaven and they got into the papers back home. That was unfair, because there was no water available on the train to shave. More damaging photos were taken when we had to oblige our sponsors, Tetleys, the brewers. We'd be pictured sitting on beer crates and the implication was that we were scruffy cricketers on the booze, seemingly unconcerned that we were playing badly and losing every Test. If we'd been kitted out in Armani or Hugo Boss, would that have made any difference to the bad press we received?

Ted Dexter, our chairman of selectors, got involved, saying that he'd be looking at the whole question of facial hair, whether designer stubble in the Gooch style should be allowed on England duty, and it got sillier and sillier. Dexter was on stronger ground when he said that Test cricketers shouldn't have to play in smog. That gave a few journalists and rent-a-quote MPs a lot of mileage back home, but it was a fair point made by Dexter. In Delhi, you could see the smog just above the traffic on the way to the ground, and in Calcutta the air pollution was terrible. At the close of play, the spectators pile all their rubbish up and use the stadium as an incinerator while in the morning, you couldn't have a proper practice session half-an-hour before the start of play because you couldn't see more than twenty yards in front of you. These aren't excuses for losing the Test series because there's no avoiding the fact that we played very badly, but Dexter was right to draw attention to the difficult conditions we encountered. It wasn't a case of the Whingeing Pom this time.

It went wrong right from the start on the first morning of the Calcutta Test, when Mike Atherton dropped out ill fairly late and we could only play one spinner – Ian Salisbury – because John Emburey and Phil Tufnell were out of sorts, and lacking confidence. So we went in with four seamers, and although I was pleased enough with my three for 67, the dry, firm conditions were ideal for their spinners. We were relying heavily on Mike Gatting for his expertise against spin and although he scored 33 and 81, he got almost all of those runs by sweeping and lapping. He clearly didn't trust himself on the drive and they gave him hardly anything to cut. Gatt never looked comfortable in that series against their spinners, and that was a setback to us because he had been brought on this tour to dominate them. Anyway, we lost easily after being bowled out for 167 and having to follow on. You need a minimum of 350 on the board to stay in a Test in India when the spinners are in charge and we could never do that at any stage. Their spinners were decisive in the series, with the legspinner Anil Kumble taking 21 wickets in three Tests. We didn't play them very well, remaining rooted to the crease. Our batsmen had spent hours at Lilleshall, practising against spin bowling on artificial wickets but when we got out to India, it all seemed to go out of the window. Our new coach Keith Fletcher seemed to sum up our pre-tour conviction that it would be all right on the night when he pronounced that, having seen the Indian spinners in South Africa a few weeks earlier, we had nothing to worry about. He said he hadn't seen Kumble turn one ball from leg to off – perhaps he was saving that delivery for England, because we saw a few of them.

Fletcher was very uninspiring on his first tour as replacement for the retired Micky Stewart. His body language was poor, he appeared indecisive and he had trouble remembering his players' names, a rather important asset in a coach. He was a great success as captain and guru at Essex, but he was too similar in outlook to Gooch. We needed someone positive like Micky Stewart who would kick us up the backside but also encourage. Instead, Fletcher looked for excuses, saying at the end of the India series that the wickets back home in domestic cricket didn't help us to play spin bowling well. Yet on that trip, the likes of Gooch, Gatting, Graeme Hick and Neil Fairbrother were acknowledged to be fine players of spin. The truth is we played shockingly.

We kept shooting ourselves in the foot on that tour. On the eve of the Madras Test, Graham Gooch had some prawns in a Chinese restaurant at our hotel and was so ill he couldn't play the following day. What was he doing taking such a chance ? It was crazy, and it made us look like a bunch of amateurs. Everyone knew about the dangers of Delhi Belly, and yet there was our captain pressing the self-destruct button. We also didn't get the best out of Gooch's successor, Mike Atherton, on that tour. After missing out of the first Test through illness, he wasn't even used as one of our four fielding substitutes at Madras. It didn't make sense to have Robin Smith opening instead of Athers, and you could tell Mike was fuming. He was right out of it, reading his book on the coach, very uncommunicative, contributing little in team meetings and not really part of the social activities. He may have been only 24 at the time, but he was tough enough already to get through a very difficult tour for him. I wonder if his treatment in India hardened him up even more and contributed to the 'Iron Mike' image when he took over as England captain.

There were so many illogical decision. Paul Jarvis had been the best bowler on tour so far, yet he was dropped for the last Test in Bombay in favour of Phil DeFreitas, who had moaned his way through the tour, wanting to go home when there was a risk of violence. DeFreitas didn't take a first-class wicket on the entire tour and his negative comments did nothing for team spirit. The selection of Richard Blakey ahead of Jack Russell was a debatable decision. I read a comment from Allan Knott that Richard was the best wicket-keeper/batsman available for this tour; I thought I was seeing things. Jack was a gutsy batsman, good at standing up to the spinners, full of 'over my dead body' determination and a left-hander, a handy way of combating the legspinner. Yet he got left behind and Blakey failed with the bat, with scores of 0, 6, 1 and 0. In my opinion, Alec Stewart should have kept wicket in all the Tests in the absence of Russell, with Atherton opening if Alec had been in the field for a long time.

But the biggest selection blunder was picking Gatting ahead of David Gower for the tour. Now I admit that Gower was one of my favourite players, in fact there were times when we played against each other in county cricket that I was sad when he got out. He was also still good enough at the age of 35 to do it at the highest level. It was illogical in cricketing terms not to pick him. David was experienced in Indian conditions, he played the spinners very well, and he was also left-handed, which might have posed a few problems for Kumble. Gatting, to the surprise of many, looked like a fish out of water against the spinners, barely getting much bat on anything and David's temperament would have been a godsend out there in tense situations, with fielders pressurising you. It had to be personal between Gooch and Gower, there could be no other valid reason for leaving him behind. Sadly, it must have been a hangover from the Australian tour of 1990–91, because in my opinion David Gower should have played every Test match when fit during this period. Leaving out Russell and Gower for the 1993 India tour was one of the biggest cock-ups in my time as an England cricketer. We did make things difficult for ourselves at times!

We never pulled together in the same direction on that trip. Phil Tufnell added to his reputation as a difficult tourist, but he could have been handled more sympathetically. Tuffers got wound up because he couldn't win lbw decisions when the batsmen missed a straight ball and any bowler can relate to that. He was brattish in his reactions to umpires and he ought to have counted to ten at times, but all he really needed was an arm around his shoulder and a quiet word of consolation, then encouragement. There was no point in him going to Keith Fletcher for help because he would have been shown the same unsympathetic response as by Gooch. That was the weakness in having Fletcher and Gooch operating in harness. I'm not sure we've ever got the best out of Tuffers. He's different, he should be given a little leeway, but instead successive managements have just wielded the big stick. On the Australia tour of 1994–95, I was really disappointed at the impersonal way Tuffers was treated by our management, when he was going through an emotional, turbulent time over his private life. No one took him aside, and said, 'I understand what you're going through,' instead he was left to stew in his own juice. As a result he cracked up at the end of that tour and had to spend a night in hospital. That must have been a terrible time for him.

Chris Lewis, another of those enigmas, was also on this Indian tour and he flattered to deceive. He got a hundred in Madras, but it was in a losing cause. That sums up his career. How many times has he produced a spell of bowling or an innings that actually wins a match for England? I think Graham Gooch ended up believing he was just a little precious, that he liked to be praised too much. Of all his England team-mates, I probably know Chris better than the others, but he still baffles me at times. When he came out on his first England tour, to the West Indies in 1990, Micky Stewart asked me to room with him with the request to 'straighten him up' and I could see what Micky meant. I like Chris, but he could be irritating – leaving things behind, for example, or inconveniencing others. In the Caribbean, Goochy, Allan Lamb and Micky were at a loss to understand him. He's very fashion conscious and would spend a lot of time preening himself, putting netting on his hair so that he'd get waves in it. The management didn't grasp that, but that's because they didn't understand black culture. Black guys spend a lot of time getting ready, putting oils on our skin after a shower to get some moisture, and that might appear odd to those who are in and out of the shower and ready. Chris likes his own space, hates smoky bars, doesn't drink and dislikes standing around, talking aimlessly. He likes to go dancing and he's a very snappy dresser. All this has often been beyond the understanding of our tour management, but you're only talking about tolerance, letting the guy be, as long as he's not a disrupting influence, and I don't think he's ever been that. Chris has felt over the years that people don't like him, which I believe has held back his cricketing development, but I prefer to see it as people not understanding him.

No one seems to be able to get the best out of Chris Lewis. In his early days as an England tourist, I'd ask him why did he bowl his quickest overs towards the end of play rather than when it's more meaningful, and he'd say that he couldn't bowl as consistently fast as me because it's not natural to him. That was missing the point, though. After this India tour, I thought his hundred would kick him on as a Test all-rounder, batting at number seven, bowling consistently and fielding superbly. He started to lift weights in an attempt to get stronger, so that he'd bowl faster, but something always held him back. I can't put my finger on it. Chris talks well on the game, he can be very pleasant and articulate, but too many of his team-mates fail to get through to him. Consistency seems to be his undoing, although when he moved to Surrey that looked an ideal, high-profile move for him, giving him that extra spark of confidence to get him back in the England team. His decision to move back to Leicestershire surprised many of us in the game. He obviously has captaincy ambitions, but his restless moving around the counties can't help his credibility. I still like him and rate his ability, but can anyone manage at last to unpick the lock?

You could ask the same question of Graeme Hick, another to get his maiden hundred on the Indian tour, but again in a losing cause, in Bombay. I thought Graeme was set for a big future after that hundred, but he's been in and out of the England team ever since. Before he first played for England in 1991, he had so much pressure on him, as he ticked off the qualification years. He was billed as the Great White Hope, and then the West Indies got into him, followed by the Pakistanis the year after. He needs a lot of encouragement, and I remember Graham Gooch having a long talk with him in his second Test at Lord's when it looked as if Hicky was struggling with his confidence already. I'm not sure Goochie thought he could play the real man's game. Some, like Alec Stewart, Nasser Hussain and Mike Atherton, thrive on it, while quieter lads like Hicky, Graham Thorpe and Mark Ramprakash have to be told 'Just go out and do it – forget what the press have written, they're not bowling at you.'

Graeme Hick is a gentleman, a nice, quiet person and an excellent team-mate, and yet sometimes I've seen that flash of steel in him and been pleased. When someone hits him in the rib cage, he needs to say, 'Come on, you ******, give it to me!' and really mean it. That's what it's all about at Test level.

SEVEN

DRAMAS WITH DERBYSHIRE

The 1993 season ended on a high note for me as I helped England beat Australia in my only appearance of the series, at the Oval, and then was picked for the West Indies tour – but the real dramas that summer came at my county. It was one of the most traumatic seasons in Derbyshire's history, with massive financial problems leading to staff redundancies, an administrative shake-up and uncertainty about our playing futures. We also had to make do throughout the season without an overseas player. Our vice-captain John Morris asked to be released from his contract because he wanted to be captain, and finally our long-serving coach Phil Russell emigrated to South Africa, ending an association of almost thirty years with the club. That's more than enough for any group of players to contend with, and we could have been forgiven for under-performing. Yet we won a trophy, the Benson & Hedges Cup, and the manner in which we pulled that off shows how important team spirit is. All those players who took part in that successful cup run can be rightly proud of how they pulled together against the odds, eventually triumphing in the Final over one of the strongest and most talented of teams, Lancashire. It was a fantastic effort, with Kim Barnett and Phil Russell working wonders to hold things together during all the uncertainties.

We got wind of our financial problems at the end of May, when we were playing at Chelmsford. Kim told us to assemble for a team meeting one evening and there we were addressed by Mike Horton, the new chairman. He told us that our chief executive, commercial manager and accountant had been made redundant and we'd be lucky to get paid at the end of the month. The annual loss was now £120,000, the overdraft at the bank £400,000 and they were beginning to ask searching questions. The treasurer had resigned, and so had Chris Middleton, who'd done the job for eight years, always speaking up bravely for the little clubs against the fat cats. Chris felt responsible as chairman for the financial mess and did the honourable thing by resigning. The players always knew that with such a low membership, Derbyshire would inevitably struggle financially, but we hadn't grasped the extent of our problems until now. The club had been left a legacy of £400,000 by a retired farmer, and the plan had been to leave that for future development, on long-term projects, but it looked as if there was no choice now and that money had to go towards paying off the debts. Mike Horton promised us that we'd all get our salaries eventually, but asked us to be patient and understanding. It was a very difficult situation, and the new chairman was to do a tremendous job in turning things round over the next few years.

Derbyshire had caught a big cold over our overseas player for the 1993 summer. Ian Bishop was our man, a fast bowler who had been a great success in recent years, an impressive professional who set very high standards. But Bish had a bad back. In April, our chief executive Bob Lark travelled to Trinidad to seek reassurances and he got them. Yet by the end of that month, it emerged that Bish couldn't make it for the entire season and we had to pay his salary for the whole summer. It was also too late to register another overseas player, so we were stuck. No star to help us on the field and money down the drain. I suspect the Bishop Affair didn't help Bob Lark's cause a great deal when heads started to roll at the club. Somehow, the players managed to rise above these problems; we bonded and stuck together. The team spirit was very special for a time and it pulled us through.

We had a few incentives to beat Lancashire when we came to the

Benson & Hedges Cup Final in July, but one of them had stemmed from our county match against them at Derby a fortnight earlier. Wasim Akram had bowled devastatingly in the second innings to win the game, running through us with late swing, just like he'd done against England the year before. The ball-tampering allegations were still swirling around and we certainly wondered what was going on in our dressing-room that day, as Wasim sliced through us. In the first innings, he had been smacked around the park by Kim Barnett and Chris Adams, going for five an over, but now he was cutting the ball back 45 degrees, and proving unplayable. The last man to be dismissed in our second innings was Ole Mortensen and he ran after the ball down to fine leg, saying he wanted to have a look at it. He kept it, handed it over to our captain and the club took the major decision to send the ball to Lord's, asking for their comments. The implication was obvious from our camp, that the ball had been tampered with and the papers went to town on it. At international level, the matter had been swept under the carpet, but if it was creeping into county cricket, the Test and County Cricket Board had to be seen to be taking action. In the end, they wrote back, saying there was nothing suspicious about the ball's condition. That caused a bit of a stir in our dressing-room, and it certainly raised the temperature between the sides, with the Lord's Final just a few days away. On the one hand, Lancashire felt we had accused them of cheating, and they had been subsequently cleared, while we denied we'd been moaning and felt it was a legitimate complaint. It was set up for an acrimonious match.

There certainly appeared to be a score to settle between Chris Adams and Wasim Akram when they locked horns before lunch in the Final. Adams had hit a few shots off Wasim in the county game and the Pakistani's blood was up after the suspicions raised by our camp. So we were watching the encounter very closely and were dismayed to see Wasim bowl a beamer at Chris. With someone as fast as Wasim, a beamer is very serious. You should never bowl a beamer deliberately because it could kill someone. With a fast bowler, there is precious little time for a batsman to react when it's whizzing towards your head. We've all sent down an accidental beamer at some time – I did to Allan Border in my first Test – but the convention is that you apologise instantly, go down the pitch and check that the batsman's all right. Above all, you must make it clear it was unintentional. Well Wasim Akram didn't when he hit Chris Adams that day at Lord's and that really stirred things up. He made a very swift gesture with his hand and walked back to his mark. The apology wasn't instant and it wasn't visual, and there was a suspicion that the beamer had been deliberate. During the lunch interval, we were still seething, and Adams was even more angry. In the players' dining-room, he squared up to Wasim, and the players had to be separated, with Chris being led back to our dressing-room. They were both spoiling for a fight and even though it was nipped in the bud, the incident stoked up the fires even more for the rest of the match.

I think that encounter gave us even more incentive to beat Lancashire. Although we were 66 for four at lunch, and in trouble, Dominic Cork played brilliantly for his 92 not out, showing his big-match temperament on the wider stage for the first time, and Karl Krikken improvised superbly for his unbeaten 37. I reckon Lancashire underrated us when they batted, sure that with their depth all the way down the order they could rely on one of their big hitters to see them through. But Mike Atherton batted far too long for his 54, he didn't change gear at all, and then got out when he should have anchored the innings to victory. We were delighted to see him stay in for so long. Neil Fairbrother, one of the best one-day batsmen in the game, was the obvious danger man, but we had hatched a plan against him in the recent Sunday League match. I had him caught at deep backward point in that game, so we set out to tuck him up there at Lord's. He managed to slap me away in the air a couple of times, but he never broke free and couldn't nail down the win. The final over came and with wickets in hand, and Fairbrother and DeFreitas at the crease, you'd have backed Lancashire, but

Frank Griffith kept cool and bowled excellently. They couldn't get him away, panicked and we ran out winners by six runs. Brilliant! A sweet win after all our problems in May and the recent aggro with Wasim. Everybody raised their game an extra notch and the celebrations were rather wild.

It was good to see Dominic Cork show his all-round capabilities and fighting spirit to a national audience, terrific for underrated pros like Alan Warner and Frank Griffith to have their deserved day of glory, and for Karl Krikken to state his credentials as a fine wicket-keeper-batsman. That cameo innings of 37 not out was typical of Karl, he loves getting up the noses of the bowlers, never letting them settle into a line, always trying something outrageous. Karl's full of nervous energy, like Corky or Derek Randall, and when he bats, he never stops chattering at the fielders, getting under their skin. He's the same behind the stumps. A great encourager, noisy and confident, he makes sure the batsmen can't settle. Karl may not look that pretty with the gloves on, but he's highly effective. He has great hands, never seems to drop anything and his reactions are razor sharp. He has regularly stood up to the stumps when Cork or DeFreitas are bowling, taking some brilliant stumpings down the legside. Karl should have been on an 'A' tour by now, and I think the only thing that's held him back has been the fact that he appears awkward and ungainly. If you ask around the county circuit, a lot of good judges will tell you that the current wicket-keeper with the best hands is Karl Krikken. He deserves a chance.

So we had something to show for our efforts from a very difficult summer. It was sad, though, to see Phil Russell leave us at our time of triumph, an achievement that owed such a lot to him. As coach since 1977, he had been responsible for the development of players like Barnett, Morris, Adams, Cork, Krikken and myself. Phil backed his judgement, he had a special eye for young talent and he moved with the times. He'd been at Derby for 28 years, as a player and then coach, but he wasn't rooted in the good old days. Phil liked constructive discussions rather than rows in the dressing-room if we'd had a bad day, and he tried hard to understand us. But the job in South Africa, as groundsman-coach at Kingsmead, Durban was too good an offer to turn down, so he left. Two years later, we met up again in South Africa when I toured with England. That was one of the rare happy times for me on that trip. Phil was so good at spotting things I was doing wrong. When I was on England duty, he'd ring me up during the lunch or tea interval, to tell me I was rushing to the crease too much, or dipping my head at the moment of delivery. He was far better for me than any of England's coaches during my career.

Unfortunately, Phil Russell's departure created a bit of a power vacuum that was enthusiastically filled by our captain Kim Barnett. Kim had been in charge for a decade now, and Phil had been able to clip his wings to a certain extent. The committee came to be dominated by Kim, and he adopted a black-and-white view of everything, including the players. You were either in Kim's camp, or seen as an outsider. He didn't seem to understand that players like myself just wanted to play cricket and stay out of the politics. Four years later, in 1997, I would suffer from Kim's desire to control everything at the club but before that, we kept losing fine players because of the situation at Derbyshire. Chris Adams, Peter Bowler and John Morris all left in frustration at Kim's reluctance to hand over the reins of captaincy to someone else. That's why Johnny Morris went to Durham in 1993, with a year still left on his contract. He wanted to have a go at the captaincy, feeling rightly that he had no influence at all as vice-captain. I can understand Johnny's frustration at being the number two, with no input to the captain, but I believe he was living in a dream world if he thought he was captaincy material. Johnny found batting too easy, he didn't have to work hard at his game. As captain, therefore, he wouldn't be able to crack the whip of discipline on players who lacked his great natural talent. At times, he could be as cocky off the field as when he batted, and he didn't treat the young pros at the club with a great deal of respect and consideration. When they graduated to the first team,

Above: My first representative match – for Yorkshire Schools Cricket Association at St Peter's School, York, in 1981. I'm fourth from the right, in the back row.

Left: My beloved grandparents who did so much for me – Dorrel and Maudlyn.

Right: A proud moment. Bowling Geoffrey Boycott with an inswinging yorker while playing for a Yorkshire League XI in April 1984.

Left: The scorecard didn't lie, even though I felt I was dreaming!

Left: My early bespectacled years at Derbyshire.

Below: My father Albert (left) with a family friend, Francis.

Left: It was great meeting my cousin, Danville, on the England tour of the West Indies in 1990.

Opposite: Kim Barnett (centre) leads our celebrations on the balcony at Lord's, after we had won the 1993 Benson & Hedges Cup against Lancashire.

Right: With Margaret Beckett, my local MP who did so much to overcome the red tape that allowed me to qualify for England in 1987.

Above: Michael Holding was a great inspiration to me, firstly, when I was growing up in Jamaica, then after joining him on the staff at Derbyshire.

Above: Phil Russell, my first coach at Derbyshire. A great help to me over the years, he forecast I'd play for England one day.

My England debut at Trent Bridge in 1989 against Australia was painful.
The contact lenses came later!

Left: Yorking the great Viv Richards in the Jamaica Test of 1990 – the game that put me on the map.

Below: Graham Gooch offers a few words of consolation. Ours was an up and down relationship when he was England captain.

Below: On my way to my best wicket haul to date, 10 for 137 against the West Indies in Trinidad during the second Test of that 1990 tour.

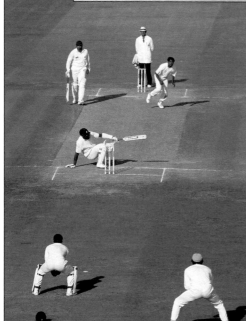

Above: After letting down Robin Smith in Trinidad when I left him stranded on 99, I got him through to his hundred a few months later in the 1990 Old Trafford Test against India.

Left: Getting the treatment from Pakistan's Aqib Javed in the 1992 Old Trafford Test.

Below: After umpire Roy Palmer warned Aqib for intimidatory bowling against me, there were disgraceful scenes of dissent from the bowler and captain Javed Miandad.

Above: I've never pretended to be a master blaster – especially against a bowler of Wasim Akram's class!

Left: Courtney Walsh giving me some severe treatment during the Jamaica Test, 1994.

Right: India v England, first Test, Calcutta, 1993 – and proof that my fielding has improved!

My beloved grandmother, Maudlyn, and I on my return to Jamaica for the 1990 England tour.

The happy couple. With Jenny outside Chatsworth House during one of my 1997 benefit functions.

they remembered suffering at Johnny's hands, and that would have counted against him if he'd been captain. I believe Chris Adams would have been a sounder bet because he was a better communicator than Johnny, but he too was blocked by Kim's influence at the club and the accumulated frustrations led to Chris' departure to Sussex in 1997.

While Derbyshire tried to sort out their chronic financial problems in 1993, the Ashes were again at stake, and I watched the Australians' dominance with mounting frustration. By the end of the series, Graham Gooch had handed over the captaincy to Mike Atherton, who had seen off the challenge of Alec Stewart. I thought that a mistake because Athers had no experience of the job apart from Cambridge University, and they didn't often find themselves in a winning position, where the captain needed to show a great deal of flair. Counties who played against Oxford and Cambridge just saw it as a chance to build up confidence and polish up their averages. There was a strong case for robbing such matches of first-class status. So here we had a Cambridge captain, aged 25, lacking experience in the job at county level, being thrust into the England hot seat against the Australians when we were 3–0 down in the series. Clearly one for the future! Only a few months earlier, he had been undeservedly sidelined in India, yet now he was England captain. At least he was worth his place in the side. Athers had become a genuine Test opener, with the ideal game plan and temperament for the role, but all this 'Future England Captain' stuff from his supporters in the quality newspapers did him no favours – although it got him the job, I suppose. Alec Stewart was the preferred choice for me. I liked his aggressive, hard-nosed attitude, his positive body language. Alec had played grade cricket in Western Australia for winter after winter, from the age of seventeen, competing on equal terms with tougher customers than Athers would meet while captaining Cambridge. There was a feeling that Alec might be too brash on the field to suit the England captaincy, after picking up a fine for dissent in the Sydney Test of 1990, and showing disappointment at some decisions which went against him earlier in the year during the series against India – but I was there on both occasions, and he honestly didn't go over the top. Nothing as serious as Athers' misdemeanours a year later against the South Africans, when he got embroiled in the 'dirt in the pocket' affair and then was fined £1,000 for dissent. Some sections of the press tried to build the captaincy contest into a class thing – the Toff against the Oik, one headline summarised it – and I thought that a disgraceful slur on Alec and his family. Mercifully, he was big enough to rise above all that nonsense, dedicate himself to playing for England first and foremost and prove an excellent and loyal supporter to Mike Atherton throughout his years as captain. Purely from a selfish point of view, I believe Alec Stewart would have been better for my England career; I liked the way he encouraged his team-mates on the field, especially the bowlers.

I was more concerned at the time about getting back into the side, whoever was the new England captain. I'd watched the Tests all summer whenever I could, and felt there was a sameness about our pace attack. We were looking for accuracy and meanness, but lacked devil. The Aussies batsmen looked far too comfortable against fast-medium bowling on good wickets, and they hammered us, building up huge scores, then bowling us out twice. Game, set and match. My county form was good, with seven wickets in the Gloucestershire match, and six for 57 against Sussex, and Derbyshire's rota system had kept me fresh and raring to deliver. So the call came out – send for Devon! It was the Oval, after all, and I was looking for us to get some payback on my favourite ground. We won the match and I got six wickets, in the process bowling the quickest I've ever known.

In their first innings, I worked up a good head of steam right away and fired out three of their first four batsmen, leaving them 53 for four. I had Mark Taylor caught in the gully, Michael Slater caught at silly mid-on, as he was late on the hook, and David Boon tucked up, held at short leg. For the first time in the series, they were looking apprehensive, coming out to bat wearing all the arm guards and chest protectors they could find. It was exhilarating to see them hopping about on a bouncy pitch, instead of playing forward all the time on featherbeds. I got on fine with Athers in the field, because he knew I was on a high and just wanted to get at them, while Graham Gooch was very demonstrative towards me. Every time I got a wicket he was clambering all over me , and I did wonder why, if I was that good, he hadn't picked me earlier in the series when he was captain. When they batted again, I bowled a spell against Slater and Taylor that was the fastest I've ever bowled, even quicker than the following year at the Oval, when I blew away the South Africans. Slater actually backed away from me, and that was very gratifying, because he had such quick feet that you would have thought he'd get into position swiftly enough. When Dean Jones joined us as Derbyshire captain three years later, he mentioned that spell to me and said that he'd never seen Slater give himself room against a quick bowler. That just confirms what I felt at the time, that I had him rattled. I've bowled against Slater several times since then, and he only trusted himself to play the hook shot once – at Adelaide in '95, when he top-edged it and was caught superbly by Phil Tufnell at long leg. The rest of the time he has ducked under the bouncer – and I consider that a real compliment from such a dashing, quick-footed and gifted batsman.

After getting into my stride against Slater, I had Allan Border caught behind off a faint edge and then dismissed Mark Waugh, on the hook. This was a very gratifying wicket. Two overs earlier, I'd dug my heels in with Athers, insisting that Mark Ramprakash should be at deep square leg for Waugh. I wanted the old 'spider and the fly' routine, just to tempt a player who loves to take on the bowlers. So I kept the ball up to Waugh after that, hoping he'd forgotten about the deep square leg. Eventually, I gave him the bouncer and he hooked it straight down Ramps' throat. Waugh stood there, dumbfounded and I could tell he'd forgotten about Ramps, because he was looking to get on the front foot . Who said fast bowlers were stupid? Time and again in Tests, I have asked

Goochie or Athers for a man on the hook, only to be told it was a waste of a fielder. I knew what I was doing, but they didn't believe me. It's not as if I'd tell them how to bat against Shane Warne or Allan Donald.

My next wicket was the one that's been highly prized by every bowler in Tests throughout the nineties: Steve Waugh. He's so good at sucking you into bowling where he wants it. A lot of fast bowlers over the years have thought he doesn't fancy the short stuff, because he opens up on the back foot and looks a little tentative. Yet he likes it dug in at him, it helps him adjust to the pace, and he loves to drop the wrists on the short delivery, to steal a single. The way to get him is by pitching it up, trying to swing it late. I got him that way at the Oval, plumb lbw with a swinging yorker, my first ball of a new spell. After getting Waugh out, we knew we could win, and we bowled them out with an hour to spare. I was delighted that my old sparring mate, Angus Fraser got the Man of the Match award for taking eight wickets, and it's amazing to think that Gus only got back in the side because Martin Bicknell failed a fitness test on his damaged knee. It's always reassuring to see Gus at the other end, because he gives you consistent control, doesn't go for many runs and will never give up. He and Steve Watkin were terrific foils for me in that Oval Test, and we cleaned up all twenty wickets between us. My six wickets were each one of their top batsmen, and any strike bowler would settle for that. It was also good to hear strong support for me at the awards ceremony from the match adjudicator, Bob Willis. He said it was good to see me back in the side. I heartily agreed!

Inevitably, some cynics said that the Aussies were already on their way home psychologically, and that made it easier for us. They were due to fly back that final night, but the last thing they wanted was a long flight home, having lost a Test to the Poms. No one who made those suggestions can ever have played against the Aussies. Winning is everything to them. They would have loved to stuff us by 5–0, rather than the eventual 4–1 margin. If you still have doubts, don't forget that both captains were called in for a quiet word on the first evening by the match referee, Clive Lloyd. He told them to tone down the verbals, that there was a bit too much aggro out in the middle. The Aussies were trying all right! It was a good victory for us, but a deceptive one, and it started a trend that I know perplexed and annoyed Mike Atherton. After the Oval '93, we seemed to save our best performances for matches in series that we'd already lost or drawn. We won in Barbados in '94, Adelaide in '95 and the Oval in '97, while we pulled the series back against South Africa at the Oval in '94. There's no point in a fine collective performance in a dead rubber, you need to be out of the blocks right from the start of the series. We lacked that during the Atherton years. Perhaps our individuals pull out that little bit extra at the end of a home series because they're playing to get on the winter tour: certainly England have a far better record at the Oval than Lord's, earlier in the summer. I just love playing at the Oval, the wicket suits me and the crowd are very voluble and supportive of me.

That Oval performance was certainly instrumental in getting me on the coming winter tour to the Caribbean. Under a new captain, I hoped for a repeat of the 1990 experience.

EIGHT

ILLY'S NEW BROOM

The 1994 tour to the West Indies wasn't as successful for either England or myself, compared to four years earlier. We lost the series 3–1, I had to come home for a month for a knee operation and didn't do myself justice overall. But the most significant moment of that tour for me was the day when it was announced from Lord's that our new chairman of selectors was to be Raymond Illingworth. I had met him in my early days with Sheffield Caribbean, when also representing a Yorkshire League XI. He was manager of Yorkshire at the time, and he made an enquiry about me, wondering where I'd been born. When he discovered it wasn't in Yorkshire, he soon lost interest. A few years later, he was again to lose interest in me, but not before a series of humiliations that made me seriously think about giving up the game.

We lost the first Test in Jamaica after collapsing from 121 for nought to 234 all out. You can't do that and expect to stay in the game. We tended to fold at key times in that series, with the West Indies, as usual, taking their wickets in bunches after lying low for an hour, regrouping, recharging the batteries and then hitting us with refreshed fast bowlers. Our inconsistency must have been trying to Mike Atherton on his first tour as captain, but he didn't help himself sometimes with his leadership in the field. He frustrated me in Jamaica when I honestly felt I had Brian Lara in deep trouble, only to be taken off prematurely. We'd heard such a lot about Lara around the Caribbean on the last tour as well as this one, and although he took a hundred off us in '90 for Trinidad, that owed a lot to our bad bowling that day. We thought he was very talented, but nothing exceptional. After he scored 375 in the Antigua Test, we were prepared to revise our original opinion of him! Anyway, at Sabina Park we had them on the run at 23 for three, and after firing out Richie Richardson and Desmond Haynes, I felt full of aggression and pace.

Lara came in at number four and straight away, I had him looking tentative. I nearly had him caught by Chris Lewis at point, diving forward, and he didn't know where he was during those early overs from me. It was a great duel, and the knowledgeable crowd knew what was going on, with the attacking batsman being put through the shredder by the fast bowler, who had it all firing properly. Obviously, I wouldn't have been able to keep up the speed and hostility for too long, but Lara could have gone any delivery, and we needed to nail him then. I'd bowled well at him in the one-day international in Barbados, tucking him up around his rib cage, frustrating him because he couldn't get his shots going. Finally I had him caught at mid-on for 9. I wouldn't have been so rash to believe I had the sign on him, but he was there for the taking when I tore into him in the Test at Sabina Park. At one stage, clearly rattled, he took a time out, calling for the physio, Dennis Waight to bring out some eyedrops. He just wanted time to compose himself, rather than sort out his eyesight. I'd been digging the ball in at him, at speed, and he looked very unsure of himself. Having gone through the gears, I was in overdrive. Then Athers took me off. I said despairingly to my captain, 'I've got him, don't take me off now,' but he replied, 'No, you've had your spell, I need you later.' Yet this was the time to be flexible if we wanted to get rid of their best player and have them four down for just a few runs. It's true I was coming to the end of my spell in conventional terms, which would be six or seven overs, but this was an occasion when the normal treatment of a fast bowler shouldn't have applied. I was still fresh, on a high because I was making Lara struggle. If I'd got him then, there might not have been

103

any need to have me back for another spell later on, because they would have probably been all out cheaply. The crowd seemed as disappointed as me that the duel was over, but Athers wouldn't budge. It seemed as if he wanted to appear strong-willed for the sake of it, without realising that you've got to know when to go for the jugular, and throw the usual formula out of the window. That spell against Lara was one of the best I've ever bowled and I honestly deserved his wicket.

There was another side to Atherton's captaincy which was admirable, though. As an opening batsman, he really led from the front on that tour, showing a physical and mental bravery that set the standard everyone else should have aimed for. This was one impressive aspect of the 'Iron Mike' persona. At Sabina Park, he was subjected to a calculated assault by Courtney Walsh which was designed to break his will. It's a typical West Indian tactic to try to expose the opposing captain as a batsman, because that tends to weaken morale. It often worked. Not with Athers, though. Walsh kept peppering his rib cage, ripping his fingers across the seam, trying for the fend-off to short leg. Athers stuck at it superbly and although he was eventually out before the close, he won the respect of the opposition.

There was a marvellous moment when after Athers had been hit in the ribs for the umpteenth time, the television cameras caught him grinning wryly. He actually seemed to be enjoying the torture in a perverse kind of way. It was hugely impressive and increased his authority as captain in the eyes of all of us in the England dressing-room. For the rest of that series, his was the wicket that was most prized by the West Indies.

My respect for that side of Athers' character was even higher after Walsh also put me through the mincer at Sabina Park. I was hardly in the Atherton class as a batting technician, but Walsh decided I had to have the same treatment. It came after Andy Caddick and I had added thirty-odd for the last wicket. I'd whacked Curtly Ambrose for four, then when Walsh came on, I drove him straight for a stylish boundary – if I do say so myself! That didn't please Courtney and he started to aim at my body. Bowling around the wicket, and ignoring the stumps, he just concentrated on my body with the short ball. One ball ripped the cloth of my helmet's peak and I was physically shaken by now. The umpires, Ian Robinson and Steve Bucknor did nothing about it, they just let him carry on with the assault. Now I know there's no honour anymore between rival fast bowlers when they bat, and that I've bounced a few tail-enders myself, but he should have been pulled up after a while. I could understand his frustration, because our little partnership had held them up, meaning the game would now go into the final day. Perhaps I'd ruined Courtney's social plans! All he had to do was keep pitching the ball up, and I'd have a whack and almost certainly get myself out, which is exactly what happened when he managed to locate the stumps eventually. I'd been looking at umpire Robinson a long time, but I never complained. It didn't seem right, though, it was too cynical. I haven't had the pleasure of bowling at Walsh since Sabina Park '94, but when that does happen, he'll get some of that back. He's in my category as a number eleven batsman, so we'll see how he plays it. Cricketers have long memories for such things.

That proved to be my last Test of the series, because a knee operation took a month out of the tour. I'd felt a twinge just before I was about to bowl and it started to swell up after the game ended. It felt tight at the back of the hamstring and it hurt when I swam, so the sensible option was to have an operation back home. The surgeon cleaned up the rough stuff at the back of the knee and found nothing serious. That was a big relief to me and after rehabilitation, I was back at the end of March, in time to watch the Trinidad Test. Back for the ignominy of seeing us being bowled out for 46. That was a shattering blow, because we should have won that Test. We'd made it difficult for ourselves by dropping Shivnarine Chanderpaul twice, early in his innings, and he got past fifty, with good support from the tail. We ought to have been chasing no more than a hundred, but instead it was 194. We were still favourites, but all that changed in Ambrose's first over, when he had Atherton lbw first ball, and Mark Ramprakash ran himself out off the fifth ball. Total panic in our dressing-room, with the other batters suddenly realising that they'd better not have that shower yet, but get the pads on. Ambrose and Walsh knew they had only fifteen overs that night, so they could really slip themselves and come back refreshed next morning. They sniffed blood and we folded to 40 for eight at the close. Keith Fletcher, our coach, looked as if he'd seen a ghost and the whole team was shell-shocked. Fletch didn't move from his seat from the moment Ambrose started that first over. He should have cracked the whip with our batters, talking to them, telling them they simply had to stay in that night and forget the runs. The minds had to be cleared, we needed to be told that the West Indies would not fancy having to take ten wickets on the final day, defending a low target. All we needed was a solid start. Instead they ended up only needing to take two wickets on the final day.

Back at the hotel that night, all the West Indian supporters, players and the hotel staff were understandably elated, and you could sense they were pleasantly amazed at the collapse. We walked around like zombies, trying not to catch the eyes of anyone, especially the English supporters. What could anyone say? We were all traumatised. I felt so sad for those eleven players who experienced that humiliation, and when we somehow bounced back to win the next Test, in Barbados, I was elated for them. We'd made just one change – Phil Tufnell coming in for Ian Salisbury – and when the celebrations started in Barbados, those of us who hadn't played made a point of standing back and letting those eleven guys take all the plaudits. I remember saying, 'That took real character, guys – go out there and celebrate.' There are times when only those who have been through the rollercoaster of abject defeat followed by a great win should be in the spotlight.

Everything was all against us at the start of the Barbados Test, especially after we'd just suffered another hammering, in Grenada, against the West Indies Board XI. History was also against us, because England hadn't won a Test in Barbados for almost sixty years. Yet we ended up victorious, spurred on by thousands of England supporters who contributed to a brilliant atmosphere inside the Kensington Oval.

The England players always love Barbados, because our families come out at that stage of the tour and the Rockley Resort, where we stay, is very homely and relaxing. I'm sure that helped contribute to the way we fought back, but the crux of the matter was the opening stand of 171 by Alec Stewart and Mike Atherton. It was absolutely essential to regain some self-respect from day one, and I cannot praise those two enough after we had been put in. We had a platform to build on, and the other batters must have felt they couldn't let the openers down. Stewie got two hundreds in the match, playing beautifully while I was thrilled for Gus Fraser, who got bounce and carry on a good pitch to take eight for 75, brilliant figures for a great team man. On the last day, we needed to get Lara out quickly and Phil Tufnell obliged with a brilliant catch off a mishook. Yet again Tuffers proved that he wasn't as bad a fielder as the press had suggested. I remember one marvellous effort from him at Hobart on the Australian tour of 1990–91, when he dived and took a magnificent catch at square leg off my bowling to dismiss Greg Matthews. Tuffers had been shaken by all the media sneering and the derogatory banners in the crowd, allowing those negative vibes to affect his fielding. I could relate to that!

After Barbados, our bowlers found it hard work in the Antigua Test, where Brian Lara scored his amazing 375. It was such a flat pitch. Winston Benjamin moaned to me, 'I've never bowled forty overs in an innings in a Test, they should dig up this pitch!' and it wasn't a fair contest between bat and ball. Lara was totally in command. I'd had my doubts about him during that spell of mine at Sabina Park, but by the time we got to Antigua he looked a fantastic player. He was so focused. During the breaks for lunch and tea, he was on the outfield, having throwdowns, checking he was still timing the ball and moving his feet. All this when you're not out 200 odd! It was almost as if he knew this was his best chance of achieving something special. When he was 320 not out on the second evening, I was convinced he'd break Sir Gary Sobers' record of 375, and he did. Our bowlers were sick of the sight of him by then, but total respect to the man. He had the temperament, the desire to add to his phenomenal ability.

So with another overseas series lost, it was time to see what Ray Illingworth proposed to do about it. The early omens weren't good. It was odd that the new chairman didn't send a message of congratulations to us after the win in Barbados, because he must have known what character the boys had shown to bounce back after Trinidad. Then he waded in via the media, saying that time was running out for several of the established England players. Clearly he was going to be a 'hands on' chairman, unlike Ted Dexter, who may have said some baffling things at times but was always loyal to us in public, and very supportive in private as well. Illingworth was going to be a big challenge to Atherton's authority as he wielded the new broom.

From the first Test of that 1994 summer, I knew we were heading for disharmony under Illingworth. His first session with us during the Trent Bridge Test wasn't impressive or constructive, as he seemed determined to ruffle a few feathers. He told us that mobile phones and sunglasses were banned in the dressing-room and on the balcony, that we had to be concentrating fully on the cricket. He also got rid of the team's spiritual adviser in a petty gesture. The Reverend Andrew Wingfield-Digby had been working with us for the past three years, and he was good to have around as an outlet for anyone who wanted to talk to him. He never put any pressure on any player, he was a good bloke and a caring person. But Illingworth told the press, 'If any of the players need a shoulder to cry on, they're not the ones to stuff the Aussies next winter.' That was just big man's talk, empty words. Andrew was never involved as a shoulder to cry on, he just helped some players with their confidence. But the chairman had to be seen to be making an impact. He certainly did that with his team selection for that first Test. He picked Craig White, even though Athers said he'd barely seen Craig play. Steve Rhodes came in for Jack Russell as the wicket-keeper, while Richard Stemp was also in the squad. So the Yorkshire Connection was fairly strong in Illy's first squad, and some of us had to flick through the *Cricketers' Who's Who* to find out more about White. A super bloke, Craig, and a talented cricketer, but Illingworth's choice of him clearly sent out certain signals to the captain. He was stamping his authority on Athers right from the off, and was going to exercise a lot more power than previous chairmen of selectors. We were all hoping that Athers would persuade Illy to keep out of the way during play, but unfortunately, he was in our dressing-room a lot of the time during that Trent Bridge Test. You'd walk off the field, and there he'd be, telling you where you'd gone wrong. Keith Fletcher was completely sidelined right from the off. Illy had captained Fletch when they'd played for England, and he quickly re-established his authority over him in 1994, all those years later. The decision to recall Mike Gatting and Graham Gooch for the New Zealand series must have dismayed the captain, who had wanted to rebuild with a young team and players who he'd grown up and toured with. Yet Graham Thorpe and Mark Ramprakash missed out on the chance of some morale-boosting runs against New Zealand after taking all the flak in the West Indies. Not only was that unfair, but illogical. Gatting and Gooch weren't the future for English cricket, and Gooch's double hundred at Trent Bridge was irrelevant. The captain was being handed sides that he didn't want, and he was going to have to face up to it.

I took just two wickets at Trent Bridge, bowling poorly on a very slow pitch. So I was pleasantly surprised to be retained in the squad for the Lord's Test. I thought 'At least Illy's going for continuity, that makes a change.' So I came to Lord's feeling confident and I bowled well in the nets on the Tuesday and Wednesday. Geoff Arnold, our bowling coach was sufficiently impressed to say that he'd recommend to the chairman and captain that I should play. An hour or so later, as we practised again at the Nursery End, Athers called me over and said, 'Dev, you won't be needed tomorrow, you can pack up and go off to your county game.' I was stunned and asked why. Athers replied, 'Look, I'd like you to play, but Illy insists,' and he looked away, shamefaced. They wouldn't even let me stay overnight, have a warm-up with the boys in the morning, then wish them good luck and finally rejoin my county after making sure there were no late injuries to the seam bowlers. I had no problems with Paul Taylor, who replaced me, but surely it made sense to keep options open until the last possible moment. Illingworth had spoken, though. I realised a place was being reserved in the near future for the injured Darren Gough, who had started the season bowling with pace and heart, and it certainly did him no harm in Illingworth's eyes that he was a Yorkshireman. But any England player should be treated with more respect than I was that day. The press were buzzing around me, to get a reaction to the snub, and I had to be diplomatic. On the way out of the pavilion, with my kit packed, I saw the chairman by the office door a few yards away. He didn't say a word, but the look on his face could be summarised as 'That's sorted him out, now who's the boss?' If only he had put himself out and said something like 'Look Devon, I reckon it's going to turn tomorrow, so we're going in with another spinner' or something like that. Just show me a little respect. Why get rid of me so early? What harm would be done by letting me stay on till the next morning?

I drove off to Cardiff, where Derbyshire were due to play Glamorgan, and all the way down there, I was fuming. Why treat me with such professional disrespect? Was that the end of my England career? If so, what a humiliating way to end it. I was very disappointed with Athers. He didn't even try to soft-soap me, saying that I'd be back, to keep taking wickets for Derbyshire, etc etc. It was clear it was no longer his team, that he was being dictated to by the chairman. With the Ashes tour coming up, he was obviously keen to hang onto the England captaincy, even if it meant doing what

Illingworth told him, and being disrespectful to players. In that Lord's Test, Paul Taylor bowled just six overs in the second innings and didn't get the new ball, while Craig White hardly bowled. That was Athers' way of showing dissent – he wouldn't bowl those he didn't rate. This became one of the features of his captaincy from that time onwards.

That day was the lowest point of my career to date. Getting no support from my captain made it worse, especially after he'd admitted that he wanted me to play. A month later, I gave Athers my support when I added my voice to those who didn't want him to resign after the 'dirt in the pocket' affair. I rang him up on his mobile phone when he was lying low for a few days, and told him he should see the job through. He was the best man for the job then, with Gooch and Gatting too old and Alec Stewart obviously not in favour.

Mind you, to this day, I still don't know if Athers was guilty of ball tampering during that Lord's Test against South Africa. When I first saw the incident on the television, I thought nobody in his right mind would try to tamper with the ball in front of so many, but on the replay I wasn't so sure. It certainly didn't look very good as he applied dirt to the ball from his pocket. Perhaps he was just pre-occupied, unaware of what he was doing, too busy wondering what Illy was saying about his field placings! Anyway, I told Athers that it looked a silly thing to do, but he should stay on and ignore the resignation calls. He did so, but at a cost. He was now in Illingworth's debt, after the chairman had worked hard behind the scenes at Lord's to save Athers' skin. Illingworth was to impose himself even more on the captain after that, with sad consequences for a number of players, including myself.

I had no qualms about giving Atherton the support he should have given me a month earlier. I have to admit, though, that I had great pleasure dismissing him lbw at Blackpool in July, as we bowled out Lancashire for 83 on a flat pitch. I was bowling well now, making it clear that I wasn't going to lie down and take that June humiliation.

With South Africa 1–0 ahead in the Test series, the familiar cry arose as we went to the Oval, trying to square it. They did send for Devon, and I made history.

NINE

THE HISTORY MAN

We cricketers usually say we take little notice of statistics because they can be deceptive and are often picked selectively to stand up what may well be a contentious point. You'd be surprised how interested you get, though, in cricket history when you've just taken nine for 57 in a Test match! I certainly became involved in the mass of statistics that rained down on me on an August Saturday afternoon at the Oval after I led the England team off the field, having taken all those wickets. It was the greatest cricketing day of my life and I'll always treasure the fantastic support I got from the crowd during that innings, and the affectionate warmth of the reception as I walked up the steps to the pavilion. To round off a perfect weekend, we hammered the South Africans the following day to win by eight wickets, squaring the series. It was great to be back.

If you believe in fate, consider the events leading up the Oval. I had been bowling well for Derbyshire for some time, and I just had this feeling that I'd be brought back for the Oval, as I made my way to Hove for the match against Sussex. I made a point of packing my England gear in my car before I left Derby, hoping that I'd be going on up to London from Hove on the Monday night before the Test. My Oval boots were also packed, just in case. They're made by Ian Mason, my Sutton Coldfield cobbler, and although expensive, they're beautiful. Consisting of kangaroo hide and soft leather, with lots of padding around the insole and ankle, they give great support.

I wear them if the outfield is dry, to absorb the pounding on the feet, and they always get an outing at my favourite ground, the Oval. It just feels right to wear them there. So I had a sixth sense that I was going to be recalled, and a few hacks from the national newspapers came down that weekend in Hove, dropping hints to me. After being kicked out so humiliatingly from Lord's in June, I felt I had a lot still to prove – and I certainly wanted to prove Illingworth wrong.

I was named in the squad on Sunday morning and I couldn't wait. My morale was high as I drove to London next day after taking seven wickets in the match, getting bounce and making the ball cut back sharply off the seam. I'd also helped Derbyshire win the match with a dramatic last-wicket stand and my 15 not out gave me a lot of pleasure. Matthew Vandrau and I came together with 28 needed, up against a handy attack of Franklyn Stephenson, Paul Jarvis, Ed Giddins, Ian Salisbury and Eddie Hemmings. No problem. I smacked Stephenson flat over mid-wicket for six, almost demolishing an ice-cream van in the process, and I even managed to hit the winning runs. It was great for all our supporters who had come down for the match, and Sussex, who were going for the championship, were very sick about losing. So I couldn't have been more buoyant for the Oval Test. Somehow, Sussex were a good omen for me, because I usually do well against them.

It was great to join up again with the England boys and I was perfectly happy that the chairman had little to say to me. He'd made it quite clear what he thought of me two months earlier at Lord's. He made his presence felt, though, on the first morning – or should I say, he made his absence felt. I wasn't told I was playing until 10.15, a quarter of an hour before the toss of the coin. This was because Illingworth hadn't turned up to tell his captain who was to have the last place. It was between me and Phil Tufnell, and when I asked Mike Atherton who was selected, he replied, 'I don't know, the chairman hasn't arrived yet – it's either you or Tuffers.' What a farce. Tuffers and I were standing around like spare parts, laughing at our helplessness. The England captain had to be told by his chairman who was to play! It was no way to prepare England players for a Test match. Illingworth was just trying to impose his style and ego on all of us, especially Athers, putting him in his place like a little boy. Eventually, he turned up, didn't say a word to me and told Athers that I was to play. The chairman should have known what such uncertainty does to a player, but he probably thought we needed toughening up.

So within a few minutes of getting the glad news and commiserating with Tuffers, I was putting on my special boots, trying to clear my mind of the latest Illingworth humiliation. We were bowling. I took one for 81, but bowled better than those figures suggested, having a few catches dropped. But the most significant development for me that day was a major disagreement between me and my captain about how I should be bowling. It came after I had hit Jonty Rhodes on the head, as he ducked late into a ball that wasn't that high. I almost appealed for lbw because the ball didn't bounce as much as I'd expected. The ball cracked Jonty loudly on the helmet, and it looked terrible. I went down the pitch to have a look at the damage and the dent on the left side of the helmet was sizeable. There was one complication. I knew Jonty was an epileptic and the sight of him curled up on the ground was distressing and worrying. I'd never been concerned before about dishing out the treatment to any batsman, but this was different. I couldn't remember ever hitting someone just above the temple, and with his medical history, you had to be worried for him. In the end, the news was good. Jonty stayed in hospital overnight, had a scan and reported nothing worse than concussion. While he was being led away, a few of our guys came up to say, 'Don't worry about it, Dev, it wasn't deliberate' and they were right. I switched off from that incident straight away, and was raring to get at the rest of the batsmen. We needed to get just a couple more wickets, because with Jonty in hospital, that meant they only needed to be nine down to be all out.

For some reason, the ball started to swing and I was doing it at pace. Brian McMillan was joined by Fanie DeVilliers, and I was sure

I had the latter caught at second slip, off one that swung and left him late. It was out, no question, but umpire Ken Palmer said it was a bump ball. Human error, one of those things, and I still felt I could get DeVilliers any ball. Then my captain intervened. Athers told me to bounce DeVilliers, saying I was bowling too much like a gentleman. He told me to bowl bouncers, while I pointed out that the ball was swinging so much it was just a case of getting it in the right place and there'd be a nick. I said bouncers would be wasting our chance, that we needed to get them nine down tonight and then they'd be all out, with Rhodes absent. Athers wouldn't have it and took me off, telling Darren Gough to bowl, without even giving him the chance to warm up. Goughy was told to bowl bouncers and he went for sixteen in his first over. I didn't get another bowl that night, and they finished on 326 for eight. We'd let them off the hook and I was seething. So was Athers. He stormed off the field, without waiting for anyone else. In the dressing-room he said, 'Dev, why didn't you do what I told you?' and we had another sharp exchange of opinion. I said that DeVilliers would be thinking like a tail-ender, getting onto the back foot, waiting for the bouncer, while the full ball would expose his footwork and he'd soon edge the swinging delivery. To be fair to Athers, he eventually saw my point and apologised. It must have been a frustrating end to a difficult day for him. It's not often that the England captain has to hang around waiting for the boss to come along to say which bowlers he can have in his team.

It didn't end there, though. The next morning our bowling coach Geoff Arnold had a go at me as we were working together on the square, with me bowling into his glove. He said to me, 'You've got to do what the captain says,' and I had to repeat the gist of my views from the night before. I pointed out that Athers eventually saw my point and that I wouldn't tell him how to open the innings, so what was wrong with me sticking to my guns? But Arnold persisted and I got fed up with it all. I walked away from him, saying, 'Just leave me alone, I'll take six wickets tomorrow.' I got that wrong as well!

So to that amazing third day. My day. It began with Graham

Gooch sounding a rallying call on behalf of our captain. Athers had been given out lbw first ball the day before, and made it quite clear he thought it a poor decision. With a slow shake of the head and a meaningful look at his bat, it was obvious he felt he had nicked the ball onto his pad. But it wasn't a very bright thing to do to make his views so obvious, especially as the match referee was Peter Burge. He had been the official earlier in the series at Lord's, when Athers fell foul over the 'dirt in the pocket' affair. After that, it was a reasonable assumption that Burge was waiting to hammer our captain if the opportunity arose during this series. For an intelligent guy, Athers showed a lack of common sense by making his dissent so public and he received a £1,000 fine from the match referee. So with Athers the centre of attention on the Saturday morning, his predecessor did well to get us all together when the captain was out of our dressing-room, telling us to get behind him and give him our total support.

Then I had my little innings of four. Not even long enough to be a cameo and it ended with me slogging to mid-on, the usual kind of dismissal when I bat. But it was a long enough innings to get me even more fired up to hand out the tough stuff later that day. When I walked out to bat, some of their close fielders started on me, shouting, 'Come on! Let's hit him on the head!' Obviously they hadn't forgotten that I'd hit Jonty Rhodes on the first evening, although they conveniently ignored that he'd actually ducked into the ball. That didn't bother me. DeVilliers was the bowler, and he wasn't very quick anyway. I might have been more concerned if Allan Donald had been waiting to greet me! So I was assuming that I'd get one up in the blockhole, the double bluff with the bowler expecting me to be on the back foot, waiting for the bouncer. Instead, DeVilliers did bowl me a bouncer. I never saw it. It flew into my helmet grill, straight between my eyes. The South African close fielders enjoyed that, especially Brian McMillan and Darryl Cullinan, who were always up for the chirrup. 'Give him some more of that!' they were shouting and that really got to me. I turned round to the fielders behind the wicket and uttered the ultimate in subtle putdowns: 'You guys are f*****g dead! All you guys are f*****g history!' Powerful stuff, I think you'll agree – straight out of the school playground. It served its purpose though, getting extra adrenalin surging through me. I was spoiling for a fight by now. Allan Donald, a nice guy, came up to me at the end of the over and asked me if I was all right. He backed off after I told him where to go. It wasn't like me, but the cackling from the slips had got me going. They'd pay for that.

We were all out soon after, and we had a few overs at them before lunch. I was straining at the leash, almost foaming at the mouth. A sizeable bump was coming up on my head, but after a couple of tablets, a glass of water and a lump of ice on the spot, I was ready to roll. The irrepressible Darren Gough was pumping me up – 'Come on Dev, you give it to them!' – and with so much handclapping going on in the dressing-room, I could feel such strength from my team-mates. I couldn't fail. History was about to be made.

The most significant delivery of the 99 balls I sent down that day was the first. It went exactly where I wanted it, and came out of my hand at precisely the right time. I hit the crease at the right instant, with my left foot landing just where I wanted, and the ball climbed at great speed past Gary Kirsten, to be taken high to his right by our wicket-keeper, Steve Rhodes. My follow through took me almost into Kirsten's face, and I made it clear to him he was on the line. When I watched the TV video of that spell, David Gower said on air after that ball, 'I do believe Devon means business here.' Well spotted, David! Off the third ball of the innings, Kirsten went back, the ball hit the bat handle, and I caught it in my follow-through, almost colliding with John Crawley at short leg. First blood and a wicket maiden first over after my first two deliveries to Hansie Cronje zipped across his face like lightning. He was up on his toes, clearly worried about the pace and bounce. I couldn't wait for the next over.

In my second over, I nailed Peter Kirsten with the bouncer, gambling he'd go for the hook. He did, top-edged it and Phil

118

DeFreitas took a magnificent catch at long leg. Then it was Cronje's turn – bowled middle stump by one that cut back into him. He played the perfect forward defensive stroke, but he was about half an hour late on it. The earlier, short-pitched deliveries had set him up, so that when he did go forward, it would be tentatively. So they were 1 for three at the end of the second over, and the Oval crowd were going berserk. From the first ball, they were taking me to the crease with their roars and clapping. I could hear the din as I ran in, but not a sound when I was about to deliver the ball. It was uncanny, I was getting the adrenalin surge at precisely the right moment, while staying calm when I needed to. Why isn't fast bowling always as easy as this? I came off at lunch to a standing ovation, and I was inspired by that affection and support. After a quick shower and drink, I was just pawing at the ground to get at the batsmen again. No interest in food … why is that clock moving around so slowly?

Kepler Wessels was the next to go and it was an enjoyable dismissal. I decided to go round the wicket and tried to tempt him with a line that was short, outside the off-stump. I then pitched one up, and he went for the drive, but it swung late and he edged to Steve Rhodes. It may have looked a terrible shot, but I feel I'd softened him up well. Then Brian McMillan edged me to Graham Thorpe, who took a good catch at slip. Goughy had hit McMillan a couple of times on the hand, and he was looking to try and give himself room on the offside. He couldn't get out of the way of one that lifted and left him. Apart from that, it wasn't much of a ball! Then I really got one to swing to have Dave Richardson plumb lbw. It turned him round, it swung late and quickly towards off and it would have taken out middle stump. Craig Matthews was next to go, off the best delivery of all. It ripped him in two, jagged back, kissed his gloves and Steve Rhodes took a superb catch down the legside, leaping high to his left. So it was now 143 for seven, I'd taken all of them and we were wondering if I would get all ten. I'd never taken eight wickets in an innings before in first-class cricket, so there was no time like the present. Then Goughy intervened, getting Darryl Cullinan caught at slip for 94. I was just glad we'd got him because he'd been playing so well, but I still told Goughy he was a spoilsport!

My eighth wicket came when Jonty Rhodes played a tentative stroke to one just outside off-stump. He wasn't quite there for the stroke, his foot movement was late and I suspect the bang on the head I'd given him two days earlier was responsible. Enter Fanie DeVilliers, the bowler who had given me a lump on my forehead a few hours earlier. He certainly didn't fancy getting the strike, especially when I said to him as I passed him at the non-striker's end, 'Look, it's your turn soon – you won't get away from me.' You do say some daft things when you're a pumped-up fast bowler! I didn't get one ball at him, though, because I bowled Allan Donald off his pads with a quicker ball, as he gave himself a bit of room. So I'd done it – nine for 57 in 16.3 overs. I can remember almost every one of those 99 balls, particularly my rhythm and the smooth way I managed to release the ball at the right moment. It was a fast outfield and any edges off me through the slips went to the boundary. Cullinan stroked me for a few fours as well, but getting wickets regularly kept me going. I never felt the slightest bit tired. I was just above it all, it was the eeriest feeling. Walking up those pavilion steps doffing my cap to the crowd was the proudest feeling for me. I felt vindicated in my whole approach to bowling, justified in my frequent comments that fast bowlers are devastating when they get it right. You need luck to take nine wickets in an innings, when the other bowlers are rightly busting a gut at the other end to get into the action. They had some ill-fortune with some dropped catches, while some beauties were taken off mine. I do believe I've bowled just as well, but had bad luck. The Perth Test of '95 springs to mind when I finished with nought for 93, bowled very fast, yet had about six catches dropped off me.

Everybody was so excited afterwards. I did interview after interview and that night I couldn't sleep. I watched the game on the TV highlights and it still looked tremendous. The important thing now was to knock off the runs and win the match, so the satisfaction would be doubly great. This we did, with comfort, and the celebrations started in earnest. It meant more to me than when I took eleven wickets in the Trinidad Test of 1990, because that game was left drawn. Here, I had been the matchwinner. At the presentation ceremony, when I'd been given the Man of the Match Award, I bumped into the Prime Minister, John Major, a huge cricket fan and regular visitor to the Oval. He smiled and joked, 'Devon, I've come back from France from holiday to watch two days of cricket and you go and rob me of it. I've just got here for the presentations! Very well done!' As I prepared to do a TV interview after getting my award, our coach Keith Fletcher said to me, 'Don't forget to give Geoff Arnold a mention for his help.' I found that rather amusing in this instance, because Arnold's advice in that Test had simply been to do what my captain said, rather than trust my own instincts as an experienced fast bowler. I preferred to mention the support of my team-mates and the brilliant way the crowd lifted me. The South Africans appeared to have been alarmed at facing me, but I honestly believe that's always a possibility when a fast bowler gets everything right. Viv Richards had told me some years earlier, 'Look, Dev, no one likes batting against that extra speed. The trick is not to show it and also to take them on, it's make or break.' It was my day, everything was perfect. I've been asked since several times if there was an extra incentive for a black man bowling at white South Africans, after all those years of apartheid. I was obviously aware of the situation in South Africa, but this day was special for me as an England player. I had no personal animosity in the long-term against any of those guys, but I was fired up for other reasons. Their glee when I was hit on the head was a factor, so were my disagreements with Atherton and Arnold, the fact that I love bowling at the Oval on such a true, fast wicket, plus the nonsense on the first morning when I had to find out if I was playing, and also my simmering resentment at the way I had been treated at Lord's in June. All of that went into the pot, then add the extra spice of the fantastic crowd support, and the ball coming out of my hand just the way I wanted

– and you have history. The statistics show that it was the sixth best analysis in Test history, and I made a point in finding out who had better ones. Jim Laker's ten for 53 was the best-known, and the other four ahead of me weren't quick bowlers either. So my analysis was the best-ever by a genuine fast bowler. The nearest from another strike bowler is Colin Croft's eight for 29 for the West Indies. So I'll settle for that!

As it all slowly sank in over the next few weeks and I savoured the day, I actually allowed myself the luxury of thinking that I'd now get an extended run in the side. Perhaps my opinion on when was the best time for me to bowl might be respected, now that I'd shown that I could win Tests. I should have taken more notice of two moments during that historic Test. They both involved Ray Illingworth. In the first innings, as I was preparing to go out on the field, I was going through my usual routine of relaxing myself, listening to music on my personal stereo. Illy came up to me, tapped me on the shoulder and said, 'I hope that's not lullaby music.' The implication was that I was in danger of being too relaxed when I went out to bowl, rather than knowing the best way to prepare myself. It was hardly stirring, motivational talk from our chairman. Then, after taking all those wickets, Illingworth said nothing to me in our triumphant dressing-room. I saw him that night in the hotel lift. He obviously had to say something to me. His words were very supportive: 'I suppose you're famous now.' Obviously, that was meant as a joke, but a simple 'Congratulations, Devon' would have been more than adequate. I never expected something as human and mature from him as an apology for being so insensitive and dictatorial towards me at Lord's two months earlier. So many of Illingworth's actions from that summer of '94 were to prove pointers for when I was actually tempted to come home from an England tour, just fifteen months after making history.

TEN

TROUBLE BREWING

The more I think about my treatment in South Africa at the hands of Ray Illingworth, the more obvious it becomes that the signs were there in the previous two years that he'd end up alienating so many England players on that 1995–96 tour. Mike Atherton continued to be undermined by Illingworth's domineering methods and his awareness that he owed his job to him. So the captain couldn't stamp his own authority on the team, he kept having to compromise, bite the bullet and live with the chairman's interference. The signposts were clearly marked in the summer of '94, they were ever-present on the tour to Australia, and they were absolutely staring us in the face after we'd lost badly out there. Keith Fletcher was sacked as coach after the Australian debacle, and Illingworth was then given unprecedented power as chairman of selectors and team manager, with overall responsibility for coaching. Most of the England players feared the worst and we weren't wrong. Stand by for monologues about what it was like in his day and a scepticism about the new methods being adopted by other national sides. For Athers, it must have been very difficult, especially when Illy kept him dangling for a month at the start of the '95 season before deciding to re-appoint him as captain. So his status as England captain was being eroded gradually. That might explain why he failed to give me total support in South Africa when I needed strong backing from my captain. Perhaps he was too concerned about hanging onto his job to risk a major fall-out with Illingworth. Whatever the reasons, I

123

now realise that I was in Illingworth's firing line for some time before it came to a head in the early days of 1996. There were also various clues in the slow build-up to the South African tour that my captain didn't rate me all that highly or understand me enough.

There were few pluses to come out of the tour to Australia in 1994-95, apart from a great win in the Adelaide Test. A 3–1 defeat in the series didn't flatter Australia, who looked far superior to us in terms of preparation, attitude, leadership and competitiveness. We struggled in the one-day internationals, and even got rolled over twice by the Australian Academy side, made up of their best young players. The tour party wasn't the one that the captain wanted. I'm sure he'd have picked Angus Fraser if given the final say – as the captain should – but Illingworth didn't seem to rate Gus. Eventually, Gus joined the party after a lot of injuries hampered us, and he took five wickets in the Sydney Test, even though not match fit. He proved a point, as he did in the West Indies on the 1998 tour after being written off two years earlier by Illingworth when he was manager. Gus Fraser never let any England captain down.

Athers also wasn't too impressed that some of the younger batsmen were either left behind or moved down the pecking order in favour of Graham Gooch and Mike Gatting. Goochie and Gatt shouldn't have been picked for that tour; they had declined at the highest level. Illy was very keen on having their experience on hand, but Athers wanted his own group of players, as he had in the West Indies, before Illingworth became chairman of selectors. It was a tour too far for Goochie and Gatt, and their selection must have contributed to Athers' uncommunicative frame of mind. On that tour, he seemed to lack drive, there was no killer instinct from him on the field and he didn't communicate very well with us. He gave the appearance of being fed up of being lumbered with a group of players who wouldn't have all been his preferred choices. Getting sniped at by Illingworth from afar didn't help, either. At a sportswriters' lunch just before Christmas in London, the chairman publicly criticised Athers and the quotes that came back to us in

Australia were tactless and uncomplimentary. That was all the captain needed after we'd lost badly in the first Test at Brisbane, and when Illy flew out to Melbourne at Christmas to join us for a week, I imagine the atmosphere between the two of them was a little chilly. The rest of us just tried to get on with playing cricket – but we weren't doing a very good job of that.

We had a nightmare run of injuries, with so many players coming and going. Alec Stewart broke a finger twice, Darren Gough broke a bone in his foot, Graeme Hick went home with a slipped disc, Martin McCague had a stress fracture of the shin and Joey Benjamin contracted chickenpox. So did I, which meant I missed the first Test. My spots were so massive that the hotel maids were almost too frightened to come into my room. The amazing thing is that my two daughters had chickenpox at the same time as me, but Jenny kept that from me because she knew I'd have been worried about them. It took three weeks to get my fitness back and I was so down about it. After coming to Australia on a high after my Oval effort, I was really fired up to get at the Aussies at Brisbane. I was bowling well and feeling very good about my form. I got back for the Melbourne Test, where we folded badly – all out for 92 to lose by 295 runs. The game ended with a Shane Warne hat-trick, and I was the third dismissal, caught at short leg off my glove. When I came in, my partner Alec Stewart said, 'What are you going to do then, Dev?' and I told him, 'If it's up to me, I'm going to smack it.' Then it got complicated. Alec said, 'Well, he might bowl you the flipper, or the googly or even just the leggie. Just block it, Dev'. So I did, and still got out! I should have tried to swat him. I got my revenge later in the series, though.

Two-nil down, with three to play and we were becoming a laughing-stock in the eyes of the Australian public. We didn't get any supportive comments from our chairman, and our captain became more introspective, with Illingworth's negative vibes seeping in. The next Test, at Sydney came soon after Melbourne and we missed a great chance to get back in the series. It wasn't Athers's greatest Test as captain. In their first innings, they made only 116, but it should have been no more than 80 after we had them 65 for eight, with some great bowling by Gus Fraser and Darren Gough. I picked up a couple of wickets and a warning from the match referee, John Reid after I gave Mark Waugh the 'send off', pointing him to the pavilion after getting him caught at the wicket. Mark had made some derogatory comments about me in the papers, saying I wasn't all that quick and he looked forward to facing me. It stung, possibly because I'd been frustrated by my illness and our poor form so far, so I behaved out of character when I got him out. I've never done that before or since, and John Reid said, 'I know you're not like that, so just cut it out.' I appreciated his low-key reaction, because a more officious referee might have fined me.

We should have made the Aussies follow on, but we couldn't quite ram home the advantage, so we had a lead of 193. Then we batted a little too slowly in our second innings, taking 72 overs before the declaration at 255 for two left them 449 to win. The timing of Athers' declaration was remarkable, because it left Graeme Hick stranded on 98 not out. Hicky had just blocked three successive deliveries, and although we all knew the declaration was imminent, there was no question of him missing out on the chance to get his hundred. But Gooch had been muttering for a time, telling Athers that no one was bigger than the team and that we needed to declare soon. I hadn't even put my bowling boots on yet. Surely Graeme would get another over? Suddenly, Athers clapped the batsmen in and I said, 'That's a bit harsh, isn't it?' No reply. The crowd was stunned, so was our dressing-room and when poor Graeme came in, he threw his bat across the dressing-room, his face deathly white. If you'd cut into Graeme's body at that moment, you'd have struggled to find a drop of blood. All the players felt so sorry for him. The team needed a morale boost and Graeme's hundred would have been one for a start. It's not as if Hicky had been dragging his feet, he was looking at the time equation rather than how many overs were left in the day. Anyway, Athers had batted slower while getting his own

67 earlier in the innings. A quiet guy like Graeme Hick would have had a big confidence boost from a hundred against Australia. Athers has subsequently been honest enough to admit that this was one of his biggest mistakes as captain, but the damage was done. The rest of the team just slumped, as if someone had switched off the lights. We couldn't lose the match, but we needed to be really focused and firing on all cylinders when we went out to bowl at them on that fourth evening. That premature declaration knocked the stuffing out of us as they rattled on to 139 for nought at the close. Hicky was particularly low. I kept looking at him as he stood in the slips, and I hoped that an edge wouldn't come his way, because I don't believe he would have held it. His body may have been there, but his mind had gone, he was empty. We were all flat in the field when we should have been buzzing.

On the final day, they needed 310 off ninety overs, a much more gettable target than the earlier one of 449 in four sessions. Athers went on the defensive too early on that final morning, getting Phil Tufnell bowling to a packed legside field, aiming the ball outside leg stump, looking to frustrate the batters rather than bowl them out by attacking. Again, we weren't going for the jugular. Eventually we got amongst them with the new ball and Gus picked up five quick wickets. But he was overbowled by at least four overs, and I ought to have been given a blast sometime before the light closed in. The sweat was pouring out of Gus. Having not been originally selected, he wasn't at his sharpest physically because he had been playing only weekend cricket in Sydney when the call came. Then Tim May and Shane Warne came together with seven wickets down. They did well to hold out for more than an hour to get the draw. I'd have loved to be given a crack at them, but the light was too poor by then. So Sydney was an opportunity lost.

There were a couple of consolations for me, though. I picked up my hundredth Test wicket when Michael Slater dragged one on – they all count! – and I nodded in Phil Russell's direction for all his hard work and encouragement. I hoped that he too would be enjoying that moment, in Durban. I also made my highest Test score. So what if it was only 29 not out? I smashed Warne for two big sixes, one straight and the other over midwicket, and then stroked him beautifully through the covers, just like a real batsman! I was only in for eighteen balls, but I couldn't see what all the fuss was about when I faced Warne. Just smack him and don't worry what he's trying to bowl at you! When the electronic scoreboard at Sydney flashed up the news that I had reached my highest score and the crowd applauded, I remembered to wave my bat in acknowledgement of my historic feat. For some reason, they all thought it was very funny! I repeated the dose in the next Test, at Adelaide, smacking Warne out of the ground. That was a big hit and I was clearly on a roll because the Test Match Special team on BBC Radio chose the time when I got my highest Test score at Sydney as their 'champagne moment' for that Test. That meant I received a jeraboam of champagne when we got to Adelaide and it came in very handy, because we ended up celebrating a remarkable victory. When you consider the low state of our morale after the Sydney Test, that we had been knocked out of the one-day series by Zimbabwe and Australia's 'A' team, that we were down to just five fit batsmen for Adelaide – it was a great triumph. We were so short of batting depth that Steve Rhodes came in at number six and I even crept up to the dizzy heights of number ten. They needed 263 to win at four an over and at lunch on the final day, they were 16 for nought. The way we'd been bowling on the tour, it was either going to be an Australian victory, or, if we were lucky, a draw. But when the chips were down we showed great character and they batted rashly. I had Mark Taylor caught at slip, Gus Fraser got David Boon taken down the legside and Michael Slater hooked me to Phil Tufnell, who took a brilliant catch at long leg. Suddenly they were 22 for three. Then came the key dismissal when I bowled Steve Waugh first ball. I was torn between pitching it up to him or bowling a bouncer and I still wasn't sure as I ran in. So I stopped halfway and as I walked back, I decided to pitch it up. The ball came into Waugh and knocked back his off-stump. A great sight and now they were 23 for four. Chris Lewis managed to get some reverse swing going and they slumped to 75 for six. But then at last we had some true Aussie grit as Ian Healy and Damien Fleming hung around for two hours, until Chris Lewis had Fleming lbw with eight overs to go. We had six overs left when Athers brought me back to knock over the last man, and off my very first ball, I nailed Peter McIntyre plumb lbw with a quick, straight delivery. We'd played really well to force that win, making them panic by getting stuck into them after lunch. Suddenly we were back in the series at 2–1 down, with Perth still to come. It didn't bother me that 2–1 wasn't a fair reflection of the difference between the two sides, I was just delighted that the Aussie gloating had stopped for a few days at least. Adelaide '95 remains the only Test victory I've experienced in Australia.

The Aussies bounced back sharply enough at Perth, as good sides tend to do. We were hammered by 329 runs, and it was our own fault. When you drop ten catches in the match, you can't expect much sympathy. Off the fourth ball of the Test, Gooch dropped Slater in the slips off my bowling. It was an easy chance, and to add fuel to the flames, the ball went for four. Goochie said, 'Sorry, Dev, the mind is willing, but the body's a bit slow!' A tour too far, Goochie. I can't complain too much, though, because I proceeded to drop Slater twice. The first was an easy caught and bowled chance and then I spilled one at long leg off a top-edged hook. No excuses, I just lost it in the breeze. My figures don't suggest it, but I bowled very well in that game. I broke Slater's right thumb, which made me feel a little better, and I found the hard, bouncy Perth wicket greatly to my liking, not far off the Oval in my scale of affections.

That Perth thrashing was a truer reflection of the difference between the two sides on that tour. We were pretty awful all series, apart from that great final day at Adelaide and some good sessions in the draw in Sydney. Our management wasn't very impressive, quite apart from Athers still clearly having to learn his trade as captain. Geoff Arnold, our bowling coach, kept pulling out tapes of

Craig McDermott, who took 32 wickets for them in the series, and telling me, 'This is how we should be bowling,' which ignored the fact that McDermott and I were totally different types of fast bowler. Keith Fletcher, a nice enough guy, was totally out of his depth as an international coach. We got more and more fed up of Fletch going to press conferences after another bad day, saying how disappointed he was and that we needed to do better. As if we didn't know that. He needed to be more positive with his players, rather than keep pointing the finger at them. On the final morning at Adelaide, we needed John Crawley to build on his half-century and to get support from the remaining batsmen to give us something to bowl at. Fletcher's team talk before play started wasn't very impressive: 'I've seen stranger things happen, you know. We might get away with a draw.' Thanks, Fletch. In fact we got away with a win by being more positive than our coach. In 1994–95, it was absolutely fair that we got stick in Australia. We fielded badly, they ran their singles very sharply, and our physical preparation was clearly not good enough because we picked up so many injuries. It can't just be about ill-luck, you make your own luck by proper preventative training. We were just slapdash. It was all very well for Ray Illingworth to say we had to be more professional and get our strategy right, but what if the preparation by our management is amateurish? I had first-hand experience of the Australian way in 1996 when Les Stilman came over from Australia to coach Derbyshire. Les told me as soon as we first met that summer that he'd studied who I had got out in Test cricket. He had discovered at what stage in the innings I had taken those wickets and had come to a definite conclusion about the best times to bowl me. Why couldn't the England think-tank under Illingworth come up with a database like that? It's something that the Australians do as a matter of course; so does Bob Woolmer as South Africa's coach. Not until 1997, when David Lloyd started to reorganise England's approach, did we have a proper, professional awareness of how to give yourself the best possible chance to play international cricket successfully. Before that, we were just playing at it, hoping something would work out. Meanwhile, we kept performing inconsistently, getting slagged off by arrogant Aussie supporters, telling the Poms that we were rubbish. It was hard to put up much of a case against that accusation.

There was little sign of improvement at the start of our next series, at home to the West Indies in 1995. Athers had finally been put out of his misery by the chairman, who decreed that the captain would carry on. It was all rather unnecessary when you consider Athers had one hand tied behind his back over the last tour party, and that the chairman had made it clear that he was now the supremo after Fletcher's sacking. Why did he have to flex his muscles by keeping Athers in suspense? If he wanted to change the captain, just get on with it, otherwise show the present skipper some respect, the very least he himself would have expected when he captained England more than twenty years earlier. The result was that we all felt on trial when we came to Leeds for the first Test, the captain included. That's no basis for a positive approach and we were hammered by nine wickets. I can understand how much pressure Mike must have been feeling, but again he disappointed me with his safety-first approach and inability to see clearly the key moments when the game could have been tilted our way with a little more flexibility and boldness.

We batted first, got rolled over cheaply and it was absolutely imperative that we struck back early. The ball was moving around off the seam, and it was a typical Headingley situation, where runs are at a premium and the bowlers shape the outcome of the match. We had the perfect start when I got Carl Hooper out first ball. In came Brian Lara, clearly not attuned to the situation because from that first over of the innings, he started to fire off big shots. Ian Bishop told me later that when Hooper was out first ball of the innings, their dressing-room was in chaos. Batsmen were scrambling around, looking for thigh pads and all the other protective gear and no one was settled, ready to bat. Least of all Lara. Apparently, he was all over the place, looking for his gear. He certainly played like it when he finally got to the middle. Great player though he undoubtedly is, he wasn't mentally tuned in to what was needed, he was just teeing off and launching himself at the ball. He flailed away at me, and got a few runs in the third man area, but in the air. He could have been caught several times, but got away with it and I conceded 24 in those first two overs. It wasn't through typical Lara finesse, it was hit and miss, and he was vulnerable. But Athers played safe by taking me off, seemingly ignoring the fact that Lara was stepping away to leg, carving me in the air through third man. All we needed was to have the third man wider, pack the offside field and hope he got himself out in this frenetic mood. I blame myself also. I should have stopped to think it through and asked Athers to change the field, but I was over-dosing on adrenalin, enjoying the roars of the crowd, tilting at the great Lara. I plead guilty to all that, but fast bowlers have often lost it through the red mists and it was surely up to my captain to pause for a moment and see the big picture. When you're dealing with Lara, you should be thinking how soon you can get him out, rather than what it's going to cost you. We fell into their hands by going on the defensive after just five overs.

Eventually, the spinner Richard Illingworth got Lara with an intelligent piece of bowling, flighting the ball up, to have him caught at slip. By then, I was grazing in the outfield, not trusted to come back for another spell. I picked up Curtly Ambrose at the end of the innings, but my 7.3 overs wasn't a huge workload, when you consider Darren Gough could only bowl five overs due to his injured back, and the other seamers, Peter Martin and Phil DeFreitas, bowled fifty overs between them. It would have been nice to have shared the burden, but I was just frozen out, a victim of Lara's frenetic assault. That night, at close of play, neither Athers nor Illy said a word to me, and I really wished I could have talked it through with them. Of course, I respected Illingworth's playing and captaincy record, and I would have dearly loved to be able to sit down with him and talk through that spell of mine. If he'd told me I'd bowled rubbish – fine. If he could have helped me to work out how to bowl more productively in the future – even better. I would have taken constructive criticism smack on the chin. All I ever wanted from Illy and Athers was communication, straight talking, respect. If they didn't rate me, then tell me to my face. Just talk to me. I wanted to know if I'd got carried away in that first spell against Lara. Should I have reined in the aggression, tried to get the ball in a different area? The bare facts say I failed, but my instincts told me I was so close to nailing him, and that might have altered the complexion of the match. Fast bowlers like me, who aren't great performers like Lillee or Marshall, need to be switched on at the right time to channel our hostility and pace into the key areas of an innings. When was the best time to bowl me? I would have relished the chance to discuss this with Illy or Athers but it never happened, least of all at Leeds in that 1995 Test.

I had a chance to make amends in the second innings, but it was denied me. They needed only 126 to win, or, if you like, we needed to take ten wickets pretty swiftly. You might have thought that a strike bowler like myself could possibly be of use if you needed to take wickets quickly, but I was relegated to fourth choice bowler. They had lost an early wicket and Lara came in to join Hooper. Martin and DeFreitas were the opening attack and both batsmen kept looking at me, rather puzzled. DeFreitas disappeared for 33 in his four overs and even then, Richard Illingworth's spin was preferred to me. Hooper and Lara both said to me during that period: 'What's happening? Why aren't you bowling?' I was trudging from fine leg and then up to mid-on, while Athers just blanked me. I said to the two batsmen: 'You probably won't see me for the rest of the series, although I might sneak in at the Oval', and their amazed reaction heartened me. All this was going on in the middle, but the result was never in doubt, the runs were just flowing everywhere, so there was time for a quiet word. Here we had two of the opposition batsmen wondering what the hell was going on with our bowling line-up, content that they were easing to victory but making it clear to me that they were bemused that I was being sidelined. It was some consolation to have some respect come my way from Hooper and Lara. The four overs I was allowed to bowl at the end, when they were easing to victory, struck me as a complete waste of time. What was the point in putting me on near the end, when the game had been decided? That's not the time for a strike bowler. You need to be in there right away, striving for the quick breakthroughs that might just give you a glimmer of hope, not when Lara and Hooper are set, vying with each other to see who can hit the ball furthest out of the ground.

On that Sunday evening, after we had been hammered by nine wickets, I was the last to leave our dressing-room. I was so disappointed at the manner of our defeat, at my own sub-standard contribution, the feeling that we might have pressed them harder, and that the England team appeared no nearer to consistency. It seemed wrong that no one said a thing to the team in general as we sat in the dressing-room. This was the time when we needed to hear from the captain and supremo about where we'd gone wrong, how we could turn it round, what lessons we had learned from this match. It was time to get things out in the open, thrash out our differences, talk as a unit. Instead, everyone had just disappeared to their respective bolt-holes in various parts of the country. It was just like a game of village cricket – get bowled out cheaply, lose the game and slide off. What a sorry state of affairs. Where was all this new professionalism we kept reading about? I'd love to have known the thinking behind the decision to shove Robin Smith in as opener against Ambrose, Walsh and Bishop on a seamer's pitch, when Robin had hardly any experience of the job throughout his career, let alone in a Test match.

I drove away from Leeds, seriously wondering about my England future, but also about the efficiency of the new broom. It didn't really matter how Athers and Illy viewed me, but as someone who desperately wanted England to be the best, I was very pessimistic about the quality of decisions being made. Illy had put himself in the firing line now that he was in charge, and there was no evidence of the kind of progressive ideas that were needed. Athers was close to being a lame-duck captain; he was in the chairman's debt and we were drifting, because the captain wasn't going out with the XI that he wanted. Angus Fraser was dropped for the Leeds Test, and I'd stake my life on the fact that Athers would have wanted him on the park, in conditions made for Gus. I would have loved to see him at the other end to me as well. When we got to Lord's, the chairman decided to over-rule the selectors' consensus at the weekend for the next Text, so he dropped Steve Rhodes as wicket-keeper and gave the gloves to Alec Stewart. This was on the day before the Test. In the event, it worked out for him, because Alec took an excellent catch to dismiss Lara on the final day that set us on the road to victory. Yet it had to be wrong that the captain was told his team, rather than have the final, decisive say. I honestly felt sorry for Athers, because he was just there to rubber-stamp the chairman's decision after Illy had made it clear in public who was the boss. So Athers just had to lump it. Illy was obsessed with playing a balanced attack, involving two spinners, and that's why Alec Stewart had to keep wicket to accommodate five bowlers, yet West Indies had no qualms about that. They just picked four bowlers, like they have done in modern times, convinced that if the four are good enough, that will do the trick. We just delved back into the past.

I was dropped for the Lord's Test, which was no surprise, but another Derbyshire bowler made a major impact. Dominic Cork at last got the chance he deserved, and turned in the best analysis of any England bowler on debut. England won by 72 runs, and I was absolutely delighted for Corky. He had waited too long for his England call-up, although I never told him that! He had such a passion to play for England, and since 1992, when he had played one-day internationals, the steam had been coming out of his ears every time he had been passed over. I'd come back from a Test match and deliberately wind him up, folding up the full England sweater before him, saying, 'If you want this, mate, you've got to work very hard for it. You can look, but don't touch!' Dominic was the ideal bowler to get wickets against the West Indies, because they would underrate him. They'd think he wasn't all that quick, and look to whip him through the on-side, unaware that he could swing the ball away from them because he bowled so close to the stumps. He deserved to be selected, and when he did the hat-trick and scored an unbeaten fifty in the Old Trafford Test, it seemed as if we had unearthed someone who at least might aspire to Ian Botham's all-round greatness, even if he would always fall short of Beefy's prodigious efforts. Dominic enjoyed the adulation and attention, he quickly acquired an agent, and soon he was lacking direction, getting pulled away from focusing on the cricket field. He got it all out of perspective too soon after his great summer of '95, forgetting that when you come back to a county dressing-room after great international feats, you do so with humility. It all happened too quickly for Corky, it appeared an easy game to him, and his life and his cricket suffered. That was a shame for his county and country, because a committed Dominic Cork is a very fine cricketer.

While Dominic was storming the barricades for England, I was trying to regain some form and confidence for Derbyshire. I bowled well, taking 56 championship wickets at 23 apiece; a wicket every seven overs, not bad for a strike bowler. After getting ten in the match on a flat wicket at Kidderminster, I was brought back into the Test series, at – guess where? This time, though, the scales were tilted too far in the batsmen's favour at the Oval. Only 22 wickets fell in five days, and it wasn't the same for me. All the bowlers got little encouragement from the lifeless pitch. We dropped a few chances, and I spilled Carl Hooper off my own bowling – an easy chance, to my right, to which I reacted lazily. Hooper was on 1 at the time, and he went on to make 127! I did feel I bowled well, though, plugging away for 39 overs. By now, I was starting to think about the forthcoming South Africa tour. Earlier in the season, after my disappointment at Leeds, I hadn't dared think about a winter tour, but I believed that my county form would be in my favour. I hadn't gone away from Leeds to sulk at Derby, I'd worked hard and bowled quickly. Of course, the nine for 57 was in my mind from the Oval the year before, and I was hopeful that our tour selectors would realise that their batsmen would not have forgotten that day.

After the West Indies Test ended in a turgid draw, Ray Illingworth was interviewed on television. As usual, he had a fair amount to say, and when asked about my tour credentials, he said, 'I suppose we've got to take him,' which was hardly a glowing endorsement. That day, Illy had called a few players in for a chat, and I was one of them. He told me I'd be going on the South Africa tour. But he also said: 'You've got some work to do,' and I assumed he was referring to my troublesome knee that had flared up after a county match at Chelmsford. I missed the final two county games of the season to have keyhole surgery and my rehabilitation programme was scheduled to start in earnest some six weeks prior to the South African tour.

Peter Lever was also at that Oval meeting. He had been appointed the England bowling coach for the South African tour, and clearly he felt special responsibility for getting me fit. The day after I had the operation, Lever called me in hospital, asking when he and I could work together in the nets. He said that Illingworth was breathing down his neck, wanting us to get started. I pointed out that I was unlikely to be roaring into the nets for a little while yet.

By late September I was gingerly stretching and testing the knee on the outfield at Derby. Lever turned up, telling me that I had to bowl in the indoor nets so that he could have a look at me. I sent down a couple of deliveries but then had to stop as the indoor surface was proving too painful for my knee. Two days later I was asked to go to Leeds for further work with physio Wayne Morton. Wayne put me on the treadmill and then supervised some sprints, and he felt I was progressing satisfactorily. Lever and Illingworth, who were also there, didn't agree. They clearly felt I was coasting, making too much of my injury, and going on too much about the need to take the recovery period in stages in case of a setback. It didn't dawn on me until much later that Lever and Illingworth were so keen to get me fit to bowl because they had big plans for me. A technical overhaul, in fact. Without my knowledge, the battle lines for South Africa had been drawn up two months before the tour started.

ELEVEN

A RACIST SLUR

One day in the summer of 1995 as I sat watching Derbyshire bat, my team-mate Adrian Rollins came up to me and showed me this article he'd been reading in a cricket magazine. 'What do you make of this, Dev?' he asked me. When I read the front cover of the July issue of *Wisden Cricket Monthly*, and the article inside, I was astonished. No wonder Adrian, like myself a black professional cricketer, wanted some confirmation that he should be upset about what he had just read. The two-page article, by someone called Robert Henderson, was headlined 'Is It In The Blood?' and it suggested that as a matter of biology, non-white cricketers were incapable of giving full commitment to England. The words 'negroes', 'instinctive patriotism' and 'biology' were included, and the writer asked the question *'Is that desire to succeed instinctive, a matter of biology? There lies the heart of the matter.'* Not for me it didn't. I was very proud to have represented England and no one in a civilised country like ours should be allowed to suggest that someone who wasn't white might be lacking in drive and dedication.

There was one passage which I found particularly offensive. *'It is an entirely natural thing to wish to retain one's racial/cultural identity. Moreover, the energetic public promotion of multi-culturalism in England has actively encouraged such expressions of independence. However, with such an attitude, and whatever his professional pride as a cricketer, it is difficult to believe that a foreign-born has any sense of wanting to play above himself simply because he is playing for England. From what, after all, could such a feeling derive? If a player has such a lack of sentimental regard for the country which nurtured him, how much less reason have those without even one English parent or any of his educational advantages to feel a deep unquestioning commitment to England? ... It is even possible that part of a coloured English-qualified player feels satisfaction (perhaps subconsciously) at seeing England humiliated because of post-imperial myths of oppression and exploitation.'* In my mind this was a racial slur and the writer and the magazine couldn't be allowed to get away with it. I had got used to people knocking my bowling, or saying I couldn't bat or field, but this wasn't just about cricket or cricketers, it was a stick with which to beat non-whites in the United Kingdom, irrespective of their profession. I didn't believe the vast majority of people in Britain felt the same way as Henderson, and I was determined that he mustn't be allowed to say such things without being called to account.

Phil DeFreitas, my county team-mate, was pictured on the second page of the article and he was, by definition, being singled out. I told him we had to deal with this urgently. The authority and prestige that had been associated with the name *Wisden* for more than a century of cricket coverage had been damaged in my opinion, and I couldn't believe the editor had allowed such an article to appear in his magazine. As I read it, the piece attacked all black and Asian cricketers in England, suggesting there was something biological that just might prevent them playing their hearts out for England. I was particularly incensed, because even my detractors would surely acknowledge that I'd always tried my utmost. By extension, the implication was that if you were coloured, you couldn't aspire to the same professional standards as a white man. A black doctor or an Asian lawyer would be inferior. The article had said nothing about the white cricketers who had come from other countries to represent England – players like Andy Caddick, Graeme Hick, Robin Smith or Allan Lamb. It was aimed at non-whites, questioning their attitude. Somehow, the slur had to be knocked on the head swiftly. It wasn't enough to dismiss it as contemptible rubbish, because a magazine of *Wisden Cricket Monthly's* status is taken seriously in the cricket world and read by thousands. Some racists might see the article as an encouraging confirmation of their prejudices. This article wound me up in a way few things ever have in my life. I'm a fairly placid kind of a guy, who tends to see the good points in folk, but this was different – even compared to what happened subsequently with Ray Illingworth in South Africa.

I contacted the players' union, the Cricketers' Association, and was disappointed at their cautious reaction. David Graveney, the General Secretary, talked to the Association's lawyers and then told me to forget about the matter, that nothing could be done about it. The lawyer's advice was that I would only be wasting money, that the article wasn't libellous. David agreed that some passages might be interpreted as being abusive, but his opinion was, why give Henderson's views more publicity? I was hurt and dismayed at that. Having been an Association member since coming into the county game, I would have expected more tangible support. Why should I just forget it? I started seriously to doubt the whole purpose of the Association. Was it worth taking an interest in the union if one of their members was not going to get some active response to something as serious as this? At that time, the Professional Footballers' Association had been doing some excellent work to combat racism in their game, so I contacted their Chief Executive, Gordon Taylor. His response was very positive and supportive. He said that, if necessary, the PFA lawyer would be available to me, but as it turned out it never got to that because I had my own. I'd rung up the magazine's editor, David Frith, to ask what he was doing printing that piece, and he said the subject was a matter for legitimate debate. He wouldn't agree to my request for him to admit publicly that the article was rubbish and shouldn't have been published. Frith issued a statement regretting an error of judgement but pointed out that in the disclaimer which appeared in every issue of the magazine, it was spelt out that the views expressed were not necessarily those of the editor or his editorial board. Part of his statement read: '*I also believed that it was an editor's responsibility to tackle different issues, to bring them into the open so that solutions might be found. My particular hope in respect of this article was that the plight of foreign-born cricketers in this country and those with immigrant parents – whether from West Indies, Australasia, Southern Africa or Asia – might be better understood when their difficulties were considered. Publication of this particular article was, I now realise, not the best way to have gone about it. The national-identity element was drowned out.*'

Yet Frith didn't seem perturbed that such an article would give encouragement to racist hooligans who were ready to pollute the atmosphere in cricket. The idea of someone believing I didn't try my hardest really hurt. When my kids had grown up, they might have asked me why I hadn't fought that article. What's more, anyone who had been on my first tour to the West Indies in 1990 knew how much I wanted to put one over on those guys, even though I was born in the Caribbean. I was just bursting with pride to be playing for England. My kids had all been born in England, for heaven's sake. They went to integrated schools, and had white godparents. We all considered England our home, and colour wasn't an issue in our choice of friends at school. My wife, Jenny, although of Jamaican background, was born in Yorkshire. I paid my taxes here. No one was going to question my commitment to England.

One of the things that concerned me about the article was that some readers might then believe that a lot of non-white cricketers were taking advantage of the system to qualify for England under supposedly lax registration rules. So if you allegedly get in through the back door, you're not fully committed to England. Yet I came to England at the age of sixteen to study, to be with my father and it was two years later before I even played cricket. It was fully ten years later that I played for England, so I reckon that I'd been fully integrated. Cricketers like Gladstone Small, Phil DeFreitas and Wilf Slack were the same. It was interesting that white players coming

141

here from South Africa, Zimbabwe, New Zealand and Australia didn't seem to bother Henderson in his article.

My lawyer, Naynesh Desai, had briefed a barrister and he advised me that I had a strong case for libel. His duty, though, was to tell me that no libel actions are ever straightforward, and that there was always the chance that I would lose. The initial costs would be in the region of £30,000 and I risked being out of pocket by around £100,000 if the case went against me. That obviously was a concern, but I wouldn't give up, even though at times I wondered if I was getting out of my depth. I couldn't believe how this issue had taken off in the media, with so many radio phone-ins and articles in the newspapers. David Frith kept making desperate calls to me, trying to reach some sort of compromise. There was even a suggestion that he and I should meet, with Dennis Silk there to mediate. At the time Dennis Silk was on the TCCB's disciplinary committee, and although I had great respect for him, I felt it would be wrong to involve him. I knew that the owner of *Wisden Cricket Monthly*, Sir John Paul Getty, was very embarrassed at the furore and damaging publicity, and he'd be very keen to dampen down the over-heated atmosphere, but I wouldn't back down on something as important to me as this. Jenny was very resilient at the time, telling me that if we agreed to a mediator getting involved, our opinions would most probably be diluted and a gloss would be put on the case. In the first few weeks after the article appeared, I had phenomenal support from the public, plus stacks of letters, and this gave me the strength to carry on with my legal action. David Gower, my first England captain, wrote a newspaper article, criticising the piece in the magazine, which was doubly gratifying since he was a member of *Wisden Cricket Monthly's* editorial board. Ian Botham said he would gladly go to court and testify on behalf of DeFreitas and myself about our commitment to England. In the *Guardian*, that famous campaigning journalist, Paul Foot wrote a very strong piece, taking my side. The general public were fantastic. In London one day, a bus driver caused a tailback of cars when he jammed on the brakes after seeing me and shouted over encouragement. Straight after that, I got into a taxi and the cabbie went on at great length about Henderson's article, telling me to stick to my guns. Things like that reminded me that the overwhelming majority of people in Britain are fair-minded and would expect me to fight the case, irrespective of their colour. I believed in the traditional British values of fair play, and the risks were worth taking.

As the legal machinery rolled into action, the magazine's lawyers responded by saying that they would plead fair comment, that the article wasn't meant to be malicious. But in October 1995, just before I was due to go on the South African tour, they backed down and agreed a settlement. So we had to go the High Court for five minutes, to have the agreed settlement read out in open court, and subsequently I was awarded damages. Driving past the High Court that day, looking for a parking space, I remarked to Naynesh, 'Looks like there's a big case on today, look at all the press.' I didn't realise they were all there to see me and to get my reaction to the successful conclusion. After we'd parked the car, we were within a hundred yards of the entrance when a mass of photographers started running towards me. I was amazed at the media interest, and I lost count of the interviews I gave that day – but I was happy to do so, because it brought to a wider audience the dangers of allowing views like Henderson's to go unchallenged. There was one particularly enjoyable moment when the judge said to me at the end of the formal proceedings, 'Well, Mr Malcolm, I hope you do to the South Africans what you did last time.' That visit to the High Court certainly put me in the right frame of mind for the forthcoming tour. Incidentally, DeFreitas conducted his own action later and was also successful, receiving damages.

I just wanted to get the matter out of the way before I went to South Africa a few weeks later. The money awarded wasn't an issue to me, because I shared it between the Derbyshire Childrens' Hospital and the Devon Malcolm Cricket Centre in Sheffield. Some of the money went to the hospital, because they needed new equipment and funds were scarce. My daughter, Natalie had an umbilical hernia operation there and I was very impressed by the care and attention they gave her. Besides Karen, my sister, is a nurse and I love kids. It was a pleasure to do something for the hospital, and to see something worthwhile come out of that shocking article. That cricket centre in Sheffield which bears my name is my way of giving something back to the community which helped me go forward into professional cricket. It's situated in an inner-city school called Earl Marshall School, and it's there for underprivileged boys and girls of all races – Pakistanis, West Indians, Somalis, Yemenis, Bangladeshis, West Indians and, of course, for whites. The idea is to help them develop cricket skills, and with Chris Searle there as the inspirational driving force, the kids can learn so much. Chris is a former head teacher and was the founder of the Centre. He's done a fantastic, unifying job. With such a racial mix at the centre, there's genuine hope that the youngsters will grow up to respect not just their own culture, but others as well. I remember playing for Asian sides in Sheffield, and I enjoyed getting to know about their religion, how they lived their lives. Cricket teaches you respect for others. Sheffield Caribbean Club, where I first learned about cricket in any depth after coming over from Jamaica, was so important for me at a time of my life when I might have drifted, just like many other black kids. They put in so much hard work on my behalf, encouraging me to bowl fast and even organising transport for me. I still keep in touch with them and I'll always be grateful to them. So the Devon Malcolm Centre is my attempt to bind young people into one community.

Although my disgust at racism was at the heart of my libel action, I must say that I haven't experienced racial abuse much in England. There was one day at Leeds during the 1991 West Indies Test when a drunk in an executive box had a go at me. Perhaps he thought I was one of the West Indies players and he was doing his patriotic duty by calling me a black so-and-so. Some black players feel that they get too much stick from crowds in Yorkshire, but I won't hear a word said against them. I never had any problems when playing in Yorkshire, and I get a warm welcome from the crowds when playing county or Test cricket up there. You get abuse wherever you go, with someone shouting 'Malcolm, you're crap!' but I don't believe that's because I'm black – perhaps it's because I really am rubbish! It has to be water off a duck's back when the crowd is baying at you, otherwise you can't do your job. My grandparents used to say to me 'If you know better, then do better', so you must rise above the abuse and treat everyone the same, irrespective of their colour. The white man was never a demon to our family as I was growing up in Jamaica. At college, my Physical Education teacher was a white Englishman, my Spanish teacher was white and from Spain, the vice-principal was Chinese and I was taught Chemistry by an Indian. So we had no problem with race; it was up to others if they wanted to see negatives. Now I'm sure some extreme black people will see me as an 'Uncle Tom' character, soft towards whites and not militant enough, but I believe everybody should show dignity. When black kids ask me what to do when they encounter racism, I tell them to be dignified. Don't be put off by racist chants or abuse, because if you lash out, you'll then be categorised and that's what the bigots want. Mind you, the situation is much worse in football than it is in cricket. Ian Wright, the Arsenal striker, is a friend of mine, a warm-hearted guy who does a lot of unsung charity work, and at times throughout his career he has had to put up with a lot of racial taunts on the field. Wrighty needs to get over such obstacles and not be distracted. Paul Ince, the Manchester United footballer, is another who has taken a lot of racist abuse on occasions, but nothing like the awful stick that was flying around twenty years ago when black players like Cyrille Regis, Laurie Cunningham, Viv Anderson and Clyde Best were the advance party for future generations. Brendan Batson, Gordon Taylor's assistant at the PFA, was another player to turn things round by his quiet dignity.

I suppose I'm lucky to have a calm temperament, so it's easier for me to shrug off the racists than for fiery characters like Ince and

Wright. My family believe I inherited my grandmother's serenity. She ran the home back in Jamaica, keeping amazingly calm when there was so much mayhem going on around her. Maudlyn had great management skills, organising all of us with such coolness, with a smile never far away. I'm glad she passed on some of her temperament to me, because soon after winning that libel action in the autumn of 1995, I was to face the biggest test of character in my career.

TWELVE

NIGHTMARE IN SOUTH AFRICA

In October 1995 I left for the tour to South Africa, convinced that my knee would soon be a hundred per cent and that I would be a major influence in the Test series. I had no doubt that the mental scars from my nine for 57 would still be there in the minds of the South African batsmen. Three months later, I came home straight after a Test match that my own manager had accused me of handing over to the opposition on a plate, but grateful that I hadn't succumbed to the temptation to punch Ray Illingworth on the nose in the heated aftermath of that Cape Town Test. I believe that the provocation I'd suffered might have tilted many other cricketers over the edge, leading to an incident that would have finished their England careers, but I'm not a violent man and had no intention of making Illingworth's case against me look justified. When I arrived at Heathrow Airport a few days after Cape Town, the flashbulbs were popping, the notebooks and microphones were at the ready. I was the target. There would be no comment from me that day, but as I parted from those of my England team-mates who'd also flown back with me, one of them shouted over to me, 'Go on Dev, you tell them what he did to you!' It had only dawned on the lads in Cape Town that I'd been singled out by Illingworth all tour for some hostile treatment. I'd deliberately kept it from them that he was making my life a misery at times and that my captain Mike Atherton was not as supportive to me as he should have been for any of his players. The aim was to win the Test series, and for that you needed a strong team morale. That's why I kept quiet, to avoid distracting my fellow players. But I don't feel the need to keep quiet any longer.

One of the keys to the lack of trust in me from Illingworth was the precise state of my fitness at the start of that tour. He and the England bowling coach, Peter Lever, seemed sceptical about my rate of progress after my knee operation in September. Yet when I arrived in South Africa, I was still a fortnight short of the necessary gym work to get the knee absolutely right. One of the lads noticed that I was limping in those early days on tour, something I didn't realise but which subsequently made sense. Subconsciously I was favouring my left leg, to take the strain off the one that had recently undergone surgery. It's a perfectly straightforward reaction, stemming from the desire to avoid undue pressure on the vulnerable knee. All I needed to do was get some hard work in on the running machine, lift some weights with my right knee, and with the physio Wayne Morton's careful guidance, I'd be as right as rain in a fortnight, ready for the First Test a further three weeks away. But not only were Illingworth and Lever impatient with my rate of physical progress, they had radical plans for me. They wanted to re-model my bowling action. I had passed my 32nd birthday, taken over a hundred wickets in more than thirty Tests, yet it was time to 'streamline' me, and overhaul my action. Lever told me that the ball with which I had dismissed Carl Hooper in the Leeds Test a few months earlier was the perfect ball. I couldn't remember much about it, other than it bounced and had Hooper caught at slip, but Lever believed I had delivered that ball in a different way to my usual style, and that was the way forward. As far as I was concerned, it was just a case of getting the ball down the other end as quickly as possible, but the bowling coach said my arm was higher, that I was looking inside my left shoulder, rather than over the shoulder. Apparently I'd flicked my left arm quickly in the manner of Allan Donald and generated extra pace as a result. All very flattering to be compared to Donald, but I couldn't quite see it. I thought I bowled quickly because I was naturally strong, rather than flicked out my left arm, but Lever knew best. He said I also

148

needed to stand taller at the moment of delivery. It then dawned on me what Illingworth had meant during our meeting at the recent Oval Test when he told me I had work to do. He wasn't just referring to my physical condition; he meant a technical overhaul. It was a hell of a lot to take in as I was settling into my rehabilitation programme in those early weeks of the South Africa tour. Yet I thought that if it meant I'd become a better bowler, I owed it to the management to give it a go. There were misgivings, of course, because I'd always seen myself as an instinctive fast bowler, rather than a technical all-rounder like Dennis Lillee or Malcolm Marshall. It did seem very odd that Lever was basing his assessment of me on just one delivery at Leeds – a ball that, for all he knew, might have been my loosener which came out of my hand just right. I was convinced the South Africans feared me, after dominating them with a bowling action that met with my new bowling coach's disapproval. In the end, I should have been stubborn, digging my heels in right away in South Africa, but instead I gave it a go. It's ironic that, later, Illingworth thought I had been stubborn and too resistant to change. He never gave me any credit for at least listening to his scheme and trying to make it work.

Early in the tour, when we were training in Johannesburg at the Wanderers Ground, Lever kept on at me about the new action, while I tried to get through to him that I needed to regain peak fitness before I could tinker with something as important as that. I needed to be confident that my knee would withstand all the various new pressures that the overhaul might bring. Significantly, Darren Gough was also being cajoled in the same direction, but he couldn't handle it. Illingworth ended up telling him to go back to what he did instinctively, while I continued to get the heavy hand. It really should have been the same for both of us. There was no evidence available for Lever to prove that what I was doing was wrong, because he couldn't work the video recorder. I'd been told that the play-back would be very useful as I came to terms with the new action, and when I asked Lever where the video machine was, he said it was back at the hotel. None of the coaching group knew how to operate it, so I never saw myself on our video throughout that tour! It's rather important to use the video as a way to win over a cricketer who needs persuading whether it's wise to tamper with a bowling action that's got him through more than ten years of first-class cricket. They expected me just to take their word for it, rather than show me evidence of how it would improve me.

Soon, we had a tense meeting at our hotel in Johannesburg. I had been summoned there by Illingworth to explain why I had missed the bus taking some of the players out to Springs the night before to watch the closing stages of a day/night game featuring the rest of the squad. The batting coach, John Edrich had brought forward the time of departure by an hour, and I pointed out that I needed to carry on with my rehab work in the hotel gym. By the time I'd finished that, the bus had left without me. We had been warned not to venture out alone in Johannesburg, so I opted to stay in the hotel. Edrich must have reported my absence to the manager and so I had to present myself to him the following morning. He accepted readily my explanation and said, 'Right, what about this bowling action? Are you going to do it or not?' He spoke very aggressively, as if he was exasperated with me. Also present were Lever and my captain, Mike Atherton. Athers looked embarrassed, sitting there with his head down, avoiding eye contact with me. I would have liked to hear from Athers about the wisdom of this proposed overhaul, but he said nothing as Illingworth spoke to me in a hostile fashion. I said I'd continue having a crack at it and Illingworth replied, 'If it happens, fine, but if it doesn't, no one will know about it.' That suited me, but the overall tone of his remarks made me believe he was unimpressed by my progress. I lost some respect for Athers in that meeting; it baffled me that he should have looked so uncomfortable. He ought to have made it easier for me in the aggressive presence of Lever and Illingworth, but instead he just failed to speak up for me. That meeting wasn't a great omen for me, but I would be getting used to feeling isolated on that tour.

At the end of October, we played in Soweto. That was the first game of first-class cricket ever to be played in the townships, a historic day. Ray Illingworth was approached by Dr Ali Bacher, the managing director of the United Cricket Board, with a request that I should play. The feeling was that a black man representing England in the township of Soweto would have great symbolism. I knew how much work Dr Bacher and his coaches were doing in the townships, and they deserved all the support we could give them. Illingworth told me he understood I wasn't yet fit enough, but I said I'd do my best and would happily turn out if it helped the development programme. I got the feeling his arm was being twisted, but I let it pass. I had enough on my mind, because I was nervous about all the attention I was getting in South Africa. There had been a lot of murders recently, and I was aware that a black guy fielding on the boundary would be an ideal pot-shot for some extremist, whatever their colour or politics. I knew apartheid wouldn't disappear overnight, despite the recent general election that had swept the ANC and Nelson Mandela into power. Going out with my team-mates at night was an unnerving experience, because my black face stood out like a sore thumb. The boys wouldn't have understood how anxious that made me feel. Sometimes I was so worried how I'd be viewed by the black locals that I would stay in my hotel room and not dine out with the lads. Of course, I wanted to give young black kids hope of a better life and I'd do all I could in terms of publicity, but there was only so much I could say.

The game had started when I discovered why I had been asked to play in Soweto. President Nelson Mandela flew in by helicopter to set the seal on a great day for the new South Africa. We had no idea he was coming. We were in the field at the time, the game was halted and we were lined up to meet him. I was bowled over when he came up to me, shook my hand and said, 'I know you, you're The Destroyer,' delivered with that wonderful, warm smile. I was astounded that he should recognise me and highly flattered that he'd bring up my bowling spell at the Oval that had indeed destroyed his country just over a year earlier. The pride just swelled up inside me that this man – who had gone through so much suffering with such dignity – should be standing there, shaking my hand, having taken the trouble to do some research on me. He'd seen so much death and poverty, and here we were, in a stark township, talking about cricket. His easy manner allowed me to stumble through a couple of incoherent sentences and for the rest of the day, I just floated on air. I'd always refused to go to South Africa until Nelson Mandela had been released and there was majority rule. He was now leader of his country, talking to me with such natural friendliness. Apart from Jenny giving birth to my three children, it was the greatest day of my life. Then I was taken over to the press box with the President. I was totally out of my depth. It would have been nice to have received some tips on protocol, on how to handle such a situation. The cameras were trained on us and after the President had dealt with the media with his usual dignity and good humour, I was asked for my reaction. I was still so overwhelmed by euphoria that I could only offer platitudes. We were in South Africa to win the Test series, but we'd also do all we could to help Dr Bacher's development programme. I wish I could have been able to offer something more deep to summarise my feelings, but I was inadequate, so emotional. It was also a great day for my England team-mates, and I certainly wasn't the only one to arrange for a framed photo of the day Nelson Mandela came to shake our hands.

Meeting Mandela made me feel as strong as Samson. With the Oval triumph still fresh in my mind and my rehabilitation going to plan, I felt the President's visit was a positive omen for me. I'd be after those South African batsmen in three weeks' time, hoping that the great man would forgive me if I rolled them over again. Yet, within twenty-four hours, my manager had knocked the stuffing out of me, bringing me unceremoniously down to earth. I had bowled fourteen overs in the day, and with my knee still not quite a hundred per cent, there was a slight puffiness the following morning. So Wayne Morton packed it in ice at the ground before I was due to take part in the usual warm-ups with the rest of the squad. The opposition were nine wickets down, so we'd have to take the field again. But then Illingworth came in to see me on the treatment table to say that I wouldn't be staying at Soweto, that I had to go off to Centurion Park for a session with Peter Lever. Centurion Park was an hour's drive away, and the manager's directive didn't make sense to me. We needed to take just one wicket to bring the innings to a close, and surely then I could work in the nets at Soweto with Lever. Why pack me off to Centurion Park right now? I told Illingworth that I needed treatment from our physio on my knee and Wayne said I wasn't yet ready to leave. But the manager insisted, saying the bus was ready to take me, and that I mustn't hang around any longer. He clearly didn't want me around. Wayne had to curtail the treatment. I sat on a bus for an hour, feeling bewildered, and then Lever put me through a two-hour session, working on my new action. At the end of it, my knee had swollen up and was much puffier than in the morning. After I had left Soweto, Illingworth went over to the press box, and revealed that he had sent me off to Centurion Park with the bowling coach. That gave the press a big hint that the management weren't happy with me, so from now on, the public pressure on me was going to be even greater.

Why did Illingworth go public on something that was supposed to be a private matter? Was I that useless as a fast bowler? It seemed a strange time in my career to be trying to alter my bowling technique, esepecially in view of the successful bowling perform-ances I had behind me. Perhaps he felt that Lever needed to be seen to be justifying his presence on tour, otherwise questions might be asked at Lord's about the expense of having the bowling coach out in South Africa. In the meantime I had the media pointing the finger at me for alleged stubbornness, hypochondria and shortcomings as a fast bowler. This misuse of the press I regarded as a quite inappropriate manner for a manager to conduct himself. Peter Lever's admission a couple of months earlier that he'd never been injured in his fast bowling career proved that there was a lack of understanding about the recuperation period required for a fast bowler to get over a knee operation, both physically and psychologically. At a time when I needed to be restoring self-confidence as I eased back to full fitness, the effect of what was being done was to undermine me, and it was being done in public. I admit that I had bowled without fire in the first innings in Soweto, but that was due to having to experiment with my new action, as well as tread carefully, with my rehabilitation still not complete. It's not as if I had asked to play. I'd made it quite clear I wasn't fully fit. This had been accepted by Illingworth and I only played as a favour to Dr Bacher, at the request of the England management. Could it be that Illingworth was annoyed at all the attention I had received from President Mandela earlier in the game? As the only black man in the England party, I had been singled out to play by Dr Bacher and then publicly acknowledged by the great man himself. The President had been alongside me when the media questioned us, making the whole event worldwide news. It made Devon Malcolm a bigger name than just the day before, because I had been pictured alongside one of the most admired people in the world. But all of that was none of my doing. I didn't know he was coming to the game, nor did I know I was going to be the focus of so much attention. I had been in a daze from the time the President arrived at Soweto, and no one could possibly accuse me of muscling in on all the publicity. Perhaps Illingworth thought that sending me away from Soweto, and then informing the media, was a way of putting me in my place. If so, it was bizarre man management. Then things became even worse.

Soon after the Soweto game ended, I had a word with Mike Atherton about my new action. I said that nought for 32 off fourteen overs in the first innings might have appeared respectable, but I had never looked like getting anyone out. I lacked pace and fire, even though I still wasn't physically fit. The ball was coming out of my hand all right, and it was swinging, but there was little speed there. I was worried that Lever was robbing me of my natural assets as a fast bowler. What did Athers want me to do? He replied, 'I want you to bowl quickly, like you did against them [the South Africans] at the Oval,' and I said I'd struggle to do that with this new action. 'Leave it to me, Dev, I'll sort it out,' he told me and I felt reassured. I didn't want to be in the same room when Athers discussed it with the manager, because I had felt embarrassed for my captain the last time, when he seemed so diffident, leaving Illingworth to run the show. Athers called me in my room later to say, 'I've spoken to Illy, and he says "Fine. Do what you want to do, but you're on your own"' In other words, if I failed in the series using my usual style, there would be no support from the manager.

Illingworth was obviously getting infuriated by me, and he soon started criticising me, again using the press. Atherton had dealt with the press in a routine briefing, then left the room. Unknown to him, Illingworth and Lever carried on talking to the press, homing in on me. Lever discussed the difficulties he'd been having with me, finally describing me as 'a cricketing nonentity'. Illingworth was also far from complimentary about me, so the press boys had a great story. I knew nothing about any of this until one of the English tabloid reporters told me what had been said. I was horrified at Lever's dismissive description of my bowling credentials, and that our private work in the nets should now be out in the open. This was in contravention of our agreement that none of this would ever be made public. What's more, Athers had told me that everything had been sorted. I was flabbergasted. How could two members of the tour management slaughter one of their players in public in this manner? If any of the players had broken ranks on tour, in breach of our contract, Lord's would have thrown the book at us, yet it was acceptable for Lever and Illingworth to throw mud. How could you call someone who has taken over a hundred Test wickets a 'cricketing nonentity'? I'm sure I could have sued for libel, because if you have played at the highest level and taken nine for 57 in a Test match, how can you be a nonentity?

I refused to comment to the press that night, determined that I would give the management absolutely no justification for coming down hard on me. There would be no slanging match between us; I would keep my dignity at least. Next morning, at breakfast, my team-mates were hugely embarrassed. They'd all seen the papers and the 'cricketing nonentity' quotes were all over the front page. I approached Illingworth for an explanation, and he came up with the stock response – he'd been misquoted. Judging by what various sources who were at that press briefing had to say, that seemed highly unlikely. The general feeling was that Lever and Illingworth were both gunning for me. All this with the Test series just three weeks away. I had started the tour as the fast bowler in pole position, once my routine rehabilitation had been completed. Now I was fading out of contention, with the management castigating my ability and my commitment. It was also the start of the period when I deliberately set out to distance myself from my team-mates. What I was going through was too serious to debate with the boys over a drink. They all had enough individual challenges and problems on tour, and it was vital that our team morale shouldn't be blown apart because of the situation between myself and the manager and coach. They would be distracted. Whatever my difficulties, the main aim was to beat South Africa in the Test series. So I stayed in my hotel room more and more, becoming isolated and miserable. With two months left of the tour, it was set to be a long hard road ahead for me. My main hope was that my captain would come round to supporting me, and get me focused on the job ahead after I'd sidelined my critics in my own mind. That proved to be a vain hope. Athers let me down more than once.

I started to get dreadfully homesick after the Soweto game and the 'nonentity' farce. My third daughter, Stephany, had been born just six weeks before I left, and it was hard enough not to be able to see her without sitting in my hotel room, wondering what I had done that was so wrong in Illingworth's eyes. Jenny's phone bill started to soar. After I'd been publicly humiliated, she took it upon herself to be the one to try lifting my spirits. She rang me daily from Derby, telling me what was in the papers, that all our friends were angry and

156

bewildered. She told me she felt useless most of the time, especially now that she couldn't come out and join me on the tour. There had been plans for her and the three girls to come out at Christmas but that wasn't possible anymore. Jenny had been interested in South Africa since she was a student and, like me, she would never have gone there until Nelson Mandela was released and they'd held a democratic general election. She would have been fascinated by the changing political scenery, but she said that as she couldn't possibly be civil to Illingworth's face, making the journey was impossible now. Disappointing, but understandable. She was torn between seeing me and having to celebrate Christmas knowing that I was very unhappy. You always know where you stand with Jenny, so perhaps Illy was lucky she didn't come after all. So instead of joining me in South Africa, we spoke daily by phone. Jenny ran up such a huge telephone bill that British Telecom had to contact her just to check it was the right amount and that she had indeed clocked up all those units. There wasn't a great deal of profit left from my tour fee after we'd paid the phone bill!

With the management so sceptical about my bowling and my attitude, I never had a chance of playing in the First Test at Centurion Park, which proved to be a damp squib, with thunderstorms allowing just two days' play. I was reinstated, though, for the next Test at Johannesburg. This was one of the hardest games I've ever played in from a psychological point of view. I reverted to my old action, knowing that I was now on my own in Illingworth's eyes, and took six wickets. There was some good pace there and enough hostility to keep the Oval in the minds of the South Africans. I got collared in one over by Brian McMillan, when he smacked me for 6, 4 and 6 off consecutive bouncers. That was my fault. Athers wanted me to pitch the ball up to McMillan, but I had a sneaking feeling that the short ball would do him, and I was still indecisive when I ran in to bowl a couple of times in that over. I'd ignored the cardinal rule of getting it clear in my own mind before running in, and paid the penalty. Apart from that, I was pleased with my performance and even happier that Athers' fantastic defiance throughout the last day saved the Test for us. Jack Russell also gave him great support and many of us stayed in exactly the same spot in the dressing-room area throughout the last day, willing Athers and Jack on. The South Africans were shattered that they hadn't been able to finish us off, and I was certain that we could capitalise on that huge disappointment in the last three Tests. My confidence had suddenly soared and with Ian Botham saying supportive things about me on television, I was beginning to think I'd turned the corner. Ian said I'd secured my place for the rest of the series, and I certainly hoped so.

The next Test at Durban turned out to be a massive blow for me. I wasn't selected, when the conditions were ideal for seam and swing. It was devastating, because I had looked forward so much to getting stuck into the South Africans at Durban. My old county coach, Phil Russell had sent me a fax a few days earlier saying, 'Just you wait till you and Corky get on this wicket here – you'll love it.' As Phil was the head groundsman there, I assumed he knew what he was talking about. So far that season, Shaun Pollock and Malcolm Marshall had been knocking over sides cheaply for Natal at the Kingsmead Ground, and I thought the pitch would be ideal for me. In the nets during the build-up to the Test, I bowled very well. I was getting the ball to swing a lot and generating hostile pace. On the first morning, I was so confident of playing that I brought my special Oval boots to the ground. As we started to lap the boundary, before getting into the nets, Athers came up to me and told me I wasn't playing. I honestly thought he was joking. He said he had a feeling that it would swing and he was going with Mark Ilott and Peter Martin alongside Dominic Cork. Yet I was swinging the ball in the nets and although I lacked the discipline and accuracy of Peter and Mark, I did compensate with extra pace. Gus Fraser was also left out, which prompted Illingworth to remark that Athers was now growing up as a captain, because he had at last left out his great mate. What an insult to your captain, to suggest that you're influenced in team selection by a close friendship! They also selected the spinner,

Richard Illingworth, in conditions that favoured the faster bowlers, so there were a few baffled experts that morning. Not least the England players whom I spoke to as we loped around the boundary. They couldn't believe I'd been dropped. That's not meant to be derogatory to my team-mates who were chosen ahead of me. It just seemed right that I should play. So the end of the tour was now staring me in the face. In the following game, I didn't even get picked to play against the South African Students XI. I was an outcast. Six wickets at a cost of twenty apiece in the Johannesburg Test was clearly not a good enough performance to hold my place. I was totally mystified as to why I'd been left out of the side. I could handle the antipathy of Illingworth and Lever towards me, but I was very disturbed by the apparent indifference of my captain. There was no genuine effort to soften the blow, no man-to-man conversations between us. I just got the feeling that Athers was going to keep his head down, avoid confrontations with Illingworth on this tour, and hope that winning the Test series would paper over the cracks. Meanwhile the bowler who had been expected to be the scourge of the South Africans kicked his heels.

As we came up to Christmas, Jenny was all for me leaving the tour early and coming home. Everybody she met in Derby kept saying that it was a disgrace I'd been left out in Durban. She had sacks and sacks of letters – and let me say how gratifying and moving all our family found the public support at such a difficult time. Without the generosity of spirit that the British sporting public showed me, I might have cracked. Jenny could hardly get her shopping done, with so many people coming up to her, saying 'What are they doing to Devon out there?' Not one letter came that supported the England management or criticised me, which is very rare. You normally get a few more than happy to tell you where to get off. Perhaps this was one of those occasions where the public weren't fooled. One day, Jenny picked up one of the girls at nursery and the head of the nursery kept her for a time, saying how awful it must be for me in South Africa. When Jenny left in the car, she was obviously still pre-occupied and it nearly led to a terrible accident. Coming up to a roundabout, with two of our kids in the back, she didn't stop to give the oncoming car right of way. The driver had to jam hard down on the brakes to avoid a collision. Luckily that other driver was a woman, and she probably thought Jenny had been getting a hard time from her kids in the back seat, so she was very understanding. Yet my problems were weighing so heavily on Jenny's mind that she wasn't driving sensibly. That night she rang me and said that my South African nightmare might have led to some of my family being wiped out in a car crash, so what was the point in staying out there? For Jenny to say that was a real jolt, because she had always been adamant that my profession came first. When she went into labour with our second child, she was ordering me to the nets to prepare myself for a match, insisting that one of her girlfriends would get me to the hospital on time. Later, when I was unpacking my gear, she rang me on my mobile phone in the middle of her contractions, telling me not to worry, to stay in the nets, and that everything was going to be fine. So when the woman who had always backed me totally in my chosen profession started to suggest I should come home early from a cricket tour, I had to sit up and wonder at the enormity of what she was saying. Jenny felt that it was up to Lord's to sort out the matter, because they had a responsibility to me as my employers. What was Illy doing fighting me via the press and alienating me in team selection? Why did he pick me for the tour in the first place?

There was never any danger of me leaving the tour early, though, despite the soundness of Jenny's argument. It would have been a grave embarrassment to the British Government, at a time when links with South Africa were being strengthened. Apart from that, there was a duty to my team-mates, and my tour contract to honour. I still believed that we could win the Test series, with two matches still to play, and out of respect to English cricket and the rest of the guys, I would not be rocking the boat. I kept away from the boys as much as possible, because I didn't want them to be distracted by my

Above: Fanie de Villiers hits me on the
helmet at the Oval Test of 1994. That was
the moment when I got really fired up.

Below: With my head still buzzing from
the blow, I tell the South African fielders
'You Guys are History'. A few hours later
they were and I'd taken 9 for 57.

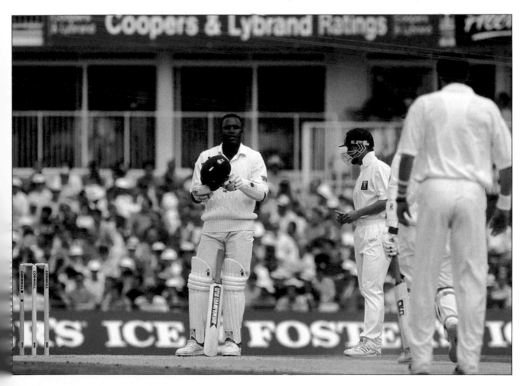

My only victim in South Africa's first innings was Peter Kirsten, bowled for 16.

Above: The second innings rout. Steven Rhodes catches Craig Matthews off my bowling for nought.

Below: The crowning moment at the Oval, 21 August 1994, when I was named Man of the Match and Series.

Meeting South African President Nelson Mandela in Soweto, 1995. My England team-mates shared my pride and pleasure.

Taking the wicket of Mandy Yachad, who was playing for the Oppenheimer XI against England in 1995 – the first wicket to be taken in an official England game in South Africa for 30 years.

My old mate Angus Fraser has been a great support to me at the other end while on England duty.

Ray Illingworth casting a critical eye over me in South Africa. Eventually, he became hostile.

I've always enjoyed Darren Gough's attitude to life and cricket.

Signing autographs in Soweto, 1995, amid the crush of enthusiastic South African school children.

The third wicket in Shane Warne's hat-trick at Melbourne in 1994 during the second Test. Malcolm c Boon b Warne 0.

Getting my own back on Warne a week later with a big six in the Sydney Test.

Mike Atherton seems pleased that I've taken the final wicket to win the 1995 Adelaide Test.

The England coach, David Lloyd, keeping tabs on me in the nets on my international comeback in 1997.

Bowling Australia's Steve Waugh with a beauty in the Trent Bridge Test of 1997.

This time I'm the suffering batsman as Glenn McGrath proves too good for me at Trent Bridge.

Above: My four beautiful girls mean so much to me! My wife, Jenny and daughters Natalie, Erica and Stephany.

Below: A pleasing moment for me as I sign for Northamptonshire in December 1997, with the Chief Executive, Steve Coverdale.

own problems. I'd get down early for breakfast in our hotel, then return upstairs, listening to my music, until it was time to go down to the lobby and catch the team bus. It was very embarrassing for all my team-mates, and I understood why they couldn't be seen to give me public support, because that would put them in hot water with the management. Besides, some of the other players had their own worries. I roomed with Graham Thorpe for a time, and he was devastated at the premature death of his first child at the start of the tour. Jenny and I nearly lost Erica, our first baby, so I could imagine how Thorpey was feeling. Mark Ramprakash was also a 'roomie' at one stage, and he was going through a tough time, getting dropped after Johannesburg after being put up the order to number three and then left to sink or swim. Mark was another who faded out of contention the longer the tour went on. Alec Stewart was very worried about the health of his mother and wife back home, and he managed to keep all that to himself. So there was no justification in me looking for sympathy from my team-mates. I would keep my dignity for the remaining few weeks of the tour, and hope that the appropriate officials at Lord's would discipline Illingworth subsequently. There would never be a stage in my life when my daughters would have to say to me 'Daddy, why did you walk out on England? Someone at school said you were a quitter.' No way, I'd never turn my back on England, no matter the provocation. Illingworth wouldn't break my spirit.

He came close to that, though, on Christmas Day. I knew I wouldn't be playing in the Port Elizabeth Test, starting the following day, but I was keen to give the boys some batting practice in the nets on Christmas morning. I was bowling at Mike Watkinson and there was a young local black bowler in the same net as me. He was rather wild, very keen to impress and I recognised the situation from my own early days as a tearaway fast bowler. When I'd been playing in New Zealand in the mid-eighties, I was invited to bowl in the nets at the touring West Indies players, and I was so fired up. When I managed to dismiss Gordon Greenidge, I was floating, so I understood why this young bowler was racing in, trying to knock Mike's head off. But he was so erratic that Mike wasn't getting adequate batting practice, and I stopped to have a quiet word with the lad. I was just telling him to slow down a bit, bowl more at the stumps, to give the batsman something to play, when Illingworth started swearing at me. He shouted over to me, 'Leave, you're disturbing the nets!' I protested that I was only trying to improve the standard in our net, but Illingworth persisted. 'Leave the f***ing net, I f***ing meant it!' Mark Ramprakash was standing alongside the netting and he was aghast at Illingworth's hostility. I told Ramps just to cool down, to concentrate on his own game, that we didn't need another player falling out with the manager, so I did what I was told. It was the most humiliating moment of my career. For Illingworth to speak to an England player like that, in public, in front of that young lad, was dreadful, so awful. I couldn't have felt lower if someone had stood me up in front of my girls and flogged me with my own belt. I crept away from the nets, utterly bewildered. Why was Illingworth so hostile to me? What was wrong with asking that young bowler to help Mike Watkinson have a better net? On the basis of what had happened during the tour, it was obvious that Illingworth had grown to dislike me. Here was fresh humiliation for the 'cricketing nonentity'. There was no excuse for this sort of behaviour; it was totally unjust and unfair. It was astonishing to be ordered out of net practice as if I was a naughty boy, a troublemaker, instead of a supportive guy trying to help a colleague.

At lunch, after nets, I tried to keep up a cheerful facade as all the team gathered round the hotel pool for a barbecue. I was one of the few who didn't have any family out there for Christmas, and it was hard keeping up appearances. Jenny would be at home, no doubt thinking about the happy Christmas Days we'd spent on England tours, and I was desperately homesick. A cuddle from the girls would have been a godsend. That afternoon, I lay on my bed in the hotel, utterly miserable. After phoning home, I put on my ghetto blaster, tried to find comfort in my favourite music, and thought to myself 'I hope none of the boys goes down overnight with some bug, because I don't believe I'd be able to play at such short notice.' I was so distraught at Illingworth's actions that logical behaviour from me would be impossible in the next few days, until I got my head around his bizarre treatment of me. It was going to be a case of lying low, counting down the days till the tour was over, longing to be with my family. I didn't tell Jenny about the morning incident, because she had enough on her plate, with three kids missing their daddy. She would find out soon enough. One of the things I recall about that dreadful Christmas Day was that by mid-afternoon I was very hungry. Perhaps I was looking for comfort eating, perhaps we'd had the barbecue too early, but I was starving by the early part of the evening. Sadly the hotel couldn't cope with the influx of Brits and there was hardly any food available that night in the dining area. So I raided the box of Belgian chocolates that Jenny had given to me before I left. Unfortunately, I'd been dipping into them over the previous few days, and there was only one left! So that was my Christmas treat – one Belgian chocolate. Next morning, I was up at five o'clock, ravenous, waiting for the staff to start cooking breakfast. And a happy Christmas and good cheer to everyone!

Somehow I got through those five days of the Port Elizabeth Test, keeping up my spirits in public. There was one morale boost for me and it came from an unusual quarter – the South African camp. On Boxing Day, Clive Rice – now one of their selectors – said to me 'Just tell me one thing, Devon. Are you playing today?' He was amazed at my answer. 'That's all I need to know,' he said and added, 'If you don't play here, how can you play at Cape Town?' That had also dawned on me. The final Test was due to start in Cape Town on 2 January, just three days after Port Elizabeth ended, so it was obvious that those who played in the fourth Test would be favourites to be there for Cape Town. I was bucked up by Clive's relief at my omission. Clearly the South Africans still feared me. They didn't see me as a 'cricketing nonentity', more the guy who had blasted them out only a year earlier.

So it came as a big surprise to both me and the South Africans that I was picked for the Cape Town Test after all. With the series deadlocked, this last Test would decide the series and I was gratified to be given the opportunity to play a part. I was worried, though, about my match fitness. The last time I had bowled in a competitive match was on 3 December during the Johannesburg Test, so it would be exactly a month later when I played in Cape Town. That seemed a crazy way to prepare me, but I wasn't going to offer any public misgivings. I was going to do everything possible to help us win the series. What would Illingworth have to say then? After just three days of the Cape Town Test I found out, in the most dramatic of circumstances.

We lost badly by ten wickets. The roof fell in on us during a hectic hour on the second day, when wicket-keeper Dave Richardson and spinner Paul Adams added a precious 77 runs for the last wicket. It was a very frustrating period of play, because when Adams came in, he could have been out at any time early on, and we would have had a handy lead of around thirty or so. I was bowling when Adams arrived at the crease, playing only his second Test with negligible batting experience in first-class cricket. He was as near as possible to being a rabbit, definitely in my class as a batsman, and he ought to have been rolled over right away. To my first delivery, he got an inside edge and the ball just missed leg stump. They got four overthrows off my bowling when Dominic Cork shied at the stumps for a possible run out, and just missed. Fair enough, these things happen. Then Adams jammed down on a yorker from me at the last instant and it ricocheted away to the fine leg boundary. Another delivery went through Jack Russell's gloves for four byes. The runs started to mount up, and our cricket was falling apart. Atherton took me off after three overs and then went on the defensive. He gave Richardson extra confidence by pushing the field back when he was facing the bowling, so he could work the ball around. Richardson, an experienced, capable batsman, was able to coax Adams along, instead of having to fight for every run against an attacking, well-placed field. We were too happy to see the strike rotated. It was unimaginative captaincy and it would cost us dearly.

It was obvious what Illingworth thought of my efforts. As we filed out after the tea interval, still trying to separate the last-wicket pair, Illingworth snarled at me: 'You haven't bowled a decent ball apart from the first two overs with the new ball.' That was very harsh to blame someone who hadn't bowled in a match for a month. Perhaps it was his way of motivating me. If so, it was a strange method to choose. I dismissed it from my mind; nothing he could do or say would stop me giving it my best shot. Yet our fielding disintegrated, all the bowlers failed to exert enough pressure on Adams and Richardson and they cracked on, amid great euphoria from the partisan crowd. That night, having lost Atherton in our second innings, we needed a big effort from our batsmen to get us back into the game. It wasn't a huge task, because if we got around 300, their vulnerable batting would be put under a lot of pressure. We were all very down about letting that last-wicket stand prosper, and I admit I shared some of the responsibility, but we were all in this together and sound batting would get us back into the match.

It didn't happen and we were bowled out for 157. They clattered their way to victory, and with it the series. The South Africans were beside themselves with excitement afterwards, whereas we just wanted to get the official ceremony out of the way and lick our wounds in private. But there was to be no chance of our dressing-room recriminations remaining private because of an astonishing tirade by Ray Illingworth.

As we trooped into our dressing-room, visibly downcast, we moved towards our individual areas. Illingworth was suddenly in my face before I even had a chance to sit down. I was leaning against the physio's table when he came eyeball to eyeball with me and snapped, 'You cost us the game!' Somehow, I kept calm, almost as if I subconsciously knew he'd have a go at me, so I was ready for him. Perhaps his tea-time admonishment the day before had prepared me for an outburst from him. I was just at the right height to land a punch on him, but instead I kept my arms folded tightly across my chest, my fists gripped tightly. I took a deep breath, just stared at him and whistled. Illingworth was purple in the face; suddenly he looked as if he was going to cry in frustration. He went over to the sink, splashed his face and walked out. The whole thing lasted about a minute. I didn't say a word and my hands remained locked underneath my armpits. In a sense I was glad that the rest of the boys had seen Illingworth's unnatural hostility towards me at close quarters. It suddenly occurred to them what I had been put through all tour. Several of the lads said, 'Dev, why didn't you just deck him?' but what would that have accomplished? I wouldn't give him the satisfaction of goading me successfully. The last person I had hit was someone in the school playground and even then, it was just the usual kids' horseplay. I may like boxing as a sport but I'm not a violent man and Illingworth's behaviour wasn't going to tip me over the edge. Having come this far on the tour, enduring so much provocation, I wasn't going to blow it with one punch.

Nothing that Illingworth could say or do would shock me any-more, but I was very hurt soon afterwards when Atherton endorsed the criticism of my bowling in that second innings. Without naming me, my captain said it was disappointing that a fresh fast bowler, armed with the new ball, couldn't get a young batsman out. Well, he wasn't talking about Angus Fraser or Mike Watkinson, he was obviously aiming that at me. I would have thought such direct criticism could have been aired privately by Athers, when tempers had cooled down. I was deeply disappointed at his tactlessness. He ignored the fact that I was rusty going into the match, that I had only bowled three overs at Adams and Richardson, almost getting the breakthrough a couple of times, that there were other bowlers on the field who also failed – and above all, that we had been bowled out for 153 and 157, both times in two sessions of play. How do you win a Test match that way? If you're going to have a pop at just one fast bowler, why not include your batters in the criticism? I wouldn't have wanted that, but why single me out? I can take my share of the flak, but it wasn't like bringing me back at the Oval, when I'd had plenty of bowling for Derbyshire before the Test. Here in South Africa, I needed a gallop after being inactive for a month. If they'd picked me at Durban, when I was absolutely right for it, then the Cape Town debacle might never have happened.

After that third-day defeat, I couldn't wait to get out of South Africa. I'd found out before the Test that I wouldn't be chosen for the forthcoming one-day series, so there was no point in hanging around. Gus Fraser was given the same news, which added up to a great piece of man-management just before a vital Test got under-way. We were building towards the World Cup in February-March, but I knew our hopes of that trophy had died when I looked around our Cape Town dressing-room and saw the disgust in the players' faces after Illingworth's blast at me. He would be in charge of that campaign in Pakistan and India, a tour that would need a great team spirit and imaginative game plan to get us anywhere near to the trophy. With him still at the helm, there would be no chance of that.

Mike Atherton was a huge disappointment to me on that tour. He was still in Illingworth's debt for saving his job after the 'dirt in the pocket' episode the previous summer, and I never got the impression that my captain would stick out his neck for me. It occurred to me that he might have been too keen to hang onto the captaincy. I was expendable, an erratic, occasionally infuriating fast bowler. I don't believe I was important enough to Athers, yet the captain has responsibility for the morale of his players, especially on tour. He must have been aware of Illingworth's hostility, of the way he treated me in the nets on Christmas morning. The captain's readiness to single me out after the Cape Town defeat made me wonder if he'd agreed with Illingworth in general about my defects. I lost a fair amount of respect for Atherton on that traumatic tour. Mutual trust was no longer there, and I'm afraid to say it has never returned.

It is baffling how little that tour management tried to resolve the differences between Illingworth and myself. Our tour manager, John Barclay seemed reluctant to get involved, yet he knew how I was being treated. Why else would he come to my room during the Johannesburg Test, at the start of December, expressing sympathy with what was happening to me? Just before I went home, Barclay said he was sorry for all the problems I'd had. That was all he ever said on the matter throughout the tour. A few weeks after I got back to England, he dropped me a note, acknowledging what a difficult time I'd had, and offering counselling through the Reverend Andrew Wingfield-Digby. It would have been valuable to have talked to the Reverend in South Africa, but Illingworth had ruled him off-limits in 1994. So why didn't Barclay intervene on tour, if he was aware of what I was going through? I suspect the strength of Illingworth's personality had something to do with that.

Never had I been so glad to see England again in the early days of 1996. I'm proud and pleased that I kept my self-respect, that all the tribulations made me a stronger person. To this day I can find no excuse or justification for the way in which I was treated on that tour. I've never spoken to Illingworth since, nor raised the subject with Atherton. Perhaps somebody will tell me one day where I went wrong.

THIRTEEN

GOING PUBLIC

When I first arrived back in England early in January 1996, I had no intentions of going public on the way I had been treated in South Africa. For a start, it would have been contrary to my tour contract, and would have led probably to a charge of bringing the game into disrepute, a fine and possible suspension from English cricket. I knew the form. Just because Illingworth had been allowed to criticise me in public didn't allow me the right to reply. So, when I took the decision to attack the Chairman of Selectors in a national newspaper, I knew what I was doing. Jenny had been in tears almost every day once the heat was put on me during the South African tour. She'd been forced to keep the kids away from the radio and television in case Illingworth popped up, giving his negative views about me. In the end, I was driven to public comment. Yet I escaped any form of censure from the cricket authorities. I'm certain that's because Lord's wanted the whole issue to be brushed under the carpet.

It took three months between the appearance of the newspaper articles and the final agreed statement from the Test and County Cricket Board which buried the whole saga; three months in which the lawyers debated which precise words could be used in the statement and several TCCB executives had to deal with the legacy of Illingworth's refusal to recognise he had treated me badly. There was never any chance of an apology from Illingworth, but the persistence of my solicitor, Naynesh Desai, ensured that Lord's and the public were better informed of my South Africa nightmare by the time the matter was put to rest in the middle of April 1996. It was totally against my principles to break cover and give public details about an England tour, but I feel I was backed into a corner and had no option. In doing so, I believe it spelt the beginning of the end for Illingworth as England's Chairman of Selectors. By the end of the 1996 season, he had finished in the job. I shed no tears over that.

On that first day back in England, I had no intention of going to the press. There was a gaggle of reporters and camera crews at Heathrow Airport to greet our flight but I kept my own counsel, determined to go through things in the proper manner. I hadn't forgotten the words of one of my England team-mates as the media scrum concentrated on me, rather than anyone else. 'Dev, you make sure you tell them,' he had shouted over to me. By then, the *Daily Express* had tabled an offer for my story, but initially I wasn't interested. Naynesh Desai warned me that going on the record would endanger my England career, and that I could also be banned from first-class cricket. All I really wanted was a private investigation by the TCCB into the affair, and assurances that officials would address themselves to the question of Illingworth's style of management. I waited for nearly a week, hoping I'd hear from someone at Lord's, until finally I rang Tim Lamb, the chief executive designate of the TCCB. I told Tim I wasn't happy with the way things had been handled in South Africa, and that I'd had various offers from national newspapers for my story of the events. He said he couldn't give me the go-ahead for that, but then he put me through to Richard Little, the director of public affairs, who was at that time in charge of media matters. Richard told me, 'We can't gag you, Devon, but please don't implicate any of the other players or criticise them.' I said I certainly wouldn't do that, nor was I even thinking along such lines. I believe Richard Little thought I wouldn't go through with my story; it was a case of 'Good old Devon, he's a big softie', but by now I was coming to the boil. I had been disturbed that no one from the TCCB had come to Heathrow to meet us; we should at least have had some sort of acknowledgement from them that we'd been out there, doing our best for England. If someone had bothered to contact me over the next few days, just to say they appreciated what a difficult time it had been for me and that there would be a proper investigation, I would have been happy and would not have gone public. But I had to make contact with Lord's, not the other way round. Things were building up inside of me, I was like a pressure cooker and asking myself all sorts of questions. What had I done wrong in South Africa? Had I said the wrong things alongside President Mandela at the Soweto press conference? Was Illingworth convinced that I'd been trying to hog the limelight? Did he want to cut me down to size?

In the end, I did that newspaper deal with the *Daily Express* out of frustration, not for the money. It was a cry for help, a way of purging myself. I wanted to get on to the next phase of my career, yet I had the distinct impression that my bosses at Lord's didn't want to hear what I had to say. All I got from them was as a result of my forcing the issue and ringing them. The *Express* articles were due to be published on a Monday and the previous Friday, I had rung up Lord's to tell them what was happening. Richard Little gave me no guidance, and made no effort to find out what was going to be in the articles, or even to see a draft. He knew I was under contract but didn't try to talk me out of it. The only concrete suggestion that Little could make was that Ray Illingworth and I should get together in a room and thrash out our differences. That was laughable. The Board only began to get worried the day before the *Express* was due to publish my articles and then Little contacted me on the Monday, expressing his concern. 'What have you done?' he asked, and after being initially hostile, he gradually backed down because he knew he'd been at fault. After that, it was between the lawyers. I had no qualms about giving my side of the story, because I felt I'd been backed into a corner. So the articles came out, while England were still in South Africa playing in the one-day international series. The story caused a stir, and no wonder. Journalistically, it must have been a dream for the paper, because it was all there – the clash between fast bowler and Chairman of Selectors, with the captain on the sidelines, staying out of it, mixed in with a bit of Nelson Mandela. My only regret was that the race card was played. The reporter who wrote the articles asked if I felt that Illingworth's hostility to me was racially motivated. Certainly his behaviour towards me had been irrational and I had racked my brains trying to work out what had motivated him. If I'd been in another form of business and had been treated so badly by my boss, I would have gone to see my personnel officer and thrown up all sorts of motives for discussion. One of them would have been the race issue, but it would not have meant I was accusing my boss of such behaviour. At no stage did I say that Illingworth had been racist towards me. I gave a rhetorical answer to the *Express* reporter along the lines of 'I don't know, you tell me.' It was naive of me, I ought to have squashed that line of enquiry flat. After all, I had Illingworth bang to rights without throwing confusing issues into the melting pot. The *Express* had a great story to themselves without a headline suggesting my treatment might have been inspired by racial considerations. The paper lapped that up, and I can understand why, but I made it easier for them by being ambiguous when asked the question. I was naive and I regret that one small section of the articles.

Immediately, my solicitor Naynesh Desai released a media statement underlining that I had not alleged I'd been discriminated against because of colour, but that I felt I had been harshly treated on the tour. Then the respective lawyers got to work – Naynesh on my behalf, and Slaughter and May for the TCCB. In the middle of February, Francis Neate of Slaughter and May met with Naynesh, and informed him that if an agreed statement could be hammered out between myself and the TCCB, then I would escape punishment. Otherwise, they would hit me with the breach of contract charge, and also one of bringing the game into disrepute. I realised I was guilty of that, but Naynesh dug his heels in for me, insisting that the agreed statement should mention my previous good behaviour for

England and that I remained eligible for Test selection. Naynesh had warned me that I was putting my England career on the line by proceeding with those *Express* articles, but he felt I was entitled to the right of reply.

I'd been frightened stiff by the prospect of either being banned for the season or never playing again for England, and the papers were now full of that sort of speculation. Naynesh was a tower of strength. He felt that the TCCB's lawyers were expecting I'd go quietly, accept my punishment, and hope the truth wouldn't come out. He believed that they were being arrogant – along the lines of 'we're doing you a favour, let's now get this thing cleared up.' The ultimatum to us didn't work. Naynesh counter-attacked, insisting that there should be some official acknowledgement from Lord's that I had been let down and badly handled. He said, 'You convene your disciplinary tribunal, and I'll bring along my witnesses, as well as Devon.' I'm sure he would have called on some of the other England players for confirmation of various events in South Africa, although I would have understood if they'd been concerned about putting their necks on the line. Naynesh asked the opposing lawyers if the press would be allowed into the disciplinary tribunal, and when he was told 'No', he said that he would brief the media every day, for as long as it takes. The prospect of publicity must have worried the TCCB greatly. The papers would have loved to have got the nitty-gritty from the tribunal, so the chances of us ever being called to one were receding. One of the problem areas in the negotiations over the agreed statement was that I had received money for my articles. The TCCB lawyers were unhappy about that, feeling I shouldn't profit from breaking my contract and therefore bringing the game into disrepute. We agreed. I never sought financial gain from going to the press, I just wanted the public to know what had happened. I found out that Illingworth was about to publish a book, no doubt giving an account of that South African tour, so that he would undoubtedly make extra money from the Devon Malcolm Affair – but I didn't want to profit. Slaughter and May suggested I donate my net fee to a chosen charity, possibly the Lord's Taverners, and I readily accepted that. So, after agent's fees, legal charges and the donation to the Lord's Taverners, I ended up with nothing. That was fine by me.

Negotiations between Naynesh and Slaughter and May rumbled on, with draft statements going back and forth. By the start of March, we weren't getting very far, apart from sorting out the question of my making money out of the articles. Naynesh told the TCCB's lawyers that the Board's unwillingness to recognise my shabby treatment meant it would be very difficult to agree on a statement. That would amount to a whitewash and I'd then be precluded from saying anything further about the matter. Yet I'd been treated like a naughty schoolboy by Illingworth; he had been abusive and tried to humiliate me several times. This had gone beyond his reservations about the calibre of my bowling – observations which should have been kept a private matter between me, the captain and Illingworth. It's not as if I'd ever been a difficult character, looking for trouble. Apart from that one moment of dissent against the Australians in 1989, I had never been in trouble. No player should have been treated this way. Slaughter and May replied that the only way the TCCB would recognise my grievances would be through an enquiry and they weren't prepared to do that.

We weren't getting very far. The search continued for a compromise. All I wanted was an acknowledgement by the Board in the statement that I felt offended by my treatment in South Africa. Surely that wasn't asking for too much? It didn't even add up to a criticism of Illingworth, simply an awareness of how upset I had been. As March slipped by, the attitude of the TCCB thawed a little. Naynesh was informed through Slaughter and May that although they still did not acknowledge my shabby treatment, they would consider any further representations we might make. It was also suggested we should make a formal complaint to Lord's against Illingworth. Naynesh's persistence was paying off. He felt that the TCCB wanted an end to the matter, because the bad publicity was piling up, after we had played so badly in the recent World Cup in Pakistan and India. The knives were out for Illingworth around the counties: Ian Botham and David Graveney were set to challenge him as Chairman of Selectors, and my case was still on the table, with great potential embarrassment for both Illingworth and the Board. The risk of my becoming a martyr in the eyes of the public must have dismayed a few at Lord's. I was set to get away with consciously breaking my tour contract because they didn't want to take action against Illingworth, which would lead to more damaging publicity.

The ball was now in Illingworth's court. Throughout March, during the World Cup in India and Pakistan, he was under pressure from the TCCB about the form the agreed statement was to take. A statement that lacked Illingworth's involvement just wouldn't wash with the public, and the TCCB knew that. He had to accept publicly that I had been hurt. The whole thing dragged on, with Illingworth digging in his heels. Yet by the start of April, time was running out for him. He had been further discredited by England's poor showing in the World Cup. If he was the saviour of our national side, why did we keep losing Tests and one-day series? Were the players on the same wavelength as him? With the county season due to start, things could become rather difficult for him as he did his rounds, looking at players. A few influential county chairmen had done their homework, talked to those who had been out in South Africa, and the knives were out for Illingworth.

On 12 April, we got the breakthrough. I'll never know how they did it, but Slaughter and May managed to persuade Illingworth to agree an additional sentence in the statement that appeased Naynesh and myself. When you read it, that sentence sounds innocuous: *'The England management has confirmed that it was never their intention to cause offence or distress to Devon Malcolm.'* Yet we felt it was a significant concession, a recognition that I had been distressed on that tour. Two months earlier, at the start of our legal negotiations with the TCCB, they wouldn't budge on any mention at all about my treatment. Now, at least, there was an acknowledgement that I had suffered. The Board's statement acknowledged that my principal motive in going to the press was not financial and that I hadn't profited financially. One paragraph of the statement was particularly relevant in my case: *'The reason why the Board imposes strict rules prohibiting its cricketers from making public statements without consent is that it believes that problems within the England team, such as Devon Malcolm's grievances regarding the tour, should be dealt with privately and in confidence, away from the glare of publicity which tends to make them more difficult to resolve.'* So in the future, I hope that neither the coach nor captain singles out one of their own players for public criticism. Such things should be handled in private. If Illingworth had told me to my face that I was a poor fast bowler, that I needed to improve in certain ways, and made positive suggestions –I would have accepted that. At least he would have had the guts to say it to my face. But criticising me in public in such damaging terms, and continuing the verbal barrage for weeks on tour, is different. I only replied in public, after long consideration, because I felt I was entitled to the right of reply. I was happy after that to let the public judge who had caused me such grief. The last sentence in the agreed statement said it all: *'Devon Malcolm remains totally committed to playing for England.'*

Significantly, my county Derbyshire took no disciplinary action against me, even though they had the power to do so. I assume that they had their card marked by the TCCB, who were understandably keen on letting the matter rest. There was another interesting side-issue from the Derbyshire angle. Two weeks after my *Express* articles, the Derbyshire CCC annual general meeting passed a resolution that a letter of support should be sent to me. I'm still waiting to receive that letter. The instruction was given to the then general secretary, Reg Taylor, a personal friend of Illingworth's. They had been on holiday together in Spain, just before the South African tour. That wasn't forgotten by me, especially when Derbyshire issued a statement after I left the club eighteen months later, pointing out that I'd always been supported during difficult times with England – but not during the Illingworth affair, as far as I was concerned. Yet the support of the cricket public gave me great strength during the spring of '96 when all these legal meetings were proceeding. They knew it wasn't in my nature to make a fuss, to wash dirty linen in public. Maintaining my dignity had always been of paramount importance to me. I had some wonderful letters, many of them from Yorkshire, that were all critical of Illingworth. One in particular came from a man in his eighties who said he'd been a county member for years and years, but there was no excuse for Illingworth's treatment of me. I've never spoken since to Ray Illingworth, he's history and I just want to get on with my life. I will never forget that my daughter, Erica, was upset for a couple of days in the backlash of that 'cricketing nonentity' jibe. She came home from school to tell Jenny that a boy had shouted to her, 'Your dad's rubbish!' Kids don't need that, do they? I never bothered reading Illingworth's book when it came out a few months after I'd escaped disciplinary action. Naynesh bought it for me, suggested I take a look, and although I took it home, I never opened it. Illingworth remains the only person in cricket with whom I've seriously fallen out, which I believe says a lot.

There was one ironic spin-off from those protracted lawyers's meetings which really tickled Naynesh Desai and myself. One of the TCCB's solicitors told Naynesh that he was going to recommend to Lord's that Illingworth should be sent away on a man-management course, dealing principally with human relations! Naynesh replied, 'What good will that do Devon? Is that a recognition of what Illingworth's done to my client?' only to be told, 'Well, it's a start.' We didn't quite see it that way, but the thought of Illy sat in class, being told how to improve his personal relations with players, had us chuckling for weeks!

More than a year after the matter was laid to rest, I received a letter that meant a lot to me because it came from the very heart of the English cricket establishment. The new chairman of the England and Wales Cricket Board, Lord MacLaurin, wrote to congratulate me on getting back into the England team after eighteen months in the wilderness. I had already been impressed by his management skills, his willingness to treat players as human beings, to integrate them fully into the new England set-up. A child in the street could have told you what the basic problems had been under Illingworth, as he traded on the players' loyalty, expecting them to keep quiet, while he sounded off about us in public. Lord MacLaurin was determined to change all that, and a couple of sentences in his congratulatory letter to me were very significant. *'I was in South Africa last year and I believe I know what you went through at that time. It shows great mental courage to come back from that setback and you fully deserve your recall to the England side.'* If ever there was a tacit recognition from cricket headquarters that I had been unfairly treated, this surely was it. The new broom had done his homework; he knew what had gone on. Even though I hadn't managed to get public recognition of that from the top brass in 1996, I felt vindicated by that letter from Lord MacLaurin.

FOURTEEN

THE LONG ROAD BACK

I knew I had no chance of playing again for England as long as Ray Illingworth was Chairman of Selectors, and he still had one more season in charge. So I was determined to get as many wickets as I could for Derbyshire in the 1996 summer, just to let people know I could still perform. That season exceeded my hopes, as I took 82 championship wickets and we finished second in the table. We had a new management team in Dean Jones as captain and Les Stilman as coach. Two tough Aussies, they had come over from Victoria with much to prove. Dean had been sacked as the state captain, while Les hadn't had his contract extended by Victoria, so they were dead set on making an impression in county cricket, just to make them sit up and take notice back home. It was to be an exciting time at Derbyshire under the new recruits, and although it ended acrimoniously the following season, with Dean resigning as captain prematurely and Les being sidelined, they were a breath of fresh air in my eyes. The team had become stale under Kim Barnett, and we needed a fresh perspective. I think we should have come closer to winning the championship under Kim than we did, and although winning a couple of one-day trophies did wonders for our morale, we hadn't done ourselves justice in the championship. The time was ripe for a change.

I was grateful to the two Australians for their support as soon as they arrived in April, because I was still suffering after my South African experience, with my confidence shot to pieces. I was having

179

anxiety attacks at the start of the season, feeling breathless and wondering if I'd ever be able to bowl fast again. In the middle of April, I went to London for the traditional pre-season lunch hosted by Cornhill Insurance, the sponsor of home Test series, and it was an ordeal for me. The England players who were there greeted me as warmly as usual and I enjoyed the banter with them. Yet I was nervous before I went into the dining area. I was shaking like a leaf, wondering what the top dogs at Lord's would say to me after going public on the South Africa tour. Richard Little spoke happily enough to me but Tim Lamb, who was sitting opposite, didn't come near me. It wasn't a comfortable experience at all, but I felt I had to go through with it, face up to my first official outing as an England player since the tour and show that I wasn't going to lie down. A week later, I played my first game since being publicly blamed for losing the Cape Town Test. I was incredibly nervous. It was at Cambridge, against the university students, and I was very unimpressive. It was a nice, greenish wicket for me to bowl on, the weather was pleasant, yet I performed like a drain, taking one for 80 off just 16 overs. I bowled short, with too much width and Will House, in particular, climbed into me, smashing a hundred off 102 balls. No disrespect meant to the Cambridge batsmen, but it was the kind of fixture in which a county bowler would expect to take wickets. That match did nothing for my declining confidence. I started to ask myself some searching questions: Was Illingworth right about my bowling? Why couldn't I roll over university students, while expecting to play again for England? Was that Cape Town defeat my fault after all?

Fortunately, Les Stilman and Dean Jones worked wonders for my morale after that. 'Deano' reminded the media how quickly I'd bowled against the Aussies in the Oval Test of '93, and told everyone who cared to listen that I was still just as fast. Over the years I'd come out well in my jousts with Deano – I broke his arm in the 1991 Perth Test and his little finger at Ballarat on the same tour – so it was good to hear public praise from such a fierce competitor. Les Stilman also spoke up on my behalf, saying that I'd been treated badly in South Africa, and that everyone should now get off my back. Derbyshire weren't too pleased with that, and Les was hauled in by the committee and had his knuckles rapped. He was told he'd be fined if he said anything more on the subject and that was significant. Derbyshire's general secretary during that period was Reg Taylor. At no time did Taylor – who incidentally was a good friend of Illingworth – issue any public comment of support for me or look into my treatment on the South Africa tour in more detail. It was left to individuals like Jones, Stilman and Kim Barnett to back me. Kim was very supportive during those months, and although our relationship was to deteriorate the following summer, when I decided to leave Derbyshire, I'd like to place on record my appreciation for his support when I was suffering at Illingworth's hands. Yet I got the impression that the club would have preferred for the issue to have faded away. When I left Derbyshire at the end of 1997, they issued a statement noting, I quote, 'the wholehearted support Devon has always been given by the club during difficult times with England.' Well, I take issue with that. My chairman, Chris Middleton and my captain, Kim Barnett supported me fully at certain times, but the club as a body didn't come out and back me publicly during the Illingworth affair. My team-mates, the management and the members were magnificent during this period, but at an official level, I believe Derbyshire decided to lie low.

It took me a month to get into some sort of bowling groove after the horror show at Cambridge, but after taking six wickets at Cardiff, I started to motor. It was a great relief to be enjoying my cricket again, without Illingworth's carping and Atherton's obvious doubts. Jones and Stilman were so positive. At our pre-season training at Ampleforth School, Les told us: 'You guys may have finished fourteenth last season, but there's no reason at all why you can't win the championship.' That was the kind of talk we needed to hear. They didn't just talk a good game, though. We were encouraged to put our thoughts down on paper, streamlining our aims. The batsmen were encouraged to think as a unit, feeding off each other's strengths while the bowlers did the same. The aim was to strengthen the team ethic, while convincing ourselves that we were good individual players. If we all improved our performances and channelled them into the right areas, then we'd automatically boost the team's results. Everybody improved their performances by 15–20 per cent. Underrated players like our wicket-keeper Karl Krikken and seam bowler Andrew Harris really came on well, with Andrew getting an England 'A' tour and Karl unlucky to miss out. The coach had told us that in the end, we alone as individuals had to do it out on the field, but he did prepare us very well. Les and Dean played the good guy/ bad guy routine very well, with Dean bawling out players at times, just to see how they'd react, and Les putting his arm around their shoulders when it looked as if they needed a more subtle form of encouragement. Dean was a very hard man, but he was still a fine batsman who lead from the front. He'd never ask another batter to do what he couldn't manage, and he won respect for his positive approach. At a time when English cricketers were being told regularly that the harder Australian approach was the way forward, it was interesting to observe at close quarters the immense mental toughness of a successful Aussie player like Dean Jones. Winning popularity contests didn't bother him as much as winning cricket matches. I enjoyed being captained by him. Initially we had a bit of a problem with setting a field to my bowling. Dean liked to be aggressive, getting in an extra slip, while I liked to have a short mid-wicket or mid-on, to make me bowl straighter. I gave him my views and he said, 'OK, fine'. He liked us to have our own opinions and to express them. He encouraged the batters to have open dialogue with him and I believe that was a big step forward. Kim Barnett had become a little stereotyped and we needed a change of emphasis.

Jones and Stilman kept boosting me throughout that 1996 season, telling me I was still the fastest bowler in England. Whenever I took a wicket they would say, 'That's another one for Illingworth' and they were great at preventing me from feeling sorry for myself. On form and fitness, I was an England contender, especially at the time when I took 32 wickets in four successive championship games, but there was no way I was going to be picked that summer. I had to bide my time and hope the new Chairman of Selectors the following summer would notice how consistent I'd been in county cricket. At no stage did I ever lose the belief that I'd ever play for England at Test level again, but it wouldn't be under this regime. There was still one major psychological test I had to surmount, though, before I could say I was really back to my best and feeling strong enough to take anyone on.

At the start of September, our home championship game against Warwickshire was televised live on Sky. We were bang in contention for the title, and this was an attractive game against the previous year's champions. Yet it was the first time Derbyshire had been live on television that summer, and I was in a terrible state on the first morning of the match. I was racked with nerves, aware that my bowling would be on display to a wider audience than just the Derbyshire membership. It had been building up inside me for a couple of days. What if I bowled badly? Was Illingworth watching, and would he be scoffing at my efforts? Unknown to me, Jenny had spotted how tense I had been the night before. During the first day, she suddenly said to my daughter Erica: 'Come on, we're going to the ground to see Daddy. Get your clothes on!' I felt so lonely out there in the middle, and it was terrific to spot my wife and daughter on the boundary edge, supporting me so publicly. I needed to get that game out of my system, to rid myself of the last skeleton in the cupboard. But there was no happy ending. I bowled badly, taking 0–62 and 2–104 and we lost the match, which finished off our championship hopes. Leicestershire ended up champions by 27 points and by the end of the season I was a tired man, having bowled a lot of overs. Yet after the horrors of South Africa and the embarrassment in April at Cambridge, I was thrilled to have taken my biggest haul of championship wickets in a season and to see us get so close to our first title since 1936. Maybe the 1997 season would be the one for us?

That proved to be a naive forecast. By the end of the following season, Jones and Stilman had gone, to be followed by Chris Adams and myself. It all fell apart, and I now see that the seeds of that breakdown were sown in our successful 1996 season. Dean Jones alienated two powerful figures in the dressing-room, Kim Barnett and Phil DeFreitas. Now DeFreitas, right from the off, wasn't impressed by Dean Jones' captaincy. If DeFreitas bowled a bad ball, he'd stand there complaining about Jones' field placing, looking for excuses. His volatile behaviour masked the fact that a good shot might have been responsible for the boundary off his bowling. We lost our first championship match to Leicestershire by six wickets, getting bowled out for 89, and immediately DeFreitas was criticising our new skipper. As vice-captain for the previous two seasons, DeFreitas obviously had designs on the captaincy – as acting captain in Derbyshire's surprise win over Kent in a NatWest trophy match in June when Jones was absent through injury, he had acquired a taste for the role, and perhaps he didn't like the brash Australian coming in over his head. Beating Glamorgan in our third game gave Deano some breathing space, and after that we went on a roll, winning four in a row at one stage – but the relationship between DeFreitas and Jones was never all that harmonious or likely to improve.

An even more damaging rift appeared in mid-summer. At the start of the 1996 season, Kim Barnett seemed to have taken on a new lease of life as he batted without the burdens of captaincy for the first time since 1983. He became involved in the team's plans, gave good input into the discussions, helped Les Stilman with the coaching and seemed perfectly happy to potter down to third man, away from the areas where the captain has to be directly involved in decision-making on the field. Kim appeared to have some detailed chats with Deano and Les, and it looked as if the transition of captaincy had worked out well. But Dean's fondness for stirring up his players, just to get a reaction, backfired on him in Kim's case. In July, we were up at Old Trafford, and Kim was told he wasn't going to open that day in the Sunday League game. That did seem a strange decision, because Kim had been an ideal opener in that competition for years, getting us off to a positive start regularly. To make matters worse, Deano hadn't told Kim personally, the news had dribbled out via one of the other players. Kim was upset, understandably so given the way he was told. It was such an unconventional decision to drop Kim down the order that the reasoning behind the move – to get the Derbyshire scoring rate moving early in the innings – really should have been explained to him. Kim got runs that day at Old Trafford in the middle order, but Deano reinstated him as opener for the rest of the season in the Sunday League, and he continued to score heavily and quickly. At one stage, Deano said to me, 'You see, my plan worked. I got Kim going at Old Trafford, the reaction was positive and he did what I wanted after that.' He was a bit insensitive to see it that way, and he should have handled Kim in a more thoughtful fashion. Yet that wasn't Dean Jones' way; that's why he had Les Stilman on board to iron out such problems. Dean liked his players to respond aggressively to his harsh style of man management, but it backfired on him with Kim. Their relationship was never the same again.

So, at the time of our greatest success in the championship for sixty years, some of our players were positioning themselves in readiness to cut short the Australian experiment that had, in my opinion, helped make us such a good side. It also meant I had just one year left of my career with Derbyshire.

FIFTEEN

STILL LOOKING OVER MY SHOULDER

When new Chairman of Selectors David Graveney and coach David Lloyd said at the start of the 1997 summer that as far as the England Test team was concerned, the slate was clean, with every player starting afresh, that was music to my ears. Ray Illingworth had finally gone, to be replaced as chairman by a broad-minded person who had the respect of the players, while David Lloyd had been a highly committed and loyal England coach for the past year. Those of us who had been in the wilderness for the past eighteen months, as well as the fringe players, could be justified in thinking they now had a chance of selection with Illingworth out of the way. Unfortunately for me, Mike Atherton still gave off negative vibes about me, so that I never felt secure in the England side during the Ashes series. I may have played in four of the six Tests, but I never felt I was entrenched. At times I had to plead with Athers for a bowl, and it was clear he didn't trust me, especially in tight situations or when runs were scarce. I'd be the first to admit that my return of six wickets at 51 apiece was far from impressive, but it didn't help that my captain clearly lacked confidence in me. To a certain extent I blame myself, because I should have asked Athers to sit down with me and try to clear the air. That 1996 Cape Town experience was still there between us, and it had never been satisfactorily cleared up. If I'd taken the initiative and asked to thrash it out with him, then we might have had a more productive partnership during the '97 Ashes summer.

That season started with a clear commitment from me to get back into the England team, and it went well from the start. In May, I took eleven wickets in the championship match against Middlesex, and both Mark Ramprakash and Angus Fraser told me it was the best they'd seen me bowl, with pace and control. Ramps said the batters just couldn't get me away. At the end of May, I was rested for Derbyshire's game against the touring Australians, at the request of the England selectors. That constituted a heavy hint! So I made it back, for the first time since January 1996 – and what a game to return to the England fold! Playing in the winning side at Edgbaston at the start of an Ashes summer exceeded my wildest dreams. I had never given up hope of playing for England again, but this was very special. The whole country seemed to be gripped by patriotic fervour, and the Birmingham crowd was fantastic, especially on the first day, when we bowled the Aussies out so cheaply, then again on Sunday, as we clattered our way to a thumping nine-wicket victory. Our supporters sang 'Ashes Coming Home' to the tune of Baddiel and Skinner's Euro 96 song, the warmth and passion from the crowd were inspiring and we responded superbly. We really felt the whole country was behind us. On that first day, I was sufficiently inspired to put in the best fielding display of my England career. I was diving around all over the place and I took a great catch down at third man, as Shane Warne sliced Andy Caddick and I held on to a difficult swirling chance. All the lads ran to me, with a mixture of amazement and pleasure on their faces and I tried to look cool – but I was thrilled. On that fourth day, during our victory celebrations, I even thrust myself forward to the front of the balcony, drinking in all the crowd's ecstasy. That was definitely not my normal style, I tend to hang back and let extroverts like Darren Gough and Dominic Cork orchestrate the crowd, but I just got carried away with the pleasure of beating the Aussies and being back in the team. Had I known how the series was going to pan out for me, I'd have enjoyed the celebrations even more.

I'd been nervous on that first morning. No matter how supportive and positive Graveney and Lloyd had been in the build-up, there comes a time when you're the one who has to cross that boundary rope and do it at the highest level. The talking has to stop and you have to prove yourself. The first wicket came my way when I went round the wicket and got Aussie skipper Mark Taylor caught at slip, tempting him with the drive. It was good to be bowling first, rather than having to wait for possibly two days, and the crowd got behind me. I got Michael Bevan caught in the gully, a pleasing dismissal, because I'd ruffled him with a short-pitched line of attack and he hadn't fancied it. Andy Caddick cleaned up the tail and amid scenes of high excitement, we were batting soon after lunch. Off ten overs, I'd taken two for 25, bowling tightly and with fire, and I looked forward to more of the same in the second innings. It was fantastic to be back. For the next couple of days, as we built up a big lead, I felt rejuvenated, loving the big-match atmosphere, especially as we were batting the Aussies out of the game.

On the Sunday, however, I started to get frustrated. Mark Taylor and Greg Blewett were putting up a great fight of it, and we didn't look like getting a wicket. Meanwhile, I was kicking my heels in the outfield, wondering when I was ever going to get a bowl. I'd had a handful of overs at the start of their second innings, then watched frustrated as Taylor got to an unbeaten hundred on the Saturday night. He was there for the taking in that second innings. He'd already had a miserable tour, had failed on the first day, and there was no doubt in my mind that another failure would see him stand down as captain. That would have been a great start to the series for England, going 1-0 up and forcing the Aussie captain's resignation. They would have been in disarray. Yet we allowed him too much on the legside in that second innings, instead of tucking him up from around the wicket, trying to get him to slice a drive. So he was reprieved, and the longer he batted, the more confident he and Blewett started to look. At one stage, they were 321 for one, and the game was slipping away from us. My captain hadn't glanced in my direction for ages, and I was seething. Clearly, he still didn't trust me;

I was his 'last resort' bowler. I kept dropping hints from the outfield, trying to catch my captain's eye as I went through endless warm-up routines, but with no success. I was too far away from Athers in the field, so I ended up having to intercede with Nasser Hussain, our vice-captain. I said, 'Tell Athers I'd love to bowl. A fast bowler needs more than six overs a day. I've been standing around in the field, doing nothing, for far too long.' It was ridiculous. Even if Athers didn't rate me, why not give me a chance? A bad delivery has been known to dismiss a Test batsman – and we needed a few wickets quickly. Eventually, thanks to Nasser, I talked myself on. I bowled a quick spell, putting Steve Waugh under pressure. John Crawley, who was fielding at short leg, kept telling me that Waugh was struggling against me, and that was a boost because I rate Steve so highly – but that spell didn't seem to impress my captain. Darren Gough cleaned up the rest of the wickets as we finally bowled them out, but I do feel I helped Goughy and Mark Ealham get wickets at the other end, just as Gus Fraser has done for me so many times. I'd only gone for two and half runs per over in my 21 overs, and I'd been under-bowled, compared to Goughy's 35 overs, Caddick's 30 and Robert Croft's 42. It wasn't as if I'd been expensive, which was the usual excuse for not putting me on to bowl.

So at the time of our great victory inside four days, I was already unsure of my role in the side or whether I'd feature all that much in the series. It just appeared to me that I might have got the nod at the selection meeting by half a vote, with the captain apparently uncertain about me. That night, we all went out to celebrate in Birmingham, and that's when I missed the chance to talk things out with Athers. I'd had it in my mind to get Cape Town out of the way, and clear up any problems between us. He needed to know that I no longer bore him any grudges for singling me out after that defeat and for not being as supportive as he might have been during my problems with Illingworth. But I was inhibited by the fact that Athers isn't a very good communicator, and there never seemed the right opportunity at any stage during those days in Birmingham.

That was my fault, I should have grasped the nettle and made Athers talk to me. I ought to have told him that it was wrong that I had to rely on my vice-captain putting a word in for me to get me a bowl, but I let it drift. By the next Test, at Lord's, I was kicking myself because by then it was clear that Athers didn't trust me any more than in previous years.

The writing was on the wall for me in the next Test at Lord's, when I bowled just seven overs in the match and didn't even open the bowling. Hardly a ringing endorsement of your fastest bowler, was it? Admittedly, it was a rain-affected match, and the Aussies batted only once, but I felt penalised because they'd bowled us out for just 77. We opened with Gough and Caddick, and clearly I was considered a luxury, because I might have been expensive. Not that I had been at Edgbaston, but why else was I allowed just two spells? When I got on, I troubled opener Matt Elliott in my first spell, only to be told after four overs by Athers that he wanted to keep me fresh – and I'm normally just warming up after four overs! When I returned for three more overs, I had Elliott dropped in the slips, and then I was banished to the outfield. Mark Ealham had the same problem with Athers, barely getting a bowl at Lord's. In my view, that was always one of Athers' main defects as a captain. He made it clear which bowlers he didn't particularly rate by just not giving them a fair go. It may be that bowlers like myself, Craig White, Paul Taylor and Mark Ealham had been forced on him in selection meetings, but he would always have the last word by making his own protest on the field. So, after just two Tests in my comeback series, I was back to square one, aware that my captain wasn't totally convinced about my own worth to the side. Why else would I get just seven overs and not open the bowling?

When we assembled at Old Trafford for the third Test, the writing was on the wall for me, and I knew that I needed to put in two excellent days' work in the nets to impress the captain and coach. I had to wait until after Gough and Caddick had finished their stint in the nets before I could have a bowl and when I did, I had Athers hopping around and getting the occasional nick. I couldn't wait to get at the Aussies, because the pitch looked green to me, with pace and bounce – it was my kind of wicket. But both captain and coach had made up their minds early on that I wasn't going to play. When I mentioned to David Lloyd that I felt the ball would go through, he said, 'It won't get above shin height,' so it was clear that I was going to be replaced by Dean Headley for his first cap. The press had been carrying that line for a few days, and that was confirmed to me on the Thursday morning, when I saw David Graveney come up and shake Dean's hand. Good luck to Deano, he bowled well to take eight wickets in the match, but I'd loved to have had a go on that surface, which did offer bounce, whatever David Lloyd said.

It's not as if I'd bowled badly in my previous Test, because seven overs is hardly a proper yardstick to judge. I was even more hurt after Old Trafford, when Derbyshire played at Cheltenham against Gloucestershire. David Lloyd came down to watch for all three days, observing the action from behind the bowler's arm, but apart from a cheery 'Awright, Dev?' on a couple of occasions, he never spoke to me. He spent a lot of time talking to Gloucestershire's Mike Smith, so it was clear to me that Mike was next in line for a call-up for the Leeds Test. It was disappointing that the coach hadn't taken time out to talk through my England efforts so far that series, because my understanding of the new England set-up was that there would be a great deal of liaison with the current players, so that the old sense of alienation and mistrust under Illingworth would have gone for good. 'Team England' was the new buzz-phrase used by the coach, whom I'd rated very highly up until this period of non-communication. If he'd told me frankly that he and Mike Atherton believed I was no longer up to the job, that would have been preferable to this feeling that I was being eased out. The hints were piling up, after all. The main thing an England player wants from the inner core of management is not to be made to look an afterthought on the field of play. It got worse as the summer went on. Just before the squad for the next Test at Leeds was to be announced, I was told by a Sky Sports cricket reporter: 'You're going to be dropped from the squad ... but you didn't hear it from me.' Thanks very much. He ended up being right and I didn't care very much for that piece of news being conveyed to me by a reporter. Where was the new, improved man-management we'd all heard about? I did not feel I was being given the respect to which I was entitled. I was also extremely disappointed that the management felt unable to talk to me directly about decisions affecting me.

We lost the Leeds Test, and I got back into the side at Trent Bridge when Darren Gough dropped out with a sore knee. Of course, I was delighted to be back; I was still taking wickets for Derbyshire and was more than happy to read the cry in the press of 'SEND FOR DEVON'. When we're in the mire, and trying to win one-off Tests late in the series, I seem to have been favoured and that's fine as far as I'm concerned, but it would have been nice to have had a proper shot at the Aussies, bowling my fair share of overs, when the series was still alive. We lost badly at Trent Bridge, but I believe a short period of play on the fourth morning was decisive, putting a totally different complexion on the whole match. That morning, we needed quick wickets to get back into the game. A bad first session would have put us out of it, but if we got quick wickets, we then had a genuine chance of getting the runs in the fourth innings. It was surely time to open with me, to go for broke. In the first innings I had clean bowled Steve Waugh with an absolute beauty – pitching off stump, holding its line and hitting off stump – and then I also cleaned up Ian Healy and Shane Warne. I felt revived, ready to roll, and full of hostility. But Athers decided to open with Caddick and Headley on the fourth morning, rather than stake everything on all-out attack. Steve Waugh was out in the first over, but that doesn't weaken my case. I believe that it was even more important then to get me on quickly, in the hope that I'd whistle out the lower middle order, then the tail. But I grazed in the outfield, while the dangerous Healy improvised brilliantly, making a rapid sixty-odd before organising the tail. In the end, we were left far too many, and we collapsed, demoralised, to lose two sessions later. Statistically, it was a heavy defeat, but cricket matches can be deceptive sometimes, and if that morning session had gone our way, we might easily have won. Athers wanted to keep it tight at the wrong time, and rather than risking his strike bowler, he watched helplessly as his more accurate bowlers were put to the sword by Healy. That was always the essential difference for me between Athers' captaincy and Mark Taylor's. Now I know that Athers has been hampered by the lack of top-notch bowlers compared to the Aussie captain, but Taylor was far better at spotting an opening quickly and responding to it immediately. Athers often appeared to be drifting tactically, proceeding as if the rota had been worked out during the previous interval, whereas Mark adapted better, played hunches, then tried something different if that didn't work. Athers never gave enough verbal or physical encouragement for my liking. When as a bowler you've been smashed to the boundary, the first person you look for in the field is your captain. Too often, Athers would make it quite clear he was unimpressed, standing there with arms folded, chewing gum, offering nothing to you. The clenched fist of encouragement and supportive words are far preferable to the averted eye. Sometimes I felt that my captain made it too obvious that it was a case of 'How do you expect me to manage these bowlers, when they keep bowling crap?' That may well have been his true feelings, but the captain of England shouldn't make that clear in public. Even if Mark Taylor lacked the brilliant services of Shane Warne and Glenn McGrath, his whole style of captaincy was more impressive than Athers'.

I was genuinely pleased for Mike that he won the last Test, at the Oval, because he looked almost at the end of his tether during that match. It was such a dramatic game, with wickets tumbling on all three days, and we were all absolutely drained on the Saturday night, after we'd won narrowly. Heaven only knows how the captain must have felt! When we all went out that evening for a celebratory drink, Athers was very quiet, and I thought then he was still going to pack it in, despite the result. But gentle persuasion from David Graveney and David Lloyd over the next few days did the trick. That only delayed the captaincy problem for six months though, because Athers eventually resigned after the Antigua Test when we lost the series 3–1 against the West Indies. Perhaps in retrospect, he should have stuck to his original decision after the Oval Test, and concentrated on sorting out his batting. He was too valuable at the top of the order to be distracted by the captaincy, something he didn't do as well as opening the batting.

During that Oval Test, I had one final example of Athers' mistrust of me in tight situations. On the Saturday morning, when we started at 52 for three, he told me that if we had to defend a small total in the fourth innings, he wouldn't be opening the bowling with me. I was flabbergasted, because taking ten wickets cheaply would be the only way we were going to win the game. I ended up pleading with him to give me an early blast and that if it didn't work, then take me off quickly and get Phil Tufnell on, to capitalise on the ball turning a lot. I said to him, 'The worst thing that'll happen is that I go for about four an over, so whip me off right away. I don't care what end I bowl from – just give me a couple of overs, please.' He wasn't convinced. But then when we were walking down the pavilion steps a few hours later, Athers suddenly said to me, 'OK, have a couple of overs.' It was ridiculous that I'd had to talk myself on, playing on my lucky Test ground, but I told him I wouldn't let him down. I got Matt Elliott out, plumb lbw, in my first over, and although I had Greg Blewett ducking for cover for a couple of overs, I was taken off after three overs. Tuffers came on, and won the game. I was delighted, but felt I'd proved a point to Athers. We needed an early breakthrough and I'd managed it, but only after some passionate pleading by myself. Should that have been necessary? I wanted the extra responsibility, but because of our batting inadequacies, leaving us with few runs to play with, I wasn't trusted. Yet even when Athers did have runs to play with, he never appeared to put all his faith in me.

So I suppose I shouldn't have been surprised when I wasn't picked for the West Indies tour, but I was. It was a bitter blow to me, because

I felt I was still the quickest England could call on, and my experience of conditions out there should have counted in my favour. I was still racking up the wickets for Derbyshire, with my tally in the past four seasons higher than any other England-qualified pace bowler. Athers may have given up on me, but I wasn't going to throw in the international towel just yet. That would keep until the following summer, because I now had other urgent problems to sort out at Derbyshire as the 1997 season ended. The parting of the ways was becoming inevitable.

SIXTEEN

MY BREAK WITH DERBYSHIRE

When I left Derbyshire after fourteen years to join Northampton-shire in December 1997, various misleading statements were issued by the club's officials and the new captain, Dominic Cork. I kept my head down at the time, knowing that many of the members who had been so supportive to me over the years must have been disappointed at my departure, especially after they had rewarded me so handsomely during my benefit year that was just ending. I saw no point in getting involved in a war of words with the club, which would be damaging and could end up with my views being taken out of context. As in a personal relationship, a breakdown with your cricket club is complicated, and can't be assessed in just a few glib sentences. Yet I know the true background, whereas others on the opposite side of the fence who have been quick to condemn me have been pursuing their own agenda and it suits their purposes to gloss over the real reasons behind my departure. I won't allow that. The Derbyshire supporters and members who have been marvellous to me for so long are entitled to know the facts.

In November 1997 I confirmed I was leaving Derbyshire. The club issued a press statement which I considered to be grossly unfair. In this statement, the club pointed out its sadness and disappoint-ment in the light of the whole-hearted support I had always been given *'during difficult times with England'*. Well, to be frank, my most difficult time with England was during and after the soul-destroying 1995–96 South Africa tour, and at no time did

Derbyshire come out in the open and criticise Ray Illingworth's treatment of me. It was left to a few individuals employed by the club – like Kim Barnett and Les Stilman – to speak up on my behalf, and that wasn't viewed very favourably. The statement also pointed out that I had been granted a benefit in 1997 after just eight years as a capped player, instead of the customary ten. The implication was that I'd just been hanging on for a benefit, then cleared off for a nice new deal with Northamptonshire. That was a very damaging allegation and I resented it.

When Kim Barnett had been made captain more than a decade earlier, he had introduced a rota system to keep his fast bowlers fresh in the hope of prolonging their careers. Kim also persuaded the club to award fast bowlers benefits earlier than batsmen, because usually our careers are shorter due to physical strain, and there was a risk that some of us would miss out on a benefit because we wouldn't manage ten years with the club after being awarded our county caps. That system had been in place for several years before I had benefited from it in 1997. Both Alan Warner and Ole Mortensen had benefits eight years after being capped, so I was just the latest in the line. It was totally unjust to imply otherwise. The club statement went on: *'It will be a huge disappointment to his many fans and to all the club's supporters that he is leaving in a very profitable benefit year while claiming that the unrest of the 1997 season is his reason for moving.'* The word 'claiming' suggests that I was drumming up some thin excuse for getting a better deal elsewhere, whereas the reality was that my position in the dressing-room had become an embarrassment to the club. When a senior player tries to blackmail you into signing a statement condemning the captain Dean Jones and coach Les Stilman in return for supporting your benefit – that is much more than just a claim of unrest. When you are left out of a crucial meeting of senior players to decide how to dispense with the services of Jones and Stilman – that's rather more serious than a little tiff. I believe the club was simply using me as a smokescreen to cover up the true story behind the disintegration of team spirit in our dressing-room in 1997. It was player power that forced out Jones and Stilman, a course of action I had always been against.

A few weeks later at Derbyshire's annual general meeting, the new captain, Dominic Cork, made things even worse for me. He had been asked why both myself and Chris Adams had moved to new counties and I was angry when I read his reply: '*We can't compete with the contracts some people are offering, but that doesn't bother me. I'd prefer a player who is motivated by pride and commitment to Derbyshire, to somebody who is in it for the money.*' Now I can't speak too much on behalf of Chris Adams, who had just concluded a lucrative new deal with Sussex, but I'm pretty certain that his frustration in recent years had stemmed from failing to get England recognition or the Derbyshire captaincy, and he was also a big fan of Dean Jones and was dismayed by the power struggle that forced out Jones. I don't believe that money was the major factor in Chris's continued disillusionment at Derby. He and Kim Barnett had never really got on, and with Kim so entrenched at the club, with such a strong power base, Chris felt frustrated. That's all I can say about Chris Adams. As for me, those words of Dominic Cork's were a shocking distortion of the true picture. Before the meeting, Cork had been quoted on local radio and the *Derby Trader* newspaper as saying that he was trying to persuade me to stay. I can say categorically that at no stage since the end of the season had I either seen Cork or talked to him. As for commitment and pride in playing for Derbyshire, surely even my harshest critics would admit I'd always tried my hardest. I've known no other way. In the season just ended, I'd taken sixty championship wickets at 21 apiece, and in the last four seasons, a combined total of 259 wickets in the championship. In 1997 during my benefit year, a time of great distraction for any player, I'd still shown my usual pride and loyalty to the club. Getting out there and doing the business in the middle was still my prime motivation and everyone on my benefit committee will tell you that. The implication from Cork was that after lining my pockets from my benefit, I'd shown little gratitude to the Derbyshire public and had moved on for even more money. Now he knows, as well as the cricketing public, that a benefit is a reward for past services, a way of the local supporters showing thanks and appreciation for what a player has done for the club. It's not a method of tying the beneficiary to the club for a few more years. There are countless examples in county cricket of a beneficiary either retiring or moving on to another club after his benefit year, yet I would have been very happy to stay on at Derbyshire. I planned extensions to my house, a couple of miles from the County Ground, which doesn't indicate I was looking to move on. Throughout the winter of 1996–97, I was looking for an extension of my contract that was due to expire at the end of the 1997 season, but the club wouldn't commit itself. A new two-year contract, with a modest increase in pay after three good personal years, would have been ideal for me, but the club treated me as a commodity. I asked again once the '97 season started and still I got nothing positive back. I was told that my form would suffer during a draining benefit year, but it didn't because it was important still to perform at my best. By the time we'd got to June and the Dean Jones saga had come to a head, the appropriate officials had enough on their plates without being concerned about an extension to my contract and, for that matter, I was now having second thoughts about staying on. It wasn't until September that various incidents had combined to make up my mind to go. I bitterly resent Dominic Cork implying that I was only interested in one final lucrative pay-day after fleecing the Derbyshire public. There had been so many times in the past decade when I could have left Derbyshire for more money. When I returned from the West Indies in 1990, another county offered me a deal four times better than my contract at Derbyshire, but I never considered leaving. It wasn't a case of hanging on for my benefit, because I'd only just been capped, and the county would have ensured I was suitably rewarded in that area. Quite simply, I owed Derbyshire everything for giving me the chance to play county cricket and that was always my reaction throughout the nineties when other counties inquired if I wanted to move on. Each time, I would have picked up a lot more than I was getting at Derby. The irony behind Cork's remarks is that he had threatened to move counties during the '97 summer. Having been groomed for the captaincy at Derby for a number of years (due to Kim Barnett's influence, and when Phil DeFreitas took over for the rest of the summer after Dean Jones' departure) Cork was not pleased. It was common knowledge at the club that Cork was set to move on – I believe he was having talks with Nottinghamshire at the time – and the offer of the captaincy for 1998 came just in time to keep him. So it was just laughable of him to try to question my motives for leaving Derbyshire.

The crux of the matter is that, along with Dean Jones, Les Stilman and Chris Adams, I eventually had to leave because of Kim Barnett's influence and power at Derbyshire. That's also why Peter Bowler and John Morris had left a few years earlier. With Kim's choice, Dominic Cork, now installed as club captain, his influence was set to last. The signs had been there some time before. Soon after Cork became an automatic first-team choice, it became obvious that Kim was grooming Dominic for the captaincy, with Kim eventually taking over as coach when his playing days were over. When Jones and Stilman arrived, I could tell that Kim was a little disconcerted that his influence might be eroded and after finishing second in the championship in 1996, the Australian partnership had gained credibility. When Les Stilman started to talk about putting down roots at Derby and developing the coaching network throughout the county, Kim must have seen the flashing alarm lights. His plans for an expanded role at the club would be in jeopardy if Stilman continued to gain support in the committee room. That's when Dean Jones played into Kim's hands. Deano's brash style of man man-management didn't appeal to every player, particularly Kim, Cork and DeFreitas. The last two had captaincy designs and Kim was determined to push Cork. As captain, Kim was very set in his ways. He was very black-and-white in his assessment of players' abilities and characters, seeing it all in one-dimensional terms. You were either with Kim or against him, in his eyes – and as he had such power in the committee room, that led to an unhealthy dominance by Kim at the club. I had always respected him for his playing ability, and the way he had helped my career as captain, as well as standing up for me publicly. With me, it was a case of staying out of all the jockeying for power and influence. I'd never had any desire to do anything other than play my cricket to the best of my ability, be a supportive team-mate, then go home to my family. It was only when Kim's plans at the club began to affect me that I changed my attitude towards him and Dominic Cork.

Cork had been upset by Dean Jones' attitude at the start of the 1997 season, when the captain made it clear he was getting frustrated at a run of injuries that was keeping such a talented bowler out of the side. Initially, Cork's problem had been diagnosed as a groin strain, but there was no improvement and Deano typically said it was a long time to be out with just a groin problem. He didn't believe in holding back on an opinion, like a typical Aussie, and Cork took offence at the suggestion from his captain that there were other reasons why he wasn't getting onto the park. Deano started to ask questions about Cork's fitness. After a second medical opinion, the problem was diagnosed as a hernia and Cork felt vindicated. Kim Barnett supported Cork's injury situation, so two powerful people in the dressing-room had further cause to be alienated by Jones. DeFreitas was another. As vice-captain for the '97 season, he could see an opening there for him if Jones was toppled. He hadn't been a fan of him in the previous season, when Deano had made it quite clear that English cricket was soft and that the players had to act like adults and take such criticism on the chin. Deano had also been very keen on promoting young players like Andrew Harris, John Owen and Kevin Dean, and a few of the established players started looking over their shoulders, believing there was too much turbulence going around, courtesy of this straight-talking Aussie. For my part, I thought that Deano was right in his analysis and his directness didn't bother me at all. Les Stilman was an excellent foil to him, a good communicator who cared about the players, with some imaginative ideas about spreading the net in the search for young talent and a healthy readiness to get us thinking about wider issues. But the Australian connection was threatening the ambitions of three senior players in our dressing-room – Barnett, Cork and DeFreitas – and Jones and Stilman's days were numbered after a few weeks of the 1997 season.

The whole thing blew up early in June, culminating in Dean Jones walking out with three months of the season left and Les Stilman marginalised, stripped of any involvement with the first team for the rest of the season. The matter was appallingly handled and I, with others, was baffled as to why the then chairman, Mike Horton, did not resolve the problem before going on a lengthy trip. For me, I still sided with Jones and Stilman. Perhaps that's why I wasn't invited to a meeting of senior players which sealed Deano's fate. It took place at the County Ground on Monday 8 June, and I knew nothing about it. I'd been involved in the Edgbaston Test until the day before, but when I drove into the ground the following day, and saw all the players' cars, I wondered where they all were. I found out that evening, when Dean Jones rang me, telling me he was going to leave. While I was away at Edgbaston, we had lost badly at Chesterfield on a flat pitch to Hampshire, and it appeared there had been a lot of finger-pointing, and harsh words. At the meeting in Derby, Kim Barnett turned up with a dossier containing all sorts of complaints against Jones that he'd been compiling over a year. It appeared that various players had been offended by Jones' manner. Dean felt it was chockfull of out-of-context quotes, alleged snubs and silly over-reactions from players who shouldn't have been so sensitive – and said so. But when it was clear he was getting no support at the meeting from any senior players, he decided to resign. That night, I pleaded with him to see it through, but he was adamant. His family didn't need it, they were already packing and certainly Deano didn't need it. He had come for the professional challenge, not for the money, and he saw no point in staying, because he'd be banging his head against a brick wall. He was right. I wish that I'd been included in that meeting, because I would have spoken up on behalf of the two Australians, but I presume that's the reason why I was kept out of it. Clearly it was premeditated, because Barnett had this dossier to hand. You don't suddenly call a serious meeting like this just because you've just lost a championship match. This had been brewing since the previous season.

So, with a final blast at the players' attitude, Dean Jones left. And it got grubbier after that. The statement drafted by Jones made predictable newspaper headlines – as he knew it would – and Kim Barnett was annoyed at that. He thought it damaged the reputation of the players castigated by Jones and felt the players should be entitled to the right of reply. To me, that was a ridiculous over-reaction. Dean Jones was fully justified in having a pop at the players who had forced him out, and the members and supporters ought to have known the truth. Yet I was determined to stay out of it in June, at a time when I had forced my way back into the England side, and with my benefit also occupying so much of my time. During the Lord's Test, Barnett forced my hand. We were off the field through rain, and I had a call on my mobile phone in the dressing-room. It was Kim Barnett. He was organising a statement by the players, saying the record should be set straight, and that Jones and Stilman were responsible for all the problems. The statement was in response to Jones' parting shot as he left the club, and also it would call for the replacement of Stilman. I was stunned that Kim thought he could involve me in all that, and asked for time to think. He told me to call him later in the physio's room at Derby, where no one else could hear the conversation, and then I talked to David Graveney and David Lloyd, who'd been sat with me on the players' balcony when I had the original call. David, who was the Cricketers' Association general secretary, said I shouldn't sign the petition if that was the way I felt, and David Lloyd was in agreement. Fundamentally, I was in the Jones/Stilman camp and deplored the way the club was being destabilised by Kim Barnett. A meeting had been organised between the parties involved that I hadn't been told about, and now he was looking for my support against Jones. I wouldn't play ball, and told him so when I phoned him back. His reply amazed me: 'Well, it's your benefit.' The inference was clear – Kim Barnett would use his influence to get the Derbyshire players to boycott my benefit functions from now on, and I would therefore suffer financially. As if that would change my mind! I told him I'd cancel straight away all benefit functions featuring any possible participation by the players, like golf days and cricket matches, but I had no intention of going against my principles. Derbyshire would get one hundred per cent support on the field from me, no matter who was in charge, but I disagreed with the plotting against Jones and Stilman. I told Kim I wouldn't be blackmailed and he said, 'That's up to you now.'

As soon as the Lord's Test had finished, I drove to Lincoln to meet up with the Derbyshire players for a NatWest trophy match the following day. I could tell immediately that their attitude had changed towards me. There was none of the usual banter, no curiosity about gossip from the Test match, no one asking me if I wanted a drink at the bar. The barriers were up. We then went on to Southend for a championship match against Essex, and DeFreitas called another meeting, once he'd ascertained I was going to London on that Saturday evening for one of my benefit functions. Eventually, they issued their statement, saying that Jones' remarks were out of order, that they weren't at fault, and they were looking forward to the next season. I'm glad they didn't say that the statement was unanimously drafted by all the players on the staff. I had no intentions of lying to the members.

So, from the end of June, I was socially ostracised by the players, and hardly any of them attended my benefit functions. I ended up putting my requests in writing to them, rather than seeing them trying to make excuses to my face, making them look awkward. Time and again DeFreitas would organise a practice session when he knew it would clash with one of my benefit functions, so that I'd go there without an advertised player. There were many embarrassments, but I just concentrated on the cricket, and shelved any decision on my future until the season was over and I could think clearly about the situation. But the day that Kim Barnett blanked me stuck in my mind, and made me feel there was little future for me at the club.

Kim and I both trained at Breadsall Priory, which was near to our respective homes, and one day after his call to me at Lord's, we arrived at Breadsall at more or less the same time. As we met in the car park, I said 'hello' to him, and he walked straight past me, without a word. This after fourteen years together on the staff. We also lived round the corner from each other. This was serious and distressing, but I wasn't going to seek rehabilitation from a colleague who was quite prepared to let me down and try to blackmail me just because I disagreed with him.

By the end of the season, Les Stilman was a broken man. He had been sent to Coventry by the senior players, hardly got the chance to work with the second XI, and he told me he wasn't sure that he had the confidence anymore to coach cricketers. It was inexcusable for Les to be treated like that; he was seen as guilty by association with Dean Jones. As for me, the parting of the ways was confirmed by one single incident at the end of the season. As part of my benefit year, I had a cricket day arranged in Guernsey. It was a prestigious day, organised down to the letter by my benefit committee, featuring some classy companies who would expect something worthwhile in return for their money. It was a six-a-side competition, with each company side having a well-known player in their ranks. My committee had recruited Chris Lewis, Mark Ilott, Johnny Morris, Chris Adams and Phil DeFreitas to join me in Guernsey, and with all sponsorship arranged, it had the makings of an enjoyable couple of days. I was concerned about DeFreitas' participation, because he had hardly been all that co-operative in the previous two months, but he was certainly up for this one. On the Sunday, 48 hours before we were due to fly to Guernsey, he confirmed to me that he was looking forward to the trip, and that he'd see me at Heathrow at midday. He'd be in London, seeing his parents, and would travel to the airport independently so there was no need to organise transport for him. On Tuesday morning, as I travelled down to Heathrow, my benefit co-ordinator Marion Bingham rang me on the mobile to say that DeFreitas was still at the club, and showing no signs of leaving. Was he still scheduled to be in Guernsey? It was a question I wanted answering. She tried talking to him, but the club physio, Ann Brentall barred her entrance into the indoor school. She said he was having his fitness programme and wasn't to be disturbed. It seemed an odd time of the year to be unduly concerned about your fitness, but DeFreitas couldn't be prised away to come and speak to my benefit co-ordinator. Even the club physiotherapist made things difficult for me. That was the last straw. So I had to pull onto the hard shoulder of the M1 motorway and try to enlist an England player at ridiculously short notice. Finally, I managed to enlist young Johnny Owen, who had just been released by Derbyshire. Johnny knew he didn't exactly qualify but that I was desperate. I managed to get his airplane tickets organised, his dad drove him down to Heathrow and he made the 7.15 flight to Guernsey, with minutes to spare. I was very embarrassed at having to make excuses to the company who had enlisted DeFreitas' services, and seething that he hadn't shown the courtesy to call me, to pull out of the trip. I shall never forget Johnny Owen's willingness to help me, nor DeFreitas' deliberate rudeness. I'm still waiting for a call of explanation from DeFreitas. Not that I need one, I knew the score from June onwards.

How could I stay at Derby after being let down like that? You need some sort of rapport in the dressing-room and clearly Barnett and DeFreitas believed I was a traitor, not in their camp. I had no hard feelings against the rest of the boys for going with the flow. I had never been interested in power struggles, but I knew it would be impossible to patch things up now; things had gone too far since that call at Lord's from Kim Barnett. I'll always be grateful to Kim for many things, especially during our early times together, but his influence at Derby has been damagingly wide. After changing alongside Dominic Cork for a few seasons, it will feel strange not to be the recipient of so many of his hyperactive activities, but he made his bed accordingly, and willingly camped down in Kim Barnett's tent. Now that he's Derbyshire captain, he'll have to behave more like an adult than an over-tired kid. He must grow up quickly, and learn some man-management qualities if he wants to take the dressing-room his way. Cork's a highly talented cricketer, with a lot of physical bravery on the field, yet he could fade away from the England scene if he's not careful. He has put a lot of influential people's backs up with his bumptious attitude since his brilliant Test debut in 1995 – so now's the time to see if he has developed some maturity. He's fancied being county captain for some time now, ever since Kim Barnett took him under his wing, and the extra responsibility will be the making or the breaking of him. I honestly wish him well. England needs Cork at his best, because he's a match-winning bowler, who gets the best players out. He's also a very talented batsman when he puts his mind to it. Now that Mike Atherton is no longer captain, another barrier to his rehabilitation in the England fold has been removed. I never believed Athers had total faith in Corky like he did with Angus Fraser, and he certainly became alienated by some of Cork's extrovert behaviour.

I just hope that the county captaincy will curb Dominic Cork's tendency to sound off out in the middle as well as off the pitch. Some of his antics when taking a wicket have made him look ridiculous. And he must be careful about making any more ill-advised statements about the circumstances that led me to leave Derbyshire. I took great exception to his efforts in muddying the waters at the annual general meeting and it's important that Derbyshire supporters know the truth. I never wanted to leave until it became clear that my position was going to remain an embarrassment on both sides. Now that I've made a clean break, I'm very happy and looking forward to three good years at Northampton. They've made it clear that I won't be over-bowled, and will be looked after as well as at Derbyshire. The move will prolong my career, and I was pleased to hear from Northants that they agree with me that I've still got a fair amount of mileage left on the clock. I'm not due to play at Derby until the 1999 season, and by then I hope all the wounds over my departure will have healed. I certainly hope the supporters won't show me any hard feelings. After reading my account of those traumatic months in 1997, they'll now have a fairer picture of what really happened.

SEVENTEEN

'THAT'S JUST DEVON'

I can understand how I've frustrated so many of my captains over the years. They also must realise how often I have frustrated myself, when being unable to synchronise my natural speed with accuracy, never giving the batsmen a moment's peace. The great fast bowlers of my time – Holding, McGrath, Ambrose, Walsh, Marshall – have all been able to do that, but even other acknowledged greats like Donald, Waqar Younis and Wasim Akram can be very expensive when something goes slightly astray in the mechanism and the ball comes out wrongly. Now I wouldn't pretend to be in their class, but I do get upset when I hear people say, 'Devon's radar's gone.' Graham Gooch used to trot out that phrase when he first captained me for England, and I've seen it written countless times in the papers. I think it's patronising, with the inference that one delivery from me is just as likely to hit short leg on the back of the head as curve away to the slips. No one knows better than myself that I've had an erratic career, and I accept my fair share of responsibility for that, but I do feel that at crucial times, I've lacked the support of my captain and that there's been no strategy to get the best out of me. This has led to an insecurity that's never left me since 1990, when I returned from the West Indies confident I could be England's premier fast bowler for the next few years. Over that period, I've rarely felt I was going to be in the side for the next Test, and I defy anyone to be at their best when so unsure about their place. At times, I felt one bad spell would get me dropped for the next Test.

Perhaps it's due to the English obsession with line and length, the desire to frustrate batsmen whom it's hoped will then get themselves out. Certainly there's no middle ground with me. I won't sit back, settle for bowling maidens and hope to improve my figures. That's not my job, I have to blast batsmen out. That brings its own particular problems with field placings. Due to my speed, nicks go for four, rather than down to third man or fine leg for one. So the captain gets worried about the escalating scoring rate, even though I'm not bowling badly. At Lord's in 1997, Matt Elliott was troubled by my pace on the rare occasions that Mike Atherton trusted me with an over or two. Several times Elliott went to hook me and I did him for pace; I remember one hook shot being gloved to the third man boundary. Off a slower bowler, it would have been either a single or a ballooned catch to point or gulley, but the pace of the delivery told against me. We had been bowled out for 77, so Atherton couldn't afford to keep me on, with runs coming at a fair lick, even though I wasn't getting any luck. So I bowled just seven overs in the entire innings. I've often envied fast bowlers from other countries who are used to bowling with a big score behind them. Then it doesn't matter so much if you have a bad spell or concede a few through bad luck. The captain can persevere with you, knowing that plugging the gaps isn't as important as getting ten wickets as soon as possible. That's been one of the secrets of Australia's success against England in my time. They've kept racking up big totals against us, which helps feed their natural aggression as competitors. I've often had to bowl at the start, defending something around 200, and one bad early spell will see me confined to the outfield where I would graze for long periods. There's often been some tension between bowlers and batsmen in the England team – we think the batters don't give us enough to bowl at, while they believe we are sometimes erratic and expensive – but there's no doubt that a fast bowler in particular has to feel confident that the flow of runs doesn't necessarily mean he's bowling badly. A strike bowler mustn't bowl negatively. Others do a valuable job in boring batsmen out, but

I wouldn't want to be a line and length merchant. As a youngster in Jamaica, I remember vividly the excitement of seeing the fast bowler in action. The hush as he ran in, the whoosh! as the arm came over, and the batsman hopping around an instant later. Things seemed to happen when the fast bowler was on, and that surge of power and adrenalin has never left me when I've been operating at my best. The problem is that you're often expensive when not taking wickets, so the pressure is really on right from the start of the innings. A minimum of two wickets in my opening spell is my target, otherwise I start to wonder what my captain's thinking. It can be so difficult to relax and let it happen naturally when you're not sure of your place in the side.

I don't want to appear a whinger, as if everyone else apart from me was at fault for my erratic England career. I have deserved to be dropped on several occasions, when I simply haven't delivered. At times, I have bowled very badly for England – among those that spring to mind are Barbados 1990 in the second innings, Lord's 1990 against India, Trent Bridge '94 against New Zealand and, lest anyone forgets, Cape Town '96. There are many other occasions when I've failed to do my job, and I hold my hands up. My bowling average in Tests of 36 is expensive; it should be around 28. When I see the averages of Fred Trueman (21), Brian Statham (24), Bob Willis (25), John Snow (26) and Graham Dilley (29), I accept I should have been less expensive. When it's not working for me, I don't have a tight, efficient infrastructure to fall back on, which enables me to bowl competently while trying to regain that elusive spark. This is something Ian Botham had. He could be expensive when trying for all-out attack, going through his varied repertoire, but there was always a solid base for him to fall back on. He had been well coached in his teens on the MCC Groundstaff, then by Tom Cartwright down at Taunton, so that almost everything was in place for him as a bowler when he first played for England at 21. He could return to basics at will, whereas I came into the professional game late, at the same age as when Beefy made his England debut. All I had

211

to go on was the raw material of being naturally quick, which stemmed from my powerful physique. Phil Russell, my first county coach, didn't want to tamper with my natural ability to bowl fast, and I believe he was right. That got me into the England team, and I believe I've been England's fastest bowler throughout the past decade – yet the decision not to complicate my bowling has meant I've lacked basic efficiency. I need good rhythm, to deliver the ball at just the right instant. Yet I have often been too tense, so that I spray the ball down legside or fall away in the delivery stride. One of my main defects has been a tendency to drop my head at the moment of delivery, so that I lose accuracy. I also sometimes fail to follow through with conviction, something Michael Holding drummed into me in my early days at Derby. When that happens, the ball doesn't come out quickly and when I try to compensate with an 'effort' ball, I tend to release it at the wrong time, and it can go anywhere. At times I press too much through anxiety, and I have to tell myself not to tear in at the stumps. I run for thirty yards, with the last fifteen a sprint, so it's very easy for the precise mechanism to splutter now and then. Yet I don't believe it's simply a case of 'Devon's radar's gone again' – fast bowling is exacting, hard work, and fatigue can chip away at the mechanics. I have a God-given talent to bowl quickly and although I could easily back off and conform, I'd be less effective. I console myself with the fact that if I'd started earlier in professional cricket, I'd probably have been bowled into the ground and finished by now. The enlightened approach to fast bowlers in my time at Derby has also helped prolong my career.

I may not have the classic fast bowler's action – rather too much strength and effort, rather than the coiled spring – but I have been able to bowl fast consistently. You have to be strong-minded to resist attempts to change your style and hang onto what other bowlers would love to be able to do. When Norman Cowans first played for England in 1982, he was our quickest bowler around, even faster than Bob Willis. Yet he was made to adapt, reduce his pace and bowl like any other seamer. He became a more reliable bowler but ended up playing just 19 Tests. Gladstone Small, with 17 Tests, was the same and although David Lawrence's England career lasted just five Tests, due to that awful knee injury, I wonder how many more he would have clocked up before the pressure to conform reduced his effectiveness. Knowing his independence of mind, 'Syd' would probably have told the coaches where to get off, and that wouldn't have done him any favours. So, of all the black fast bowlers that came through in the eighties, through to the next decade, I've lasted the longest and bowled the fastest for consistent periods. I would say that on the England scene only Greg Thomas rivalled me for speed for a short period, but he managed just five Tests and had a short first-class career. In focusing on this point about consistency, I'm not trying to build myself up, more to point out that fast bowlers come and go, that it's very hard work, and you need mental strength and clarity of purpose to keep going. The sheer quantity of cricket in England drains you physically and after just one season of international cricket, the young fast bowler runs the risk of fading away. Unless the young English fast bowler is protected, he'll disappear. No wonder Bob Willis and John Snow coasted through county cricket; they knew best how to prepare themselves for bowling at Test batsmen on flat pitches. In contrast, someone like Glenn McGrath has played a minimal amount of State cricket, compared to what we face in England. In the Caribbean, the climate and cricket history encourage youngsters to aim at being a fast bowler. The tradition of great fast bowling is inspirational. and the coaches all strive to keep the production line going. The amount of fresh fruit and fish available out there makes a healthy diet easier and cheaper than in England, which helps you keep naturally fit. An English youngster who has the aptitude to bowl fast is tempted to say 'forget it' when all the games keep piling up, the weather isn't conducive to going flat out and the niggling injuries start to appear. When I first started at Derby, I was playing second XI, three-day cricket in midweek, and then a Sunday game. I found it really hard work and after telling the physiotherapist about my back and knee pains, I was told, 'Don't worry, it's just growing pains.' Very sophisticated! If I hadn't had so much passion for cricket, and a strong physique I would have probably given it away, and concentrated on athletics. A lot of English kids have fallen by the wayside without anyone in a position of authority knowing about it. Many pay no attention at all to their bowling shoes, so that when they bowl on the hard surface of an indoor school, the jarring on back, knees and ankles takes its toll. It costs a fair amount to get a decent pair of trainers with good support for the ankles, and without that, the injuries to a teenage fast bowler just gather. So, at the age of nineteen or so, he can't bowl quickly anymore. In the West Indies, they train outside in the fresh air, bowling on grass, without heavy pressure on the limbs. It's the same in Australia. In England, it's a better career move to be a batsman.

So I may not be a great fast bowler, but at least I've had a long career in an exacting role. That's the fundamental point to bear in mind when I've been criticised for being stubborn, or unreceptive to advice at England level. Graham Gooch wrote in his autobiography that when he was captain, the only way to get through to me was in fact to tell me the opposite of what he wanted, and I'd follow that line instead. That hurt me. The implication was that I was either too pig-headed to listen or too often in a world of my own. I recall the incident that probably brought Gooch to the conclusion that I was stubborn. On the 1990 tour to the West Indies, I was bowling well in the nets to Gooch in Trinidad. I was jagging the ball back into him, making him hop around. He told me to swing it the other way, and try to beat him outside the off-stump, but I was feeling in great nick, bowling really well. So I stayed with the line that was troubling Gooch and proceeded to blast out his off-stump twice, with deliveries that jagged back at him. We basically agreed to disagree that day – but I still got him out twice with my area of attack. Yet that helped create the image that I never listened, that I just went my own sweet way, that I was a wild card. That damaged me. I think Gooch's successor, Mike Atherton inherited the same generalised view of me and there were certainly times when he appeared to lose patience with me, as a result of which I was banished to the outfield. I actually think the opposite has been the case with me, that I've listened to far too much advice. Confusion then sets in and I try to disregard what some might be saying, and take in the rest. Perhaps I ought to have been more stubborn and just said, 'Leave me alone, I know what I'm doing'. I should have done that straightaway when Peter Lever and Ray Illingworth tried to change my bowling action in South Africa. I was too set in my ways to go for such a radical overhaul, having taken over a hundred Test wickets with my own natural style, but I was willing to listen to anything I thought might improve me. I was equally confused on the tour to Australia the previous year, when the bowling coach Geoff Arnold gave me advice that conflicted with that from Keith Fletcher, our team coach. During the Adelaide Test, I worked on the side of the square with Arnold, and he said he was delighted at how much I was swinging the ball. Then 'Fletch' came up and told me, 'I don't believe you're putting in as much effort as you should.' So I replied, 'I've been told I'm swinging it like a boomerang. That's because it was delivered slower. How do you want me to bowl – quickly or with swing?' Fletch told me to bowl fast, so I went out and knocked over the tail in the first innings. Then Geoff Arnold had a word with me about swinging it, so I did that in the second innings and took four wickets, to help us win the game. Yet there was no consistent bowling plan for me: we had two experts pulling in different directions, with me stuck in the middle. No wonder I often ended up doing what I thought was best.

I do envy the guys coming through now to the England side, because there seems a greater professionalism under David Lloyd. There's an awareness of the psychological challenges in playing for your country, of setting yourself goals and utilising advice on how to achieve those targets. It's a great idea to bring in a sports psychologist to help the lads focus on the positives, rather than dwell on the possibility of failure. Now I'm sure some of the old-timers who played successfully for England will say all this is nonsense, that you should be motivated enough in being selected to play for England, but anything that helps you take the field in the right frame of mind must surely be encouraged. I just wish some of these progressive ideas were on hand when I first played for England. At no stage on tour did anyone sit down with me, and have a serious one-to-one chat about where I was heading as a cricketer, and how I could attain the goals I wanted. A tour is the best time to have these discussions because there is time available, and for those who are out of the side, it's a morale-booster, and a welcome alternative to the monotony of net practice and twelfth man duties. The only England tour I went on where we had refreshing talks was my first, to the West Indies, but that was round the dining table when we ate out together, rather than as individuals having a frank, private discussion with the coach or captain. Those dinner table chats in the Caribbean were great for team morale, they definitely acted as a bonding tool, but I wish they had been extended on subsequent tours to take in each player, baring his innermost thoughts to one of the management. No one ever seriously asked for my opinion when I was on England duty, and there have been times when I wanted to give my view on something, but I never felt the door to a frank discussion was ever open. So all I could try to do was go out and do my best for both myself and the team. Yet the absence of a constructive chance for discussions contributed to my feeling of insecurity, that I was always on trial.

I would have welcomed the chance to defend myself against the various generalisations about me that have been bandied around, if we'd had the opportunity to thrash out our feelings in a private talk. I'm sure that Athers and Goochy would have felt encouraged to give it to me, straight from the shoulder. Why did I seem so stubborn at times? Why wasn't I consistent in my bowling spells? Where was the pace in that last spell the other day? What's my attitude to injuries – am I concealing some niggle that's bothering me? Why do I appear soft at times, not psyched up? I'd point out that you have to be yourself on the field. It's never been in my nature to kick the footholds in disgust like Angus Fraser, or eyeball batsmen like Dominic Cork. I've always been a disciplined person, conscious that the TV cameras are on me, aware that members of my family might be watching me and determined not to let them down. That's just me, it's not a ruse. I won't be over-expressive just for the sake of. I try just as hard as any England cricketer, but I don't make a fuss of it. In the nets, I really buckle down to the job. I back myself against the batters, it's a real challenge to me. I simulate a match situation, working out where my fielders are. I keep a tally of the times I make them play and miss, or get them out. It's deadly serious to me. I can't understand how bowlers can coast in the nets, then expect just to switch it on out in the middle. On England duty, I've had some great jousts in the nets with Alec Stewart, Graham Thorpe and Mark Ramprakash in particular, three batsmen who also take it deadly seriously, and won't reduce their commitment and concentration. Confidence is such an elusive asset, and I try to hang onto whatever plusses I've gained in the nets when I go out to the middle. Commitment is the main thing for me. At the end of my career, I'll be able to look in the mirror and tell myself that I always tried my hardest – even in the nets.

I'm sure I must have appeared an enigma to Gooch and Atherton on occasions, their fastest bowler who seemed to lack aggression at times, without that snorting fire in the belly that seems to be the preferred way for fast bowlers to psyche themselves up. Yet if I came out with all that, it would just be synthetic. I need to concentrate on what I'm doing, rather than attempt psychological intimidation. As openers, Gooch and Atherton must have copped a lot of verbal as well as physical aggression from opposing fast bowlers, and I'm sure they would have loved to have had a guy in their team who would happily give it back with interest. I'm not one of those. I prefer to settle for physical intimidation, which I believe worries a batsman far more than histrionics. The only time I've been concerned about hurting a batsman was when I hit Jonty Rhodes at the Oval in '94, and that was only because of his history of epilepsy. Even then, my concern was wiped out within a minute and I got back to the job. When I first came into professional cricket, I was more than happy to see the batsmen being physically alarmed, and if I hit them – well, they had a bat and enough protective equipment at their disposal. I remember a second XI match at Leicester in 1984, when I hit a youngster smack in the mouth; the ball shot up off a length, went through his visor and made a mess of his face. Next day, he looked a terrible sight. I wasn't at all concerned. That's part of the fast bowler's armoury and the batsmen should be able to look after themselves at professional level. When a batsman puts on the helmet, that takes away the duty of care from a fast bowler. At the Oval in 1993, I hit Mark Taylor in the chest with one that jagged back at him, with good pace. It made him gasp, and I walked down the wicket to say, 'Take pain!'. I was delighted to see that he'd been ruffled by me. When I hit New Zealand's Trevor Franklin on the head in the '90 Lord's Test, I wasn't perturbed by the sight of blood under his helmet. You can't be genial when you've got the ball in your hand.

It may be that Athers and Goochy just didn't understand me. It has always meant more to me to win the game, than take a wicket, so that I save my celebrations till afterwards, when I can savour that sweet moment. When I look at the old videos I appear almost shy when everyone's jumping around me after I've got a key wicket, but that's because I'm not a particularly expressive person. I see Chris Lewis or Dominic Cork celebrating like a footballer – and I just think they look daft. I don't think running around with your shirt over your head like a goalscoring footballer is the ideal way to underline that you're just doing your job. The pleasure I get from bowling fast and well doesn't have to be demonstrated in such extrovert fashion. I love the adrenalin surge when it's all working properly, and the cylinders are firing. I want the ball in my hand, to hit the crease at exactly the right moment, and follow through positively, after the ball has left my hand at exactly the right instant. As a fast bowler you can tell more or less straight away if it's going to work for you – not that it means you'll then take five wickets – and it's a terrific feeling to know instinctively that the batsmen are going to spend a lot of time hopping around. I love getting a wicket from a top-edged hook or one that takes the glove, because that's also stemmed from discomforting the batsman, making him flinch. Just like any other fast bowler, sometimes I've got carried away with excessive use of the bouncer. Getting the red mists is an occupational hazard for the fast bowler, but the great ones are able to channel that aggression more productively than the rest of us. I'm very careful not to bawl out a fielder when he's dropped a catch off my bowling; after all, I've got a bit of history myself in that department!

If I had my time over again as an England fast bowler, I'd definitely want to play more one-day internationals. I was categorised too early as an express bowler, better at bowling sides out than containing batsmen. Too expensive for one-day cricket, they would say. Yet I average just 25 in one-day internationals and 28 in limited-overs games for Derbyshire. Admittedly, I only played ten times for England in one-dayers, but I usually gave us a good start by getting rid of batsmen early. At the Oval against New Zealand in 1990, Alec Stewart our wicket-keeper said it was the quickest I've ever bowled. They couldn't lay a bat on me that day. We played the Kiwis in another one-dayer a few months later in Adelaide, and I put John Wright through the mincer. I had him caught off a no-ball at slip, and my first seven overs went for just fourteen. I came back at the end, took a little bit of stick, but still finished with two for 39 in nine overs. A few years later, Dermot Reeve told me he couldn't understand why I hadn't played in more one-day internationals, that the selectors ought to have looked at my economy rate, my average and the good players I got out. Dermot was a great student of one-day cricket and knew that the best way to win these games was to bowl out the opposition cheaply, rather than just seek to defend. A glance at my one-day record for Derbyshire would have been instructive. Early on, I was a typical Caribbean fast bowler – bowl a bouncer after getting hit for four. So predictable. But I started to put my fingers across the seam, so that the ball didn't come on to the bat quite so quickly, and I got a lot of wickets with that slower delivery. There was a necessity to mix it up a little, because with the bouncer penalised by a no-ball, the quick bowler had to choose from a different armoury in one-day cricket. When Derbyshire reached the Benson & Hedges Final in 1988, I was our most economical bowler, with figures that included five for 27 in the quarter-final, one for 25 in the semis, and one for 25 in the final – hardly the analyses of a spendthrift fast bowler. I was just as economical in 1990, when we won the Sunday League and in our successful Benson & Hedges Cup run in 1993. It's annoyed me to be dismissed as a luxury in one-day internationals and thankfully, Derbyshire didn't share that view.

Watching England on the recent West Indies tour has only hardened my resolution even more to get back into the England side. I would have fancied myself in the one-day internationals for a start. We had no one quick enough to get their batsmen onto the back foot, limiting their range of strokes, in the way that Ambrose, Walsh and McLean did to our boys in the one-day series. On good pitches, international batsmen just hit through the line and you need to be able to limit their range of front-foot shots. England need a quick bowler to provide an alternative to the clever medium-pacers like Mark Ealham and Matthew Fleming who mix it up well, but can still be taken apart, because they lack pace. A fit Darren Gough would have been ideal, and his late departure from the tour with a hamstring injury was a severe blow. I was devastated not to be picked for the West Indies. I had been in the side for the last Test at the Oval, which indicates surely that I must have been in the frame, and when David Graveney rang me with the bad news, I told him I was stunned, and asked why. David said the business at Derby hadn't helped my cause, and that shocked me. I told him that in my opinion, I had done very well to have taken 75 first-class wickets, in what was not only my benefit season, but also a very testing time personally, with my problems at Derby. Given all that, plus my experience of Caribbean conditions, I felt I had been harshly treated. It wasn't an angry exchange of words – I have too much respect for Grav for that – but it was a frank discussion, and honest opinions were offered. Despite my admiration for Gus Fraser, I had taken a lot more wickets than he had in recent seasons and when Grav pointed out that Gus had taken wickets out in the Caribbean, I had to underline that I had also enjoyed some success out there! It seemed to me that Gus had taken my place, and after his great success in the Test series, when he took 27 wickets, his selection was justified. Yet he and I had operated together successfully in tandem and could have done so again. When Goughy dropped out on New Year's Eve, many of my supporters had hopes that I'd be drafted in, but Grav had already told me that any replacements would come from the 'A' tour squad, so Chris Silverwood was brought in. I had told Grav that I'd keep fit throughout the autumn and early winter, just in case I was still in the frame, but after not being invited to any of the training sessions, I knew I was out in the cold. I'm not sure of the wisdom of taking two young fast bowlers to the Caribbean – Ashley Cowan and Chris Silverwood didn't get many opportunities or even threaten for a place in the Test team – and I believe that was a tour for experienced players.

I next saw David Graveney three months later, in Sharjah, when England did so well to win that one-day tournament. I was on a family holiday in Dubai at the time, and I popped along to the ground to see the England boys. David was the tour manager, and he greeted me with, 'Dev, I was worried you were going to stick one on me after our last conversation!', which was at least made us both laugh. We sat and chatted for long time, and David was kind enough to say how much he appreciated my frankness and positive attitude to being dropped for the tour. I reiterated that I'd be training hard throughout the winter, ready for the new season, determined to make him look at me again. There were no hard feelings between us, and I hoped to get a more enjoyable phone call from him some other time. The England boys were fantastic to me when I stuck my head inside the dressing-room. It could have been a little embarrassing, but the new captain, Adam Hollioake, broke the ice straight away.

Spotting my floral shirt, a typical Caribbean effort, Adam said, 'Dev, where did you get that shirt from – it's a stinker, mate!' We all fell about laughing, and I had a great time with the lads. I think Adam's a great bloke, a natural communicator, who leads from the front. He does some brave, bold things on the field, makes his players believe they can do anything and consults readily out in the middle. He is a far better one-day captain than Mike Atherton, because he's more flexible, livelier and more imaginative. Despite our 4–1 defeat in the one-day series out in the Caribbean, I still feel the same way. There was no point in Athers being out there for the one-day series after resigning the captaincy. Adam wanted to keep the Sharjah team intact, which was understandable, and Athers was surplus to requirements. After all, he was the one who opted out of Sharjah to work on his batting technique and get some rest.

With Athers no longer captain, I feel I've got a better chance of getting my England place back. No other bowler has come roaring out of the traps so far this season to suggest that I'm out of contention. It has never crossed my mind that I've played my last game for England. I may be in my 35th year, but I still have a lot to offer. The body is still talking positively to me, and I'm so glad that I wasn't burned out too early in my career, before I had the chance to develop full fitness and be able to cope with all the niggling strains. I feel I've got the body of a thirty-year-old fast bowler, with a lot of petrol still left in the tank. The move to Northamptonshire has given me a new lease of life, and the presence here of the South Africans this summer gives me an extra incentive. I owe them a few bruises after my traumatic tour there in 1995–96, and I'm desperate to get the wickets I feel I would have got in that series given the opportunity. I'm on a three-year contract at Northampton, the last year optional, and I know that when I can't bowl fast anymore, I won't be able to settle for being just an average medium-pacer. That's just not me. That will be the time to go. I know that Northants will ensure I don't get over-bowled, but I want to play in every available championship game, and the limited-overs ones as well. I'm particularly keen to prove that in the Sunday League, I can combine a good strike rate with a satisfactory economy rate. If I do get back into the England side, I'll be 35 and only Bob Willis among English fast bowlers was still being selected at that age in recent decades. That would make me very proud and it would prove a lot of people wrong. Everywhere I look, I see fresh incentives.

CAREER STATISTICS

by Wendy Wimbush

DEVON MALCOLM – CAREER MILESTONES

1984   Debut for Derbyshire Second XI

        23 May: First-class debut v Surrey at Chesterfield

        First wicket: C J Richards (109)

1986   June: 5 wickets in an innings for first time: 5–42 v Gloucestershire at Gloucester

        6 July: Sunday debut v Kent at Derby

        30 July: NatWest debut v Nottinghamshire at Derby

1988   10 May: Benson & Hedges debut v Lancashire at Liverpool

        25 May: Gold Award Winner in B&H Quarter-final v Middlesex at Derby (5–27)

        June: 100th first-class wicket: A W Stovold (Gloucestershire) at Derby

        50 first-class wickets in a season (1)
        56 wickets at 29.92 each

1989   30 July: 4 wickets in an innings on Sunday for first time: 4–21 v Surrey at Derby; capped by Derbyshire

        10 August: First day of Test cricket v Australia at Trent Bridge

        11 August: First Test wicket: S R Waugh (0)

1990   March: 200th first-class wicket: A L Logie (WI) Third Test at Port-of-Spain. In the same match took 10 wickets in a match for first time in a Test

        25 May: First limited-overs international v New Zealand at Oval

continued overleaf

1990   First limited-overs wicket: J G Wright

        50 first-class wickets in a season (2)
        52 wickets at 32.46 apiece

1991   January: 50th wicket in Test cricket: B A Reid (Aus)
        Third Test at Sydney

        May: 300th first-class wicket: G D Mendis
        (Lancashire) at Old Trafford

        June: 100th first-class match: second Test v West
        Indies at Lord's

1993   400th first-class wicket: S R Tendulkar (India), first
        Test at Calcutta

1994   100th wicket in Test cricket: M Slater (Aus), third
        Test at Sydney

        Highest Test batting score: 29 not out, third Test v
        Australia at Sydney

        August: 500th first-class wicket: R C Russell
        (Gloucestershire) at Chesterfield

        Scored 1,000th first-class run v Sussex at Eastbourne
        in his 187th innings

        50 first-class wickets in a season (3)
        69 wickets at 29.20 apiece

1995   June: 600th first-class wicket: S J E Brown (Durham)
        at Chester-le-Street

        50 first-class wickets in a season (4)
        65 wickets at 26.03 apiece

1996   May: 200th first-class match v Essex at Derby

continued opposite

1996	August: 700th first-class wicket: P Johnson (Nottinghamshire) at Derby
	This was also his 500th wicket for Derbyshire
	50 first-class wickets in a season (5) 82 wickets at 31.67 apiece (his best season)
1997	9 July: 7–35 in NatWest v Northamptonshire at Derby
	50 first-class wickets in a season (6) 75 wickets at 23.48 apiece

SUMMARY OF ALL FIRST-CLASS MATCHES

Season	Venue	M	I	NO	HS	Runs	Av	50	Ct
1984		7	8	1	23	40	5.71	-	4
1985		1	1	0	0	0	-	-	-
1986		9	7	4	29*	37	12.33	-	2
1987		13	16	4	9*	43	3.58	-	4
1988		20	21	5	22	119	7.43	-	1
1989		12	16	7	51	186	20.66	1	1
1989–90	WI	7	9	3	12	29	4.83	-	3
1990		16	13	5	20*	76	9.50	-	-
1990–91	Aus	10	14	2	18	52	4.33	-	3
1991		13	17	3	18	93	6.64	-	1
1991–92	WI (Eng A)	3	2	1	1*	1	1.00	-	-
1992		19	19	4	26	150	10.00	-	6
1992–93	Ind/SL	6	7	3	13	27	6.75	-	1
1993		11	14	7	19	69	9.85	-	-
1993–94	WI	3	5	0	18	24	4.80	-	-
1994		18	22	9	15*	89	6.84	-	2
1994–95	Aus	8	12	4	29	91	11.37	-	1
1995		14	21	4	25*	125	7.35	-	1
1995–96	SA	5	6	4	48*	62	31.00	-	-
1996		18	23	7	21	119	7.43	-	1
1997		19	24	9	21*	92	6.13	-	2
TOTALS		232	277	86	51	1524	7.97	1	33

* Not out

Highest Score: 51 Derbyshire v Surrey (Derby) 1989
Best Bowling: 9–57 England v South Africa (Oval) 1994

Overs	Mdns	Runs	Wkts	Av	BB	5wI	10wM	S/R
156.2	24	674	16	42.12	3-78	-	-	58.62
17	2	82	3	27.33	3-82	-	-	34.00
216.2	38	765	28	27.32	5-42	1	-	46.35
255.1	45	898	26	34.53	3-47	-	-	58.88
488.1	93	1676	56	29.92	6-68	2	-	52.30
297.5	40	1122	47	23.87	4-68	-	-	38.02
258.4	37	948	32	29.62	6-77	1	1	48.50
518.2	99	1688	52	32.46	5-46	2	-	59.80
422.4	78	1269	39	32.53	7-74	1	-	65.02
388.5	54	1451	42	34.54	5-45	1	-	55.54
74	8	279	8	34.87	4-68	-	-	55.50
451.1	64	1648	45	36.62	5-45	2	-	60.15
140	34	392	10	39.20	3-3	-	-	84.00
336.5	56	1262	41	30.78	6-57	2	-	49.29
91	8	444	14	31.71	7-134	1	-	39.00
551.3	97	2015	69	29.20	9-57	3	1	47.95
340.3	55	1133	34	33.32	6-70	1	-	60.08
461.4	82	1692	65	26.03	6-61	3	1	42.61
129	24	451	9	50.11	4-62	-	-	86.00
639.2	98	2597	82	31.67	6-52	6	2	46.78
526.1	81	1761	75	23.48	6-23	5	2	42.09
6760.3	1117	24247	793	30.57	9-57	31	7	51.15

TEST MATCH SUMMARY

Season	Opp	M	I	NO	HS	Runs	Av	50	Ct
1989	Aus	1	2	0	9	14	7.00	-	-
1989-90	WI	4	6	3	12	17	5.77	-	1
1990	NZ	3	4	2	4*	4	2.00	-	-
	Ind	3	2	1	15*	28	28.00	-	-
1990-91	Aus	5	7	1	7	27	4.50	-	-
1991	WI	2	3	1	5*	9	4.50	-	1
1992	Pak	3	5	0	4	6	1.20	-	1
1992-93	Ind	2	4	2	4*	4	2.00	-	-
	SL	1	2	1	13	21	21.00	-	-
1993	Aus	1	2	2	0*	0	-	-	-
1993-94	WI	1	2	0	18	24	12.00	-	-
1994	NZ	1	-					-	-
	SA	1	1	0	4	4	4.00	-	1
1994-95	Aus	4	7	3	29	50	12.50	-	1
1995	WI	2	3	0	10	15	5.00	-	-
1995-96	SA	2	3	2	1	1	1.00	-	-
1997	Aus	4	5	1	12	12	3.00	-	2
TOTALS		40	58	19	29	236	6.05	-	7

Highest Score (Home): 15* v India (Oval) 1990
Highest Score (Overseas): 29 v Australia (Sydney) 1994-95
Best Bowling (Home): 9-57 v South Africa (Oval) 1994
Best Bowling (Overseas): 6-77 v West Indies (Port-of-Spain) 1989-90

Overs	Mdns	Runs	Wkts	Av	BB	5wI	10w	S/R
44	2	166	1	166.00	1-166	-	-	264.00
161.4	21	577	19	30.36	6-77	1	1	51.05
118.4	38	269	15	17.93	5-46	2	-	47.46
110	16	436	7	62.28	2-65	-	-	94.28
223.5	42	665	16	41.56	4-128	-	-	83.93
42.3	3	180	3	60.00	1-9	-	-	85.00
102.5	14	380	13	29.23	5-94	1	-	47.46
57	11	170	3	56.66	3-67	-	-	114.00
28	8	71	0	-	-	-	-	-
46	8	170	6	28.33	3-84	-	-	46.00
28	4	132	3	44.00	3-113	-	-	56.00
27.4	7	84	2	42.00	2-45	-	-	83.00
41.3	7	138	10	13.80	9-57	1	1	24.90
181.1	32	588	13	45.23	4-39	-	-	83.61
50.3	7	220	5	44.00	3-160	-	-	60.60
57	13	195	6	32.50	4-62	-	-	57.00
93	19	307	6	51.16	3-100	-	-	93.00
1413.2	252	4748	128	37.09	9-57	5	2	66.25

COUNTY CHAMPIONSHIP SUMMARY

Season	M	I	NO	HS	Runs	Av	50	Ct
1984	6	6	1	23	37	7.40	-	3
1985	1	1	0	0	0	-	-	-
1986	8	6	4	29*	30	15.00	-	2
1987	13	16	4	9*	43	3.58	-	4
1988	19	21	5	22	119	7.43	-	1
1989	9	10	5	51	152	30.40	1	1
1990	9	6	2	20*	44	11.00	-	-
1991	11	14	2	18	84	7.00	-	-
1992	14	13	4	26	144	16.00	-	4
1993	9	1	-	4	19	9.85	-	-
1994	16	21	9	15*	85	7.08	-	1
1995	11	17	3	25*	106	7.57	-	1
1996	16	21	5	21	98	6.12	-	1
1997	13	18	8	21*	61	6.10	-	-
TOTALS	155	181	56	51	1072	8.57	1	18

Highest Score: 51 v Surrey (Derby) 1989
Best Bowling: 6-23 v Lancashire (Derby) 1997

Overs	Mdns	Runs	Wkts	Av	BB	5wI	10w	S/R
132.2	21	555	13	42.69	3-78	-	-	61.07
17	2	82	3	27.33	3-82	-	-	34.00
203.2	35	735	27	27.22	5-42	1	-	45.18
255.1	45	898	26	34.53	3-47	-	-	58.88
468	85	1642	50	32.84	6-68	2	-	56.16
207.2	32	789	37	21.32	4-94	-	-	33.62
277.4	44	947	30	31.56	4-88	-	-	55.53
346.2	51	1271	39	32.58	5-45	1	-	53.28
318.2	48	1130	29	38.96	5-45	1	-	65.86
278.5	48	1007	35	28.77	6-57	2	-	47.80
482.2	83	1793	57	31.45	6-95	2	-	50.77
382.1	73	1333	56	23.80	6-61	3	1	40.94
586.1	86	2407	73	32.97	6-52	6	2	48.17
373.3	52	1262	60	21.03	6-23	5	2	37.35
4328.3	705	15851	535	29.62	6-23	23	5	48.54

FIRST-CLASS SUMMARY BY TEAM AND VENUE

	M	I	NO	HS	Runs	Av	50	Ct
Championship	155	181	56	51	1072	8.57	1	18
Derbyshire Other	13	14	6	19	74	9.25	-	2
England in England	21	27	7	15*	92	4.60	-	5
England A	1	-					-	-
UK/HOME	190	222	69	51	1238	8.57	1	25
England XI								
in West Indies	13	61	4	18	54	4.50	-	3
in Australia	18	26	9	29	143	7.15	-	4
in India	5	5	2	4	6	2.00	-	1
in Sri Lanka	1	2	1	13	21	21.00	-	-
in South Africa	5	6	4	48*	62	31.00	-	-
OVERSEAS	42	55	17	48*	286	7.52	-	8
TOTALS	232	277	86	51	1524	7.97	1	33

Highest Score (Home): 51 Derbyshire v Surrey (Derby) 1989
Highest Score (Overseas): 48* England XI v South Africa
   (Kimberley) 1995–96
Best Bowling (Home): 9-57 England v South Africa (Oval) 1994
Best Bowling (Overseas): 7-74 England XI v Australian XI
   (Hobart) 1990–91

Overs	Mdns	Runs	Wkts	Av	BB	5wI	10w	S/R
4328.3	705	15851	535	29.62	6-23	23	5	48.54
285.3	47	1054	44	23.95	4-50	-	-	38.93
676.4	121	2350	68	34.55	9-57	4	1	59.70
14	0	76	0	-	-	-	-	-
5304.4	873	19331	647	29.87	9-57	27	6	49.19
423.4	53	1671	54	30.94	7-134	2	1	47.07
763.1	133	2402	73	32.90	7-74	2	-	62.72
112	26	321	10	32.10	3-3	-	-	67.20
28	8	71	0	-	-	-	-	-
129	24	451	-	50.11	4-62	-	-	86.00
1455.5	244	4916	146	33.67	7-74	4	1	59.82
6760.3	1117	24247	793	30.57	9-57	31	7	51.15

FIVE-WICKET INNINGS (31)

+ denotes 2nd innings

5-42	Derbyshire	Gloucestershire	Gloucester	1986
5-52	Derbyshire	Sussex	Horsham	1988
6-68	Derbyshire	Warwickshire	Derby	1988
+6-77	England	West Indies	Port-of-Spain	1989–90
5-94	England	New Zealand	Lord's	1990
+5-46	England	New Zealand	Edgbaston	1990
7-74	England XI	Australian XI	Hobart	1990–91
+5-45	Derbyshire	Warwickshire	Edgbaston	1991
5-94	England	Pakistan	Oval	1992
5-45	Derbyshire	Glamorgan	Chesterfield	1992
5-98	Derbyshire	Lancashire	Derby	1993
+6-57	Derbyshire	Sussex	Derby	1993
7-134	England XI	Barbados	Bridgetown	1993–94
5-59	Derbyshire	Notts	Ilkeston	1994
+6-95	Derbyshire	Gloucestershire	Chesterfield	1994
+9-57	England	South Africa	Oval	1994
6-70	England XI	W. Australia	Perth	1994–95
6-61	Derbyshire	Sussex	Derby	1995
5-65	Derbyshire	Worcestershire	Kidderminster	1995
+5-114	Derbyshire	Worcestershire	Kidderminster	1995
+6-52	Derbyshire	Glamorgan	Cardiff	1996
5-116	Derbyshire	Kent	Derby	1996
+6-89	Derbyshire	Kent	Derby	1996
5-119	Derbyshire	Sussex	Hove	1996
+5-96	Derbyshire	Sussex	Hove	1996
+5-43	Derbyshire	Notts	Derby	1996
6-74	Derbyshire	Kent	Canterbury	1997
5-50	Derbyshire	Middlesex	Lord's	1997
+6-75	Derbyshire	Middlesex	Lord's	1997
5-85	Derbyshire	Warwickshire	Edgbaston	1997
6-23	Derbyshire	Lancashire	Derby	1997

TEN-WICKET MATCHES (7)

10-137	4-60	6-77	Eng	W Indies	Port-of-Spain	1989-90
10-138	1-81	9-57	Eng	S Africa	Oval	1994
10-179	5-65	5-114	Derbys	Worcs	Kidderminster	1995
11-205	5-116	6-89	Derbys	Kent	Derby	1996
10-215	5-119	5-96	Derbys	Sussex	Hove	1996
11-125	5-50	6-75	Derbys	Middx	Lord's	1997
10-65	6-23	4-42	Derbys	Lancs	Derby	1997

PAIRS (7)

England	New Zealand	Edgbaston	1990
England	Pakistan	Lord's	1992
England XI	WIBC XI	Grenada	1993–94
Derbyshire	Leicestershire	Derby	1994
Derbyshire	Gloucestershire	Bristol	1995
Derbyshire	Middlesex	Lord's	1997
England	Australia	Oval	1997

INTERNATIONAL LIMITED-OVERS MATCHES SUMMARY

Season		M	I	NO	HS	Runs	Av	50	Ct
1990	NZ/Ind	2	1	0	4	4	4.00	-	-
1990–91	NZ	2	1	1	3*	3	-	-	-
1992–93	Ind/SL	5	3	1	2	2	1.00	-	-
1993–94	WI	1	-					-	1
	NZ	3	1	1	3*	3	-	-	-
	Ind	5	3	1	4	4	2.00	-	-
	SL	1	1	0	2	2	2.00	-	-
	WI	1	-					-	1
Home		2	1	0	4	4	4.00	-	-
Overseas		8	4	2	3*	5	2.50	-	1
TOTALS		10	5	2	4	9	3.00	-	1

Highest Score (Home): 4 v India (Headingley) 18.7.90
Highest Score (Overseas): 3* v New Zealand (Adelaide) 1.12.90
Best Bowling (Home): 2-19 v New Zealand (Oval) 25.5.90
Best Bowling (Overseas): 3-40 v India (Gwalior) 4.3.93

Overs	Mdns	Runs	Wkts	Av	BB	4wI	RpO
22	5	76	3	25.33	2-19	-	3.45
17	0	95	3	31.66	2-39	-	5.58
40	2	192	7	27.42	3-40	-	4.80
8.4	1	41	3	13.66	3-41	-	4.73
28	5	114	5	22.80	2-19	-	4.07
44	1	217	7	31.00	3-40	-	4.93
7	1	32	1	32.00	1-32	-	4.57
8.4	1	41	3	13.66	3-41	-	4.73
22	5	76	3	25.33	2-19	-	3.45
65.4	3	328	13	25.23	3-40	-	4.99
87.4	8	404	16	25.25	3-40	-	4.60

DOMESTIC LIMITED-OVERS MATCHES SUMMARY

		M	I	NO	HS	Runs	Av	50	Ct
Sundays	1986–97	64	25	10	42	134	8.93	-	7
B&H	1988–97	32	17	4	15	88	6.76	-	3
NatWest	1987–97	21	10	1	10*	29	3.22	-	1
TOTALS		117	52	15	42	251	6.78	-	11

Four Wickets in an Innings

For Derbyshire (9)

5-27	Middlesex	Derby	25.5.88	B&H
4-21	Surrey	Derby	30.7.89	Sunday
4-21	Leicestershire	Knypersley	15.7.90	Sunday
4-43	Glamorgan	Derby	23.4.92	B&H
4-36	Middlesex	Lord's	6.6.93	Sunday
4-42	Sussex	Derby	25.7.93	Sunday
4-50	Northants	Derby	23.4.95	B&H
4-34	Scotland	Glasgow	25.4.95	B&H
7-35	Northants	Derby	9.7.97	NatWest

Highest Score Sunday: 42 v Surrey (Oval) 2.6.96

Highest Score B&H: 15 v Combined Universities (Oxford) 25.4.91

Highest Score NatWest: 10* v Leicestershire (Derby) 10.7.92

Overs	Mdns	Runs	Wkts	Av	BB	4wI	RpO
471.1	14	2428	87	27.90	4-21	4	5.15
299.5	21	1320	50	26.40	5-27	4	4.40
217.5	22	847	33	25.66	7-35	1	3.88
988.5	57	4595	170	27.02	7-35	9	4.64

INDEX